W9-ABI-266

333

24-46

# Competent to Counsel

LIBRARY
BRYAN COLLEGE
DAYTON, TN. 37321

JAY E. ADAMS

PRESBYTERIAN AND REFORMED PUBLISHING CO.
Nutley, New Jersey
1971

39854

Copyright 1970 by Jay E. Adams

PRINTED IN THE UNITED STATES OF AMERICA

# TABLE OF CONTENTS

TABLE OF CONTENTS

## TABLE OF CONTENTS

## DIAGRAMS AND CHARTS

*As far as I am concerned about you, my brothers,*
*I am convinced that you especially are abounding in the*
*highest goodness, richly supplied with perfect knowledge*
*and competent to counsel one another.*

Romans 15:14 (Williams)

# INTRODUCTION

Like many other pastors, I learned little about counseling in seminary, so I began with virtually no knowledge of what to do. Soon I was in difficulty. Early in my first pastorate, following an evening service, a man lingered after everyone else had left. I chatted with him awkwardly, wondering what he wanted. He broke into tears, but could not speak. I simply did not know what to do. I was helpless. He went home that night without unburdening his heart or receiving any genuine help from his pastor. Less than one month later he died. I now suspect that his doctor had told him of his impending death and that he had come for counsel. But I had failed him. That night I asked God to help me to become an effective counselor.

In my first efforts to improve, I bought, borrowed and devoured as many of the current volumes on counseling as I could, but in these I found little help. Almost all commended non-directive Rogerian methods or advocated Freudian principles. Uneasily I tried to put into practice what I read, but I could not help wondering how as a Christian minister I could re-translate what seemed to be sin, as "sickness." I found it ludicrous to nod and grunt acceptingly in detachment without offering biblical directives. It soon became apparent that I was helping almost no one by such procedures, and I was wasting valuable time. Moreover, most of the advice offered in textbooks consisted of little more than vague generalizations, which I found practically worthless for meeting the problems of concrete counseling situations. Many of the interpretations of cases cited in the literature seemed fantastic or absurd, and to top it all, a number of writers made it abundantly plain that they themselves were able to help only a few of their counselees, and these found help only after many months or even years of weekly sessions. How then could I expect to do much? Where would a busy pastor find the time to devote to such extended counseling? Was it a good stewardship of his time; could I ever become competent to counsel?

I soon became disillusioned with the standard books and was tempted to fall into the common practice of referring nearly all counselees with serious problems to psychiatrists or state mental institutions. After all, that was what the mental health propaganda advised. As a matter of fact, stern warnings against counseling anyone with difficulties more serious than a psychic scratch studded the pages of books and pamphlets published by the Mental Health Association. Pastors were threatened with the possibility of doing serious harm to people if they did not refer. One trouble with this otherwise convenient solution, however, was that people who were referred frequently returned worse off or no better. And then, there was the problem of the non-Christian counsel given by unconverted psychiatrists. How could that be justified?[1]

When I took graduate work in practical theology, I seized the opportunity to enroll in courses in pastoral counseling taught by a practicing psychiatrist on the staff of a large university hospital. "Now, at last," I told myself, "I shall get the real inside dope." But by the end of the second semester I was convinced that he knew no more about counseling than the men in his class (almost all were pastors of churches)—and we were confused! He had a thorough knowledge of Freudian doctrine, to be sure, which he zealously taught us. He doled

---

[1]That counsel dealt always, it seemed, with values and standards—matters to which the pastor ought to consider himself more competent to address himself. Kenneth Taylor's translation of Psalm 37:30, 31 puts it well: "The godly man is a good counselor because he is just and fair and knows right from wrong" (*Living Psalms and Proverbs, Paraphrased,* Wheaton: Tyndale House, 1967, p. 49). Raymond Meiners has a point when he writes, "The Psalmist in the first Psalm calls that man blessed who walks not after the counsel of the ungodly. And yet, because the Christian church is failing to provide this wise and good counsel, men are forced to go to those who are ungodly to find the solution to their problems." He asks pointedly, "Have we been afraid that our Lord could not meet men's problems?" (*Pastoral Counseling,* Addresses Given, August 22-26, Lake Luzerne, New York, p. 4.)

out large doses of Freud unstintingly, as he critiqued the verbatim accounts of counseling interviews which we brought to class, but his "insights" mostly proved to be wrong, and his best advice when put into practice simply didn't work.

Gradually I drifted into hit-or-miss patterns of counseling growing out of on-the-spot applications of scriptural exhortations as I remembered them. Surprisingly, I became a more successful counselor than ever. Of course, age and experience might have accounted for some of the difference. Yet, I could not help but notice that the more directive I became (simply telling counselees what God required of them), the more people were helped. Spelling out and getting commitments to biblical patterns of behavior after an acknowledgment of and repentance for sin seemed to bring relief and results. Facing up to people and honestly talking over issues before they grew out of proportion seemed to be important behavior for me as a pastor, in view of Matthew 5:23, 24 and Matthew 18:15-18. As this worked well for me in most instances, in counseling I began to advise others to do the same and saw some persons helped even more. But while these and other more biblical goals and methods began to emerge in haphazard fashion, I was still a very confused counselor.

Then, suddenly, I was forced to face the whole problem in a much more definitive way. I was asked to teach practical theology at Westminster Theological Seminary. One of the courses I was assigned was *Poimenics* (the shepherding work of the pastor). As part of this course, I was expected to teach the basic theory of pastoral counseling. I had less than a year to think through the problem and prepare my lectures. Where would I begin? In desperation I began to exegete every passage I felt had any bearing on the subject. It was not long before I found I had taken on a mammoth task. The Bible, I discovered, says much about counseling people with personal problems. Such difficult questions as the relationship of madness to demon possession intruded themselves. I began to wonder about the dynamics behind the psychosomatic effects of guilt seemingly portrayed in Psalms 31, 38 and 51. Further, James 5:14-16 seemed to confirm the importance of confession of sin, as well as the use of medicine, in the healing of some physical illnesses. I began to ask myself, "If, as James teaches, one's sinful behavior is at least sometimes responsible for physical illnesses, what about the possibility of a similar responsibility for mental illness?" James raised for me the question of the *pastor's* duty to confront the so-called mentally ill. James seemed to say that patients should at least be asked to consider whether some of their difficulties might stem from sin. As a matter of fact, the question soon became "does not James speak explicitly about psychosomatic sickness?"

Not very long afterward, I found myself asking, "Is much of what is called mental illness, *illness* at all?" This question arose primarily from noticing that while the Bible describes homosexuality and drunkenness as sins, most of the mental health literature called them "sicknesses" or "diseases." Believing the Scriptures to be true, I had to say that the mental health viewpoint was plainly wrong in removing responsibility from the sinner by locating the source of his alcoholic or sexual problem in constitutional or social factors over which he has no control. Instead, God's Word said that the source of these problems lay in the depravity of man's fallen human nature. That much seemed clear. Extending this thought was only natural. One could not help asking, could the books be wrong in similarly misclassifying other problems like depression or neurosis or even psychosis, as sickness? When this sort of psychiatric heresy began to rattle around in my head, I remembered the name of a man whose works a Christian psychologist had once mentioned to me. That man was O. Hobart Mowrer.

I read some of Mowrer's works, including *The Crisis in Psychiatry and Religion,* and *The New Group Therapy,* which he had just published. These books astounded me. Mowrer had gone far beyond my own thinking. He was flatly challenging the very existence of institutionalized psychiatry. He stated outrightly that he believed the current psychiatric dogmas were false. He cited evidence to demonstrate that psychiatry largely had failed. I corresponded with Mowrer over certain points. In that correspondence Mowrer invited me to participate in his Eli Lilly Fellowship program at the University of Illinois, where he is Research Professor of Psychology. I went to the University of Illinois, where I worked under Mowrer during the summer session. That was an unforgettable experience for which I shall always be grateful. Getting away from all else and concentrating on the question of counseling for two months was exactly what I needed.

During the summer of 1965 we worked in two state mental institutions, one at Kankakee, Illinois, and the other at Galesburg, Illinois. In these two mental institutions, we conducted group therapy with Mowrer for seven hours a day.[1] Along with five others, I flew with him, drove with him, ate with him, counseled together with him and argued with him five days a week. I learned much during that time, and while today I certainly would not classify myself as a member of Mowrer's school, I feel that the summer program was a turning point in my thinking. There in those mental institutions, under Mowrer's methods, we began to see people labeled "neurotic, psychoneurotic, and psychotic" (people of all stripes) helped by confessing deviant behavior and assuming personal responsibility for it. Mowrer's emphasis upon responsibility was central. Mowrer urged people to "confess" their wrongs (not to God, but) to others whom they had wronged and to make restitution wherever possible. Mowrer is not a Christian. He is not even a theist, and we debated the issue of humanism all summer.

During that time I made a study of the principal biblical

---

[1]This was my first introduction to group therapy. I now have come to the conclusion that such group activity is unscriptural and therefore harmful.

data on the subject of counseling, with special reference to what Scripture says about conscience. That summer's experience left me with some large convictions. First, I discovered why the large majority of people in mental institutions are there. Spending so much time with such persons afforded the opportunity to get to know and understand them. Apart from those who had organic problems, like brain damage, the people I met in the two institutions in Illinois were there because of their own failure to meet life's problems. To put it simply, they were there because of their unforgiven and unaltered sinful behavior. Secondly, the whole experience drove me back to the Bible to ask once again, "What do the Scriptures say about such people and the solution to their problems?"

Reading Mowrer's book *The Crisis in Psychiatry and Religion,* as I said, was an earth-shaking experience. In this book Mowrer, a noted research psychologist who had been honored with the Presidency of the American Psychological Association for his breakthrough in learning theory, challenged the entire field of psychiatry, declaring it a failure, and sought to refute its fundamental Freudian presuppositions. Boldly he threw down the gauntlet to conservative Christians as well. He asked: "Has Evangelical religion sold its birthright for a mess of psychological pottage?"[1]

In *Crisis,* Mowrer particularly opposed the Medical Model[2] from which the concept of mental illness was derived. He showed how this model removed responsibility from the counselee. Since one is not considered blameworthy for catching Asian Flu, his family treats him with sympathetic understanding, and others make allowances for him. This is because they know he can't help his sickness. He was invaded from without.

------

[1] O. Hobart Mowrer, *The Crisis in Psychiatry and Religion* (Princeton: Van Nostrand Company, 1961), p. 60.

[2] The most recent book attacking the Medical Model is Ronald Leifer's *In The Name of Mental Health* (N. Y.: Science House, 1969). This book is in many ways superior to Szasz's *The Myth of Mental Illness.*

Moreover, he must helplessly rely on experts to help him get well. Mowrer rightly maintained that the Medical Model took away the sense of personal responsibility. As a result, psychotherapy became a search into the past to find others (parents, the church, society, grandmother) on whom to place the blame. Therapy consists of siding against the too-strict Superego (conscience) which these culprits have socialized into the poor sick victim.

In contrast, Mowrer antithetically proposed a Moral Model of responsibility. He said that the "patient's" problems are moral, not medical. He suffers from real guilt, not guilt feelings (false guilt). The basic irregularity is not emotional, but behavioral. He is not a victim of his conscience, but a violator of it. He must stop blaming others and accept responsibility for his own poor behavior. Problems may be solved, not by ventilation of feelings, but rather by confession of sin.[1]

From my protracted involvement with the inmates of the mental institutions at Kankakee and Galesburg, I was convinced that most of them were there, as I said, not because they were sick, but because they were sinful. In counseling sessions, we discovered with astonishing consistency that the main problems people were having were of their own making. Others (grandmother, *et al.*) were not their problem; they themselves were their own worst enemies. Some had written bad checks, some had become entangled in the consequences of immorality, others had cheated on income tax, and so on. Many had fled to the institution to escape the consequences

---

[1] Religious terminology in Mowrer's books must be translated. He redefines words like "sin" and "confession" in humanistic ways. He once told me that the Bible would be fine if the vertical dimension could be removed from it. Dr. Carroll R. Stegall, Jr.'s recent endorsement of Mowrer: "Dr. Mowrer at least knows where help comes from—God" (*The Reformed Presbyterian Reporter,* February 1967), is a typical instance of such a failure to "translate" and is a clear example of the kind of accommodation which Christians must avoid.

of their wrong doing. A number had sought to avoid the responsibility of difficult decisions. We also saw evidence of dramatic recovery when people straightened out these matters. Humanistic as his methods were, Mowrer clearly demonstrated that even his approach could achieve in a few weeks what in many cases psychotherapy had been unable to do in years.

I came home deeply indebted to Mowrer for indirectly driving me to a conclusion that I as a Christian minister should have known all along, namely, that many of the "mentally ill" are people who can be helped by the ministry of God's Word. I have been trying to do so ever since.

Let me append one final word about Mowrer. I want to say clearly, once and for all, that I am not a disciple of Mowrer or William Glasser (a writer in the Mowrer tradition who has become popular recently through the publication of *Reality Therapy,* a book that has confirmed Mowrer's contentions in a different context).[1] I stand far off from them. Their systems begin and end with man. Mowrer and Glasser fail to take into consideration man's basic relationship to God through Christ, neglect God's law, and know nothing of the power of the Holy Spirit in regeneration and sanctification. Their presuppositional stance must be rejected totally. Christians may thank God that in his providence he has used Mowrer and others to awaken us to the fact that the "mentally ill" can be helped. But Christians must turn to the Scriptures to discover how God (not Mowrer) says to do it.

All concepts, terms and methods used in counseling need to be re-examined biblically. Not one thing can be accepted from the past (or the present) without biblical warrant. Biblical counseling cannot be an imposition of Mowrer's or Glasser's

---

[1]William Glasser, *Reality Therapy: A New Approach To Psychiatry* (New York: Harper and Row, 1965). This book reports Glasser's work at Ventura School for Girls, Ventura, California, along with the efforts of G. L. Harrington and William Mainord. The foreword was written by O. H. Mowrer.

views (or mine) upon Scripture. Mowrer and Glasser have shown us that many of the old views were wrong. They have exposed Freud's opposition to responsibility and have challenged us (if we read their message with Christian eyes) to return to the Bible for our answers. But neither Mowrer nor Glasser has solved the problem of responsibility. The responsibility they advocate is a relative, changing human responsibility; it is a non-Christian responsibility which must be rejected as fully as the irresponsibility of Freud and Rogers. At best, Mowrer's idea of responsibility is doing what is best for the most. But social mores change; and when pressed as to who is to say what is best, Mowrer falls into a subjectivism which in the end amounts to saying that each individual is his own standard. In other words, there is no standard apart from God's divinely imposed objective Standard, the Bible. Tweedie is correct, therefore, when he rejects Mowrer's "projected solution" to the problem of sin as an "acute" disappointment.[1]

During the years that followed, I have been engrossed in the project of developing biblical counseling and have uncovered what I consider to be a number of important scriptural principles. It is amazing to discover how much the Bible has to say about counseling, and how fresh the biblical approach is. The complete trustworthiness of Scripture in dealing with people has been demonstrated. There have been dramatic results, results far more dramatic than those I saw in Illinois. Not only have people's immediate problems been resolved, but there have also been solutions to all sorts of long-term problems as well. In the avowedly evangelistic milieu within which I work, there have been conversions in counseling sessions.

Perhaps by now you are thinking, "It sounds good, but I've heard that sort of thing before—and it always turns out to be

---

[1]Donald F. Tweedie, Jr., *The Christian and the Couch* (Grand Rapids: Baker Book House, 1963), p. 109.

the same old eclecticism with a Christian coating." Let me assure you that I am aware of this problem, and that it has been my effort to reject precisely that sort of thing. A pamphlet entitled, *Some Help For the Anxious,* is a good example of the kind of eclecticism and accommodation that must be resisted.[1] On page 3 the author notes that Freudians see anxiety stemming primarily from internal conflicts. Then he mentions a second school of psychiatry that has taken a more interpersonal cultural approach. Its chief representatives, he says, are Karen Horney, Erich Fromm, and Harry Stack Sullivan. Horney said that the feeling of insecurity is at the base of anxiety. Fromm, however, believes that the aim in life is to find "meaning." Sullivan taught that anxiety comes from disturbances in one's relationships with others. Having divided the second school into those segments, the writer observes that there is a third which reflects existentialist thinking. In that category he places Ludwig Binswanger and Rollo May. He then sets forth each of their views. Finally, on page 5, he concludes:

> To summarize then, anxiety may come from threats to ourselves, threats from within or without. Anxiety may come from our past, present or future. In the past we have memories, experiences and unresolved conflicts that may produce anxiety. In the present we have bills, deadlines, work, examinations, and relationships with other people to elicit it. As we look to the future, anxiety is aroused by lack of purpose, and finally there is the awareness of death which seems to make life even more meaningless.

In other words, the author has summarized the ideas of all these different people and assumed that each is correct in his major tenets, even though there are many respects in which these positions are antithetical.

Throughout the rest of the pamphlet Christianity is interpreted as meeting the needs that people have according to the

---

[1] Merville O. Vincent, *Some Help for the Anxious* (pam., n. d.).

diagnoses of Freud, Horney, Sullivan, etc. For instance, take page 10: "What we require is a drastic changes [sic] from within. It seems to me that Christ's diagnosis of man's original condition is similar to Freud's diagnosis of man's original condition." This is a gross over-simplification that represents a total misunderstanding either of Freud or of Christ, or both. This baptizing of secular anthropological views which has frequently characterized much that has been called Christian counseling, must be rejected. Instead, Christians must get back of these views and understand their basic antichristian presuppositions.[1]

The conclusions in this book are not based upon scientific findings. My method is presuppositional. I avowedly accept the inerrant Bible as the Standard of all faith and practice. The Scriptures, therefore, are the basis, and contain the criteria by which I have sought to make every judgment.[2] Two precautions must be suggested. First, I am aware that my interpretations and applications of Scripture are not infallible. Secondly, I do not wish to disregard science, but rather I welcome it as a useful adjunct for the purposes of illustrating, filling in generalizations with specifics, and challenging wrong human interpretations of Scripture, thereby forcing the student to restudy the Scriptures. However, in the area of psychiatry, science largely has given way to humanistic philosophy and gross speculation.[3]

---

[1]Dr. Cornelius Van Til, of Westminster Theological Seminary, has shown the importance of presuppositional analysis. He has demonstrated that at bottom, all non-Christian systems demand autonomy for man, thereby seeking to dethrone God.

[2]The reader will note that case material is used not as supporting evidence, but only illustratively. Such materials must not be thought to confirm or verify biblical positions (God's Word does not need human support); I have used it rather to illustrate, concretize and clarify.

[3]Lewis Joseph Sherrill, in *Guilt and Redemption* (Richmond: John Knox Press), wrote: "We shall find the various psychologies just as

Much work yet remains to be done to construct a full and organized system of biblical counseling, but in this book I shall attempt to sketch the architectural preliminaries.

Jay Adams
Philadelphia, 1970

---

heavy with dogmas as any theological system. If dogma is statements pronounced true apart from evidence which any other competent person can verify . . . theology and psychiatry are simply pot and kettle, neither having any ground to call the other black" p. 15. The serious difference, however, is that Christian theologians have been willing to acknowledge their presuppositional faith, whereas psychiatrists often will not do so. Erich Fromm is a notable exception. He observes, for instance, that Freud went beyond the idea of healing in avowing that psychiatry is "the study of the soul of man" in order to teach "the art of living" (*Psychoanalysis and Religion*, New Haven: Yale University Press, 1950, p. 7). Masur may be correct when he claims that "psychoanalysis became one of the substitute religions for the disillusioned middle class." He continues, "Analysis is accompanied by ceremonies and rituals that resemble a religious rite. Its concepts, at best debatable, are repeated as articles of the faith" (Gerhard Masur, *Prophets of Yesterday,* New York: The Macmillan Co., 1961, p. 311). Percival Bailey is correct when he declares that "Many of Freud's psychological writings are not scientific treatises, but rather reveries" (Percival Bailey, "The Great Psychiatric Revolution," in *Morality and Mental Health,* O. H. Mowrer, ed., Chicago: Rand McNally Co., 1966, p. 53).

## Chapter I

# CHRISTIANITY AND PSYCHIATRY TODAY

On the first day of an elementary psychology course at Johns Hopkins University some twenty years ago, a professor sat on his desk silently reading the morning newspaper. The bell rang, but he didn't seem to notice it. Then audibly he began to read the headlines of the front page articles. They captioned difficult world problems, spoke of inhuman acts of man to his fellow man, and, in general, painted the typical sensational front page picture one may read every day. Presently, he looked up and said, "The world is in a mess." He spent the rest of the hour explaining how psychology is the world's one hope for straightening out that mess.

But the newspaper headlines have not improved; crime is on the increase; our streets have become unsafe; there are riots in our cities; and the mental institutions, in spite of tranquilizers, still do a thriving business. As a matter of fact, psychiatry, that illegitimate child of psychology which historically has made the most grandiose claims, is itself in serious trouble.

## Psychiatry Is In Trouble

Eminent psychiatrists have become disillusioned. In 1955 the American Psychiatric Association held a symposium on "Progress in Psychiatry." Here is the sort of statement which appeared in the published accounts: "Psychotherapy is today in a state of disarray almost exactly as it was 200 years ago."[1] In an address to the A. P. A. the next year, 1956, Percival Bailey said:

The great revolution in psychiatry has solved few prob-

---

[1]Zilboorg, G., in Mowrer, *The Crisis in Psychology and Religion* (Princeton: Van Nostrand, 1961), p. 3.

lems . . . One wonders how long the hoary errors of Freud will continue to plague psychiatry.[1]

Patients, failing to recover after years of analysis and thousands of dollars later, have also been wondering about the boasts of psychiatry. Some, getting worse, have begun to suspect that many of their problems are *iatrogenic* (that is, treatment induced). H. J. Eysenck, Director of the University of London's Department of Psychology, recently wrote:

> The success of the Freudian revolution seemed complete. Only one thing went wrong. The patients did not get any better.[2]

Berelson and Steiner, in their book *Human Behavior, An Inventory of Scientific Findings,* which is a survey of the progress of the behavioral sciences in our time, said:

> Psychotherapy has not yet been proved more effective than general medical counseling in treating neurosis or psychosis. In general, therapy works best with people who are young, well-born, well-educated and not seriously sick.[3]

Even popular journalists at last have become aware of the recent disillusionment with psychiatry. In an article in *This Week Magazine* for September 18, 1966 entitled "Farewell to Freud," Leslie Lieber concludes:

> Once bright with promise, psychoanalysis today seems hardly worth the millions we are lavishing on it each year. In the U. S. there are approximately 18,000 psychiatrists— as against about 484 in France and 1,000 in Italy. And about nine per cent at their couch-side listening posts throughout this great land are psychoanalysts. . . . Many of these doctors and patients have begun to take stock: have the benefits of psychoanalysis justified the hours of tortur-

---

[1]*Ibid.,* p. 132.

[2]*Ibid.,* p. 133.

[3]In *Time Magazine,* February 14, 1964, p. 43.

ous self-examination, the years of painfully slow probing, the $25,000 or so spent for the complete "treatment"? In short, are psychiatry and psychoanalysis worth the millions-a-year Americans lavish on it? . . . The truth is that not only is the dramatic breakthrough and cure almost nonexistent, but thousands upon thousands who have spent millions upon millions aren't at all certain whether they are one whit less "neurotic" than before they began their five-times-a-week, $25-a-session trudge to the psychoanalyst's couch. . . But much more significant than the gradual disillusionment of patients is the wholesale defection of analysists themselves from the Freudian fold. Many doctors are now sharply challenging the need for long-drawn-out excavations of the subconscious.[1]

Quoting Dr. H. J. Eysenck, Lieber continues:

Surveys show that of patients who spend upwards of 350 hours on the psychoanalyst's couch to get better—two out of three show some improvement over a period of years. The fly in that particular ointment, however, is that the same percentage get better *without analysis* or under the care of a regular physician. As a matter of fact, that same ratio—two out of three people—got better in mental hospitals a hundred years ago. . . . Patients get better regardless of what is done to them. Unfortunately the analyst often interprets improvement as a result of his treatment. It does not bother him that other people use other methods with equal effect—hypnosis, electric shock, cold baths, the laying on of hands, the pulling out of teeth to remove foci of infection, suggestion, dummy pills, confession, prayer.

But Lieber is not yet finished:

Another dissenter is Dr. Thomas A. Szasz, Professor of Psychiatry at the State University of New York, Upstate Medical Center and author of the book, *The Ethics of Psy-*

---

[1] *This Week Magazine*, September 18, 1966.

4

*choanalysis.* To quote Szasz, "the adherents of this exaggerated faith . . . use it as a shield of illusion concealing some ugly realities. . ." Thus when we read in the paper that the alcoholic, the rapist or vandal . . . will be given "psychiatric care," we are assured that the problem is being effectively dealt with and we dismiss it from our minds. I contend that we have no right to this easy absolution from responsibility.[1]

There seems to be little question, then, that much re-thinking is called for. And Christians ought to be foremost among those engaged in such re-thinking.

**The Freudian Ethic**

One achievement with which Freudianism ought to be credited is the leading part it has played in the present collapse of responsibility in modern American society. Another is Freud's contributions to the fundamental presuppositions of the new morality. Freud, taking his cue from Charcot, under whom he studied in France, adopted and popularized views of human difficulties under a Medical Model.[2] Prior to this time, "mentally ill" persons were viewed as malingerers rather than as patients. This Medical Model has been widely spread in recent times largely by propaganda using the mirror words "mental illness" and "mental health." This model has been disseminated so successfully that most people in our society naively believe that the root causes of the difficulties to which psychiatrists address themselves are diseases and sicknesses.

Harry Milt, Director of Public Information for the National Association for Mental Health, in a pamphlet entitled "How to Deal With Mental Problems," provides a typical sample of this sort of propaganda when he says, "Sympathetic understanding, the kind you give to a person when he is sick with a

---

[1]*Ibid.,* p. 5.

[2]Cf. Thomas Szasz, *The Myth of Mental Illness* (N. Y.: Dell, 1960).

physical illness" is what the mentally ill person must have. He continues:

> You make allowances because you know he's sick, that he can't help his sickness, that he needs your sympathy and understanding. The person with a mental problem is also sick and most of the time he can't help it either.[1]

Milt's idea is that there is no more reason to be ashamed of mental illness than to be ashamed of chicken pox or measles.

The extent to which the Freudian ethic has permeated contemporary thinking may be seen in its influence upon thought about crime. Some blamed Dallas rather than Oswald for President John F. Kennedy's death. When Charles Whitman from a tower in Texas picked off innocent passersby with a rifle, many said that society must be held guilty for the act. When a Jordanian immigrant assasinated Senator Robert F. Kennedy, the television was filled with indictments of the American public. The murderer himself is no longer held responsible. "He couldn't help it" has become a very popular phrase since Freud. Richard T. LaPiere charges:

> Psychiatrists have been trying . . . to dull, if not actually extract, the teeth of the law—and this is on the distinctively Freudian assumption that it is entirely natural for the criminal to act as he does and quite unreasonable for society to make him stand trial for being his antisocial self.[2]

The idea of sickness as the cause of personal problems vitiates all notions of human responsibility. This is the crux of the matter. People no longer consider themselves responsible for what they do wrong. They claim that their problems are *allogenic* (other-engendered) rather than *autogenic* (self-engendered). Instead of assuming personal responsibility for

---

[1] 1960, pp. 2, 3.

[2] *Psychiatry and Responsibility* (Princeton: Van Nostrand Press, 1962), p. 80.

6

their behavior, they blame society.[1] Society is easy to blame since what is everyone's responsibility is no-one's responsibility. But even society is now being let off the hook: ours is a "sick society," people say. Others specifically blame grandmother, mother, the church, a school teacher or some other particular individual for their actions. Freudian psychoanalysis turns out to be an archeological expedition back into the past in which a search is made for others on whom to pin the blame for the patient's behavior. The fundamental idea is to find out how others have wronged him. In seeking to excuse and shift blame, psychoanalysis is itself an extension of the problem it pretends to solve. It should not be difficult to see how irresponsibility is the upshot of such an emphasis and how many of the domestic and world-wide problems we face in our time are directly related to it. D. Elton Trueblood's indictment does not seem too strong: "The entire basis of human responsibility is undermined.[2]

As the natural outworking of this emphasis, to cite but one consequence, parental discipline has broken down. Richard T. LaPiere wrote that Karen Horney's

> concept of the need for *security* has become central in the thinking of clinical and child psychologists. . . . Her individual is by nature an exceedingly delicate organism. . . . Unless his society treats him with the utmost consideration, his sense of security is jeopardized . . . and he becomes neurotic.[3]

Parents are afraid that if indeed events in one's past may cause

---

[1]Wayne Oates, for example, says that "Mental illness" is the result of "the rejection and exploitation of the individual by the community," in *Baker's Dictionary of Practical Theology* (Grand Rapids: Baker's Book House, 1961), p. 303.

[2]LaPiere, *op. cit.*, p. 25.

[3]*Ibid.*, p. 77.

future psychological difficulties, they may injure the lives of their children by possible traumatic shocks experienced in the application of disciplinary methods. Thus the scriptural injunctions of Proverbs about corporal punishment (19:18; 23:13; 22:15; 13:24; 22:6; 23:14; 29:15, 17) largely have been abandoned.[1] Dewey's permissive emphasis, according to which the present generation was educated, fits neatly into this Freudian package.

There is another evil which stems from the Medical Model. Disease and sickness are often mysterious, especially to the layman. Disease comes from without and serious illnesses must be cured from without—by another—the expert. The sick person feels helpless, and so he turns to the physician. The physician, like the disease which invaded the patient, solves the problem *from without.*[2] Thus again, personal helplessness, hopelessness and irresponsibility are the natural results of the Medical Model. If a person's problems in living are basically problems of disease and sickness rather than problems of behavior, he has no hope unless there is medicine or therapy which can be applied to his case. Since there is no medical cure for people in such trouble, they move from despair to deeper despair.

The ethical chaos and helplessness which has resulted is seen even in the humor of our time. A modern folk song by

---

[1]It is interesting that God reassures reluctant parents that corporal punishment, properly administered, will not harm the child (Proverbs 23:13). As a matter of fact, spanking is a more humane punishment than many other more prolonged punishments which border on being more like torture than punishment.

[2]A recent study by Allport and Plos showed that the language of psychiatry had five times as many terms implying passivity and being acted upon as it had terms implying action (G. W. Allport, "The Open System in Personality Theory," *Journal of Abnormal and Social Psychology,* November 1960, pp. 301-310). The passive helplessness characteristic of psychiatric theory and practice, clearly consonant with the Medical Model, leads to hopelessness as well.

Anna Russell, for example, characterizes the period in which we live (note especially the last two lines):

> I went to my psychiatrist to be psychoanalyzed
> To find out why I killed the cat and blacked my
>   husband's eyes.
> He laid me on a downy couch to see what he could find,
> And here is what he dredged up from my subconscious
>   mind:
> When I was one, my mommie hid my dolly in a trunk,
> And so it follows naturally that I am always drunk.
> When I was two, I saw my father kiss the maid one day,
> And that is why I suffer now from kleptomania.
> At three, I had the feeling of ambivalence toward my
>   brothers,
> And so it follows naturally I poison all my lovers.
> But I am happy; now I've learned the lesson this has
>   taught;
> That everything I do that's wrong is someone else's
>   fault.[1]

Thomas S. Szasz made the following trenchant observation:

> To argue that all men, even those labeled "paranoid" should be treated seriously, as responsible human beings, is like desecrating the psychiatric flag. It flies in the face of one of the major tenets of psychiatry as a social institution, namely, that the actions of some so-called mentally ill persons need not be taken seriously—in the sense of their being held responsible for what they do.[2]

---

[1] The victim motif is common. Sylling recently wrote: "Most unwed mothers are victims of their parents' problems." This strange, unbiblical assumption leads him to conclude that "the sexual involvement on the part of the girl is almost incidental." Her real problem, he thinks, is not sin, but basic needs and desires which her parents have failed to meet in healthier ways. (In *Baker's Dictionary of Practical Theology*, Grand Rapids: Baker Book House, 1961, p. 234.)

[2] *Psychiatry and Responsibility* (Princeton: Van Nostrand Press,

No wonder then, that *Look* magazine, in a 21-page spread, called psychiatry "the troubled science."[1]

Recently (1965) the writer attended a Mental Health Institute for pastors. One participant was the chaplain from a state mental hospital. A summary of his address is as follows: "First of all, there is little you can do as ministers for people in a mental hospital. Secondly, what you can do is support the patient's right to feel injured by others. Thirdly, it is important to understand that in a mental institution people with guilt no longer are subjected to rebuke from others outside, the pressure is off, and in this way they quietly lose their guilt and get well. Fourthly, we must consider people in mental hospitals not as violators of conscience but as victims of their conscience. Finally, when we look at their erratic behavior, it seems to be sin, but it isn't; the patient is not really responsible for his actions. He can't help what he's doing; he's sick. Often he blames himself for what he can't help, for what isn't his fault, and this is a cause of his problems. Consequently bad behavior as blameworthy is taboo in a mental hospital. The usual religious approach of responsibility, guilt, confession and forgiveness is no good here. The patients' consciences are already too severe. These people are morally neutral persons, and all we can do is be ventilators for them."[2] This ver-

---

1962), p. 3. The allogenic view leads to a general degrading of the human personality. Man is viewed as an irresponsible pawn. The psychiatric treatment offered clearly grows out of the presupposition. Its manipulative mechanistic orientation reveals the unscriptural anthropology which denies the image of God (distorted but inherent) in man.

[1] *Look* magazine, February 2, 1960.

[2] The sheer determinism of this viewpoint, with its inevitable consequence, excusing the counselee for his behavior, is apparent. Lawrence LeShan says that this philosophy has led to "the therapist's attempts to excuse the patient's negative and undesirable behavior on the ground that it was determined by the past and so he had no reason to feel guilty about it" (Lawrence LeShan, "Changing Trends in Psychoanalytically Oriented Psychotherapy," *Mental Hygiene,* July 1962, pp. 454-463).

batim summary of the chaplain's speech, about as succinctly as any other, sets forth the institutionalized view of our time. Every point he made will be challenged in this book.

## Freudian Theory and Therapy

How has all this come about? What is its base? The answer lies in the fundamentals of Freudian theory and therapy. Freud saw the human being as torn within. Man, he said, has basic primitive wants, impulses or drives which seek expression. These Freud called the Id (sex and aggression). But in man, there is also the Superego (roughly equivalent to what more often has been called the conscience). The Superego is socialized into the individual by his parents, the church, teachers, etc. The Superego is the culprit in the Freudian system. According to Freud, the problem with the mentally ill is an over-socialization of the Superego. An oversocialized conscience is overly severe and overly strict. The mentally ill are victims of the Superego. The Ego, the third unit in man, is the arbiter, or the conscious self. A conflict arises when the Id desires to be expressed but is frustrated by the Superego. The primitive wants seek expression, but the overly severe Superego standing at the threshold hinders the Id from expressing itself in the conscious life of the individual. This battle which takes place on the subconscious level, is the source of one's difficulties. The Ego operates on a level quite different from that of the Id or Superego. The Ego functions on the level of responsibility, whereas the Id and Superego function on the level of irresponsibility. When the Id is repressed by the Superego, the person in conflict experiences what Freud called "guilt feelings." Guilt feelings, however, are not feelings that stem from real guilt. Since his feeling of guilt is false, one does not need to confess his sin, as the chaplain pointed out, but rather what he needs to do is to rid himself of falsehood. So, naturally enough, therapy consists of making one feel right by dispelling false guilt. The therapist achieves this by taking a stand with the Id against the Superego. He seeks to weaken,

dilute and defeat the Superego so that it stops making its vic-
timizing demands. Ventilation (an airing of one's pent-up feelings) is part of the process. Resocialization according to rea-
sonable and realistic standards is the other crucial part.

Albert Ellis' therapy clearly represents one modern application of these principles. In the A. A. P. Tape Library, Volume
No. 1, entitled "Loretta," Ellis climaxes an interview with a
strong attack upon Loretta's conscience. He threatens that
she will never be released from treatment until she does away
with her moral values. Listen to the following excerpts:

> Your problem actually is the fact that you have a lot of
> what I call "shoulds," "oughts," and "musts." ... The main
> issue—as I said before—in my estimation, is that you set up
> a lot of "shoulds," "oughts," and "musts" which unfortu-
> nately you were taught when you were very young. You
> were taught these by your father, your mother, your church
> ... But if you didn't have this concept of ought which un-
> fortunately is nicely defeating your own ends, then you
> wouldn't believe this—you wouldn't be disturbed.

After an objection by Loretta to this attack, Ellis tells her:

> Well, you're fully entitled to your views, but unfortu-
> nately as long as you maintain them you're going to sit in
> this mental hospital—now when you change your views
> you're going to get out.

Loretta, still staunchly objecting, triumphantly replies: "Well,
as long as we have air conditioning it might not be so bad."

After reading this barrage upon the client's value system,
one wonders at the incredible naivete with which one conservative Christian blissfully writes: "The pastor provides the
Christian comfort and the psychiatrist provides the needed
therapy and neither conflicts with the other."[1] Such com-

---

[1]Wesley W. Nelson, in *Baker's Dictionary of Practical Theology*,
p. 300. Cf. also Frieda Fromm-Reichmann: "It also makes it at times
possible for the patient to use the psychoanalyst as his new conscience

12

partmentalizing of roles is not an isolated phenomenon. C. Clifford McLaughlan wrote:

> It could be said that psychiatry looks to the past and tries to seek out and undo the mistakes and problems of the past. Religion looks to the future, points to what can be, after the mistakes and problems of the past have been sought out and been undone.[1]

And E. Mansell Pattison confidently asserts:

> . . . the religious beliefs of the therapist and patient are not the crucial factors in psychotherapy, but rather how the therapist handles his own and his patient's beliefs.[2]

In *Baker's Dictionary of Practical Theology,* which contains one of the latest compilations of conservative essays, one frequently (though not exclusively) encounters such bifurcating. The minister is thought to be limited in his training, abilities and tools, and must defer and refer to the psychiatrist. In short, he is not considered competent to counsel. The question never seems to be asked: is psychiatry a valid discipline?[3]

---

while revising his own moral standards which have interfered." (Patrick Mullohy, ed., *Interpersonal Relations,* New York: Science House, 1967, p. 125.)

[1] C. Clifford McLaughlan, *The Pastoral Counselor,* Spring 1964, p. 26.

[2] E. M. Pattison, "Psychiatry," in *Christianity and the World of Thought,* Hudson T. Armerding, ed. (Chicago: Moody Press, 1968), p. 343.

[3] One of the purposes of this book is to show that psychiatry (not psychology) is a usurpation of the work of the Christian minister. Psychiatrists do not operate as physicians. Their goal is personality and behavior change, and their method is value alteration. This usurpation has been achieved by declaring a host of people "sick" who are not, and thus taking them under the pale of medicine. Freud himself anticipated this usurpation of the minister's work. He wrote to Pfister about the "enormous number of adults who are not ill in the medical sense, but are nevertheless in extreme need of analysis" and predicted that "the cure of souls (the term used for pastoral care) will one day be a recognized non-ecclesiastical and even non-religious calling" (*Psychoanalysis*

If Freud's view were correct, namely, that trouble arises whenever the Id has been repressed by an overstrict conscience or Superego, then really our day ought to be a day of widespread mental health rather than a day of unparalleled numbers of personal problems, for ours is not a day of repression, but of permissiveness. If there was ever a time in which the lid was off, in which there was wide open rebellion against authority and responsibility, ours is that day. And yet unprecedented numbers are in trouble. If Freudianism is true, the most immoral people, or at best the most amoral people, should be the healthiest, whereas in fact the opposite is true. People in mental institutions and people who come to counseling invariably are people with great moral difficulties. "Moral difficulties" does not always mean sexual violations; that is only one aspect of it. Immorality of every sort, irresponsibility toward God and man (i.e., the breaking of God's commandments) is found most prominently among people with personal problems.

## The Revolution in Psychology

But a revolution has been brewing which largely is still restricted to the field of psychology. There is a growing number of young, vigorous individuals who have begun to challenge the traditional Freudian and Rogerian ideas. Some of the names in this movement are Steve Pratt, William Glasser, G. L. Harrington, William Mainord, Perry London and O. Hobart Mowrer.[1] The latter is the unofficial dean of the movement.

---

*and Faith, op. cit.,* p. 104). Thus, the institution of the Medical Model became the means of usurpation. Cf. Ronald Leifer, *In the Name of Mental Health* (New York: Science House, 1969), p. 167: "The ethnicizing psychotherapist is thus a functional equivalent of and replacement for the traditional extended family structure, the casuist, and the spiritual guide."

[1] There are, of course, many differences among them. For a concise statement of some of the more significant similarities and differences

The essence of the attack by this movement upon the institutionalized system may be summed up in a word: the new movement is antithetically opposed to the Freudian irresponsibility formulation. Mowrer asks, in effect, shall we replace the Medical Model with a Moral Model? Thomas Szasz, in his book *The Myth of Mental Illness,* answers affirmatively. In the tradition of Harry Stack Sullivan, Szasz styles his psychiatry "a theory of personal conduct." Advocates of the revolution press the issue: Shall we still speak about the repressed Id? They reply, no. Instead, they declare, it is time to talk about a suppressed Superego (conscience). They continue: Shall we seek to remove guilt feelings (that is, false guilt)? Never; instead we must acknowledge guilt to be real and deal directly with it. Psychological guilt is the fear of being found out. It is the recognition that one has violated his standards. It is the pain of not having done as one knows he ought to do.[1] Further, they insist that ventilation of feelings must be replaced by confession of wrong doing. No longer will they speak of

---

between Mowrer, Glasser and Szasz, cf. Glen A. Holland, "Three Psychotherapies Compared and Evaluated" (*The Dis-Coverer,* Urbana; Volume 3, No. 3, May 1966).

[1] "Guilt feelings" are thought of as false guilt by Freudians; i.e., guilt over the id/superego conflict rather than the violation of one's standards. A typical query at this point is, "How could Sue be guilty for wearing lipstick?" She could, if Sue had come from a home where she had been taught that wearing lipstick was sin. Now, if in college she has begun to wear lipstick in order not to look peculiar, but is doing so against her standards, she will be guilty of sin, and her guilt will be real. Even if wearing lipstick is not sinful in itself, Sue's act is sinful because it did not proceed "from faith" (Romans 14:21-23). When Sue used lipstick she thought her act was (or might have been) a sin against God, and yet she did it anyway. It is this rebellion against God for which she is guilty and about which her conscience rightly condemns her. Sue must confess her sin to find forgiveness and relief, and must not be told that her guilt is false. Later, if it is important to do so, the matter of whether Sue' standard is biblical may be discussed; but these are two distinct questions. Yet they have been confused consistently.

emotional problems, but rather of behavioral problems. They say the term "mental illness" must be replaced by words that indicate irresponsible behavior. People who were formerly thought to have withdrawn from reality are now viewed as seeking to avoid detection. The revolutionists naturally refuse to side with the *wants,* but rather make every attempt to side with the *oughts.*

The new movement cannot be set aside lightly. "Therapy" (the word is inconsistently retained by most of them) conducted by those who espouse the new view has been dramatically successful in contrast to Freudian failures. G. L. Harrington, in a V. A. hospital in Los Angeles, for example, worked with 210 male patients in Building 206. Building 206 was the end of the line. All hope for these men had been given up. Many could not even take care of their most elemental needs. Previously there had been an average of only two releases from Building 206 each year, but after the first year of Harrington's responsibility program, 75 men were released from the hospital, and the next year he predicted that 200 would be released—that is, almost a complete turnover. Glasser, in the Ventura State School for Girls in California, showed an 80 per cent success with hardened sociopaths in a structured total responsibility program. By success, Glasser means no return and no future violations of the law.[1] This writer was able to view at first hand the quick and dramatic results of Mowrer's program in Illinois.

### Freud an Enemy, Not a Friend

Freud hung out his shingle on Easter Sunday. For someone to whom every action had significance, however covert or inconsequential it may seem to be, surely such an overt act must be viewed as symbolical. That Freud thought little of religion in general and less of Christianity in particular is an historical

---

[1] Cf. William Glasser, *Reality Therapy, op. cit.*

fact. He called himself "a completely godless Jew" and a "hopeless pagan."[1] When he was a child, some supposed Christians pushed his father around and muddied his clothes. The elder man did not retaliate. Freud was ashamed and thought his father should have fought back. He vowed that some day he would get even.[2] In the eyes of some, psychoanalysis was the weapon he used.

Freud's *Moses and Monotheism, The Future of an Illusion,* and *Totem and Taboo* are books in which he gives religion a hard time. For him, Christianity was an illusion that had to be dispelled. Like all other religions, it was a sign of neurosis. Religion, he taught, was born out of the fear of the great untamed universe surrounding primitive man. At first there was no such thing as moral scruples. But since every man wanted to follow his own wishes (instinct), he clashed with others trying to do the same. In order to survive, men found it necessary to live and work together. Thus morality was the outcome of the growth of society, which could exist only by adopting codes of conduct. Conscience (the Superego) was built up because violations of the code were punished severely by the crowd. Eventually the code was said to be sanctioned by a god (or gods), thus raising the moral code in stature. Religion belongs to the infancy of the race. Man needs to grow up out of infancy, and that means out of religion. He calls the biblical accounts "fairy tales." Religion was invented, he claimed, to fulfill man's needs. When one comes of age, he no longer needs religion. Before adopting Freudian principles, Christians should know these basic Freudian presuppositions which underlie all he wrote.

One possible objection that might be made is that those

---

[1] Heinrich Meng and Ernst Freud, eds., *Psychoanalysis and Faith* (New York: Basic Books, Inc, 1963), pp. 63, 110.

[2] Wayne E. Oates, *What Psychology Says About Religion* (New York: Association Press, 1958), p. 31.

who argue against Freud have set up a new straw man, namely, Freud himself. In place of society, or particular members of society, Freud has now become the bad boy who gets the whipping. If this is so, the client again may shift responsibility from himself. The attack against Freud may seem to make him the cause of all the ills of modern society. But nothing more than an apparent similarity exists. No one says that Freud or his beliefs have caused sickness in the patient. All that can be said of Freud is that his views have encouraged irresponsible people to persist in and expand their irresponsibility. He has sanctioned irresponsible behavior and made it respectable. His views are iatrogenic (or treatment-engendering) only in that they can cause secondary complications.[1] Freud has not made people irresponsible; but he has provided a philosophical and pseudoscientific rationale for irresponsible people to use to justify themselves. Freud is a cause of the ills in modern society only as a complicating factor and not as a basic cause of those ills. The ultimate cause is sin.

## Where Does This Leave Us?

All this is pertinent to Christians. Mowrer asks, "Has Evangelical religion sold its birthright for a mess of psychological pottage?"[2] The question is a penetrating one. Every conservative counselor must consider Mowrer's question to be an implied challenge. Nearly all recent counseling books for ministers, even conservative ones, are written from the Freudian per-

---

[1]In an interesting tongue-in-cheek article entitled "Parnassian Psychiatry," Jay Silber divides current psychiatric systems into three types: lyric, epic and narrative. Lyric psychiatry, which he dubs the most "fertile" form today, has as its great task the creation of "problems, conflicts and intensities that had never before been fully realized by the patient" who otherwise might find it necessary to continue indefinitely in a boring routine existence. This is an interesting twist on the iatrogenic theme, which bears serious consideration. (Jay Silber, *Medical Opinion and Review,* August 1969, p. 61.)

[2]*Crisis, op. cit.,* p. 60.

spective in the sense that they rest largely upon the presuppositions of the Freudian ethic of non-responsibility. Where these are followed, the use of Freudian principles by ministers has served to perpetuate existing hostilities and resentments and has tended to broaden communication gaps by encouraging counselees to place blame upon others. Mental health institutes are conducted in order to persuade ministers that they cannot (more often the wording is "dare not") help the "mentally ill." The big words at such conferences are "defer" and "refer."[1] Christian school teachers feel helpless, fearing to discipline their students lest they injure them psychologically. So they tend to rely on specialists, both within and outside the system, without recognizing that in their classrooms they have one of the finest opportunities for counseling available—the daily contact affording nearly ideal conditions for change and growth. This book strikes an entirely new note, a note which is long overdue. Rather than defer and refer to psychiatrists steeped in their humanistic dogma, ministers of the gospel and other Christian workers who have been called by God to help his people out of their distress, will be encouraged to reassume their privileges and responsibilities. Shall they defer and refer? Only as an exception, never as the rule, and then only to other more competent Christian workers. Their task is to *confer.* The thesis of this book is that qualified Christian counselors properly trained in the Scriptures are competent to counsel—more competent than psychiatrists or anyone else.

Leo Steiner in November of 1958, speaking at Harvard, made this statement:

> The ministry makes a tremendous mistake when it swaps what it has for psychoanalytic dressing. . . . Where will psy-

---

[1]Wiesbauer writes, *"The main concern of any clergyman must be to see to it that the mentally ill get psychiatric help as soon as possible.'* Henry H. Wiesbauer, *Pastoral Help In Serious Mental Illness* (New York: The National Association for Mental Health, n. d.), p. 3.

choanalysis be even 25 years from now? . . . I predict it will take its place along with phrenology and mesmerism.[1]

The real issue for the minister is referral. At this point he cannot dodge the question. He must ask himself, shall I refer my parishioner to a psychiatrist or a mental institution, or can I do something for him?[2] In view of these recent changes, he must reevaluate the propaganda of the last generation and ask anew, "How much can I do?" But in order to answer that question, it is necessary for him to come to some conclusions about the true nature of the problems of the so-called "mentally ill." The question must be considered from a biblical perspective, beginning with scriptural presuppositions, refusing to baptize Freud (or Mowrer, for that matter). Such a consideration reveals that the central issue boils down to a discussion of the question: Is the fundamental problem of persons who come for personal counseling sickness or sin?[3] To that question the third chapter is addressed. But first, a crucial preliminary matter must be considered.

---

[1] "Are Psychoanalysis and Religious Counseling Compatible?" (Paper read to Society for the Scientific Study of Religion, Harvard University).

[2] Referral of any sort ought to be considered by a minister only as a last resort. The fact that a counselee has sought out a Christian counselor should itself be considered of some significance. He may have selected him as a counselor precisely because he is aware of his sin and need of forgiveness. The clergy began their concessions to psychoanalysis early. A close friend of Freud, Oskar Pfister, who was a liberal minister, typifies the capitulation that has generally taken place during the last fifty years. Cf. Heinrich Meng and Ernst L. Freud (eds.), *Psychoanalysis and Faith* (New York: Basic Books, Inc., 1963).

[3] The issue here is whether the non-medical complaints of counselees are *allogenic* (engendered by others) or *autogenic* (self-engendered).

## Chapter II

## THE HOLY SPIRIT AND COUNSELING

### Counseling Is the Work of the Spirit

Counseling is the work of the Holy Spirit. Effective counseling cannot be done apart from him. He is called the paraclete[1] ("counselor") who in Christ's place came to be another counselor[2] of the same sort that Christ had been to his disciples.[3] Because unsaved counselors do not know the Holy Spirit, they ignore his counseling activity and fail to avail themselves of his direction and power.

Counseling, to be Christian, must be carried on in harmony with the regenerating and sanctifying work of the Spirit. The Holy Spirit is called "Holy" because of his nature and his work. All holiness stems from his activity in human lives. All of the personality traits that might be held forth to counselees as fundamental goals for growth (love, joy, peace, patience, kindness, goodness, faithfulness, gentleness, self-control) God declares to be the "fruit" (i.e., the result of the work) of the Spirit. Not only is it futile to attempt to generate these qualities apart from him (as non-Christian and even some Christian counselors try to do), but such an approach is at bottom rebellion against God grounded upon humanistic assumptions of man's autonomy. By-passing the Spirit amounts to the denial of human depravity and the affirmation of man's innate goodness. The need for grace and the atoning work of Christ are both undercut, and the counselee is left instead with the husk of a legalistic works-righteousness which will lead ulti-

---

[1]John 14:16,17.

[2]The Greek word means "another of the same kind."

[3]In Isaiah 9:6, Christ, too, is called "Counselor." His words in John 14 (see previous footnote) indicate that he considered himself to be a counselor of his disciples.

mately to despair since it divests itself of the life and power of the Spirit.

## How Does the Holy Spirit Work in Counseling?

The Holy Spirit is the source of all genuine personality changes that involve the sanctification[1] of the believer, just as truly as he alone is the One who brings life to the dead sinner. It is time that Christian ministers and other counselors asked again, "Who has bewitched you . . . Having begun by the Spirit, are you now being perfected by the flesh?"[2] Why are Christians without peace turning to men who themselves know nothing of the "peace of God that passes all understanding"? How is it that Christian ministers refer parishioners who lack self-control to a psychiatrist who has never been able to discover the secret of self-control in his own life? Outwardly he may appear calm and assured, mature, patient and even suave. Can this be his actual inward condition if he does not know Jesus Christ?[3] Can he have this fruit of the Spirit apart from the Spirit?

## The Holy Spirit Works through Means

The Holy Spirit ordinarily effects his characterological work in the lives of believers through the means of grace. He uses the ministry of the Word, the sacraments, prayer and the fellowship of God's people as the principal vehicles through

---

[1] Growth away from sin and toward righteousness. In II Corinthians 3:18 Paul wrote of the growing change in which believers are being transformed into the likeness of Christ, and concluded: "for this comes from the Lord who is the Spirit."

[2] Galatians 3:1, 3.

[3] The suicide rate is significantly higher among psychiatrists than among those of any of the other sixteen specialty groups listed by the American Medical Association as a part of the medical profession. (*Bulletin of Suicidology,* December 1968, Washington: U. S. Government Printing House, p. 5.)

which he brings about such changes. How can counseling that is removed from the means of grace expect to effect the permanent changes that come only by growth in grace?

The inconsistency and tension of this problem is felt by nearly every conservative minister at some time or another. But fear and uncertainty (growing out of mental health propaganda), frustration (at not knowing how to handle complex problems), or simple acquiescence in referral as an easy way out, often win out. It is time to reexamine our stance as Christians, and the most important factor in that reexamination should be an honest consideration of the place of the Holy Spirit in counseling.

## The Holy Spirit's Work Is Sovereign

The Holy Spirit is a Person, not a force or a law. While he always works according to and in complete harmony with his will as he has revealed it in Scripture, he chooses his own times, means and occasions for doing his work. That is to say, the Holy Spirit works when and where and how he pleases. The Holy Spirit is God with us. Counselors and counselees alike must respect the sovereignty of the Holy Spirit. Expectations of clients and promises made by counselors must all be carefully qualified by this important dimension of the counseling situation. This fact should not discourage counseling, but rather should encourage the counselor since he knows that his work does not depend ultimately upon his own abilities.

But the counselor's abilities (gifts of the Spirit exercised under the Spirit's calling and direction), like the preaching gifts of the minister, should be a matter of concern to him. He cannot be sloppy about the way in which he counsels, expecting the Holy Spirit to do his work regardless of how the counselor does his. Chiefly the Holy Spirit works in conjunction with the proper exercise of the gifts he has given (although, of course, he is not bound to do so). This is because he has chosen to work through human agency, a fact which he has clearly demonstrated by giving gifts of ministry to his church.[1] The Spirit does not foolishly give gifts that he does not intend to use. The use of human agency in counseling, then, does not in itself bypass the work of the Spirit; to the contrary, it is the principal and ordinary means by which he works. But, as Paul says in Galatians 3, human activity which neither acknowledges nor draws upon the power of the Holy Spirit, rebelliously seeks to circumvent the Spirit and is thereby devoid of the power to effect what can only be brought about by the Spirit.

### The Holy Spirit Works by Means of His Word

The Holy Spirit expects counselors to use his Word, the Holy Scriptures. We shall see *infra* that he gave it for such a purpose, and that it is powerful when used for that purpose (II Timothy 3:16, 17). His counseling work is ordinarily performed through the ministry of this Word. In this chapter it is unnecessary to reexamine all of the biblical passages by which this relationship of the Spirit to the Word may be established, since that has been done frequently in books on systematic theology and treatises specifically relating to the work of the Holy Spirit. But it will be necessary to study the Scriptures to see what the Holy Spirit has told us about counseling, for this has not been done satisfactorily.

A further word, however, should be said about the Spirit's use of the Scriptures. To be led by the Spirit (Galatians 5:18), for instance, should be understood not as being led apart from, but rather by means of the Scriptures.[2] The word "led" does not refer to inner feelings or hunches, or to visions or extra-biblical revelations. The point that needs to be made is that since the Holy Spirit employs his Word as the principal

---

[1] Cf. Ephesians 4:7-13.

[2] The Holy Spirit is the one who enlightens believers as they read the Bible. In I Corinthians 2, Paul clearly states that men cannot understand the things of God apart from the Spirit's work.

means by which Christians may grow in sanctification, counseling cannot be effective (in any biblical sense of that term) apart from the use of the Scriptures. The fact of the Holy Spirit in counseling, therefore, implies the presence of the Holy Scriptures as well.[1] This fundamental relationship in itself should be decisive for any Christian who carefully thinks through the counseling situation. Counseling without the Scriptures can only be expected to be counseling without the Holy Spirit.

Frequent references to the place of the Holy Spirit in counseling will be made specifically throughout this book, but wherever his work has not been spelled out in detail, it is everywhere assumed. Since concrete methodology in counseling will often be discussed at length, it might be possible to dip into portions of the book and get the impression that the Holy Spirit has been supplanted by human techniques. But it is precisely this disjunction which is false. When the Holy Spirit moved directly in the hearts of believers at Jerusalem to motivate them by love to pool their goods for the sake of the poor, he was no more at work than when Paul organized and conducted a successful fund raising campaign throughout the Mediterranean world for the same purpose. Methodology and technique, skill and the exercise of gifts are all consonant with the work of the Spirit. What makes the difference is one's attitude and inner motivation: does he do what he does in reliance upon his own efforts, in dependence upon methods and techniques, or does he acknowledge his own inability and ask the Spirit to use his gifts and methods? Gifts, methodology and technique, of course, may be abused; they may be set over against the Spirit and may be used to replace his work.

---

[1] Note, for instance, the following verses: Romans 15:13; 15:4. "Hope" and "encouragement" (King James, "comfort," the word *paraclesis* could be translated "counsel") are said equally to come from the Scriptures and from the Holy Spirit. It is obvious that both are true, since the Holy Spirit uses the Scriptures to bring hope.

But they also may be used in complete subjection to him to the glory of God and the benefit of his children. Davison has well stated this point when he rightly warns against the attempt to secure a spiritual end by the adoption of habits, the multiplication of rules, and the observance of external standards, excellent in themselves, but useful only as means subordinate to the Spirit.[1]

---

[1]W. T. Davison, *The Indwelling Spirit* (New York: Hodder and Stoughton, 1911), pp. 167, 168.

*Chapter III*

## WHAT IS WRONG WITH THE "MENTALLY ILL"?

*Time Magazine* most vividly told the story of "The Revolt of Leo Held":[1]

There was almost nothing in Leo Held's life that could have presaged the end of it. Held, 40, a burly (6-foot, 200 pounds), balding lab technician at Lockhaven, Pennsylvania, paper mill, had been a School Board member, Boy Scout leader, secretary of a Fire Brigade, church-goer, and affectionate father. Certainly he bickered occasionally with his neighbors, drove too aggressively over the hilly highways between his Loganton home and the mill, and sometimes fretted about the job that he held for 19 years. But to most of his neighbors and co-workers he was a paragon of a responsible, respectable citizen. That image was shattered in a well-planned hour of bloodshed last week when Held decided to mount a one-man revolt against the world he feared and resented. After seeing his wife off to work and their children to school, Held, a proficient marksman, pocketed two pistols, a .45 automatic and a Smith and Weston .38 and drove his station wagon to the mill. Parking carefully, he gripped a gun in each fist and stalked into the plant. And he started shooting with a calculated frenzy that filled his fellow-worker victims with two and three bullets apiece, at least 30 shots in all . . . A hastily formed posse found him in his doorway armed and snarling defiance, "Come and get me; I'm not taking any more of their bull." . . . Puzzled officials discovered a tenuous chain of logic behind his actions. Mrs. Ram had quit a car pool, complaining of Held's driving; many victims at the paper plant were in authority over him or had been promoted while he had

---

[1] November 3, 1967.

26

not. Held . . . had feuded over smoke from burning leaves. . . . Held's stolid surface had massed truculent resentment and rage. . . . Another neighbor . . . told of a spat over a fallen tree limb that so enraged Held he beat the 71-year-old widow with a branch. She took him to court on assault and battery charges, but the magistrate threw out her case and Held's cross complaint. If the jurist "had thought a little more carefully" said Mrs. Knisely, and had seen that "here was a man who was sick and had sent him to a psychiatrist, this thing could have been prevented."

The question is, was Held really sick? Was Mrs. Knisely right? Wittingly or unwittingly, *Time* answers that question. The caption under a picture of the prostrate wounded killer runs, "responsible, respectable—and resentful." *Time* put its finger directly on the real issue. Held was not sick; he was resentful. Yet, it is a significant sign of the nearly total acceptance of the mental illness propaganda that Mrs. Knisely's first thought was, "He's sick and needs a psychiatrist." Held's true condition was recorded long ago in Proverbs 26:23-26, which describes people who harbor grudges, resentments and bitterness in their hearts. For a long while Held was able to cover the resentment with an outer gloss of tranquility and graciousness. But finally the resentment burst through. Consider these words: "Like the glaze covering an earthen vessel are smooth lips with an evil heart. . ." Outwardly Held seemed respectable; outwardly he appeared responsible; but inwardly his heart seethed with hatred. Held spoke to his Scout troop with "smooth lips." At church and as a member of the Fire Brigade he paraded in a glaze of respectability. But Proverbs says,

> He who hates dissembles with his lips and harbors deceit in his heart. When he speaks graciously believe him not for there are seven abominations in his heart.

Proverbs says that anger, hatred, resentment and bitterness bottled up within give rise to a half dozen other problems: "There are seven abominations in his heart." When resentment at last grew to the boiling point Held decided that he would kill everyone who, in his judgment, had wronged him. The passage in Proverbs concludes with the warning that although for a time hatred can be covered over, at length it "will be exposed in the assembly." That is, all the feelings and the attitudes down underneath will be revealed. In exactly that way Held eventually spouted forth his hatred in one dramatic public revelation of what he was really like. Not everyone, of course, reveals his inner resentments in precisely the same way.

## Mental Illness: A Misnomer

The case of Leo Held illustrates why growing numbers of authorities have begun to object to the concept of "mental illness," and the vigorous propaganda campaign which has been conducted under that misleading misnomer. The fact is that the words "mental illness" are used quite ambiguously. Bockoven speaks, for instance, of "the indefinability of mental illness."[1] Organic malfunctions affecting the brain that are caused by brain damage, tumors, gene inheritance, glandular or chemical disorders, validly may be termed mental illnesses. But at the same time a vast number of other human problems have been classified as mental illnesses for which there is no evidence that they have been engendered by disease or illness at all. As a description of many of these problems, the term mental illness is nothing more than a figure of speech, and in most cases a poor one at that.[2]

---

[1]J. Sanborn Bockoven, "Community Psychiatry, A Growing Source of Social Confusion," *Psychiatry Digest,* March 1968, p. 51.

[2]Compare Thomas Szasz, *The Myth of Mental Illness* (New York: Dell, 1960). Yet the pastor is called upon to become a chief proponent of the mental health view; he is urged to "help both the family *and* the community at large to accept mental illness as sickness and not as a disgrace" (Archibald F. Ward and Granville L. Jones, *Ministering to Families of the Mentally Ill.* New York: The National Association for Mental Health, n.d., p. 4).

To put the issue simply: the Scriptures plainly speak of both organically based problems as well as those problems that stem from sinful attitudes and behavior; but where, in all of God's Word, is there so much as a trace of any third source of problems which might approximate the modern concept of "mental illness"? Clearly the burden of proof lies with those who loudly affirm the existence of mental illness or disease but fail to demonstrate biblically that it exists. Until such a demonstration is forthcoming, the only safe course to follow is to declare with all of Scripture that the genesis of such human problems is twofold, not threefold.

A certain amount of confusion has been occasioned by the fact that physical illnesses may have non-organic causes. For example, worry may cause ulcers; fear may lead to paralysis. These resultant disabilities are ordinarily called psychosomatic illnesses. Psychosomatic illnesses are genuine somatic (bodily) problems which are the direct result of inner psychical difficulty. But illness *caused by* psychological stress must be distinguished from illness *as the cause of* psychological stress.

## People with Personal Problems often Use Camouflage

What, then, is wrong with the "mentally ill"? Their problem is autogenic; it is in themselves. The fundamental bent of fallen human nature is away from God. Man is born in sin, goes astray "from his mother's womb speaking lies" (Psalm 58:3), and will therefore naturally (by nature) attempt various sinful dodges in an attempt to avoid facing up to his sin. He will fall into varying styles of sin according to the short term successes or failures of the particular sinful responses which he makes to life's problems. Apart from organically generated difficulties, the "mentally ill" are really *people with unsolved personal problems.*

There is a mounting conviction that much bizarre behavior

must be interpreted as camouflage intended to divert attention from one's otherwise deviate behavior.[1] The explanation of much behavior as coverup or camouflage runs something like this: bizarre behavior some time in the past (perhaps far back in the past) was rewarded positively when it succeeded in deflecting attention from one's deviant behavior.[2] Therefore, on succeeding occasions the client again attempted to hide behind bizarre actions and discovered that frequently this ruse worked. If this occurred frequently enough a pattern of such action was established. Bizarre behavior then became the natural (habitual) means to which he resorted whenever he sinned.

However, such behavior, though often successful at the outset (frequently enough to become a deeply etched pattern and thus the first resort when one does wrong) does not continue to work as successfully as it did in the past. As one grows out of childhood and into adolescence, for instance, he finds it more difficult to hide. Now he is expected to give rational explanations for his behavior. Rather than change, the habit-dominated person will endeavor to continue to resort to bizarre behavior as his solution. But repeated failures of recent attempts at length force him to make some change. Yet, even then, he changes not the nature of his response but its intensity. So in order to continue to cover up his behavior, his actions become more and more bizarre. If the pattern is not broken, his behavior eventually will become so deviant that in

---

[1]Cf. O. Hobart Mowrer, *Crisis,* pp. 81-102 (esp. pp. 83-91) where Mowrer sets forth Tim Wilkins' "Dick Tracy Theory of Schizophrenia." In this view, the counselor is thought of as Dick Tracy rather than Ben Casey. A recent illustration of this viewpoint is found in Walter C. Stolov's work at the University of Washington's hospital in the rehabilitation of patients with severe ambulatory problems. Cf. *Medical News,* Vol. 209, No. 10, September 8, 1969, p. 1442.

[2]Bizarre behavior of this sort must be viewed (like all other sinful behavior) as the product of a "deceitful heart" (cf. Jeremiah 17:9).

the end society will institutionalize him. In this way behavior can become totally unacceptable in a very short time.

In the long run the counselee finds that such behavior, even when it hides him from detection, is not really successful. Increasingly as his actions become more bizarre he finds that his behavior tends to isolate him. His social contacts are broken off, and the society which he needs so desperately drifts away from him as he hides from it. He knows he is living a lie, and his conscience triggers painful psychosomatic responses. So at last he becomes a very miserable person, externally isolated and alienated from others, and internally torn apart.

Steve was a young man of college age whom the writer met in a mental institution in Illinois. Steve had been diagnosed by psychiatrists as a catatonic schizophrenic. He did not talk, except minimally, and he shuffled about as though he were in a stupor. Upon sitting down, he became frozen in one or two positions. At first, communication with Steve seemed impossible. He simply refused to respond to questions or to any kind of verbal overtures. However, the counselors told Steve that they knew he understood fully what was going on, that though he might have fooled others—the psychiatrist, his parents, the school authorities—he was not going to fool them. They assured Steve that the sooner he began to communicate the sooner he'd be able to get out of the institution. Steve remained silent, but was allowed to continue as a part of the group observing the counseling of others. The next week the guns were turned on Steve, and for more than an hour the counselors worked with him. Steve began to break down. His hesitant replies gave evidence that he clearly understood everything. There was no reason to believe that he had withdrawn from reality.

As Steve began to respond, the rough outlines of his problem emerged. But the third week he broke down entirely. Steve had no mental disorders. Steve had no emotional problems. Nothing was wrong with his mind or his emotions. His problem was autogenic. Steve's problem was difficult but simple. He told us that because he had been spending all his time as prop man for a play rather than working at his college studies, he was about to receive a raft of pink slips at the mid-semester marking period. This meant that Steve was going to fail. Rather than face his parents and his friends as a failure, Steve camouflaged the real problem. He had begun acting bizarrely, and discovered that this threw everyone off track. He was thought to be in a mental stupor, out of touch with reality—mentally ill.

The truth was that Steve was hiding behind the guise of illness in much the same way that a grammar school child will feign illness when he doesn't want to take a test for which he has not prepared adequately. Steve had done this sort of thing many times before, but never quite so radically. At times he would go off by himself and grow quiet and still and become hard to communicate with, and at other times he would walk off down the road and wouldn't return for hours. Over the years Steve gradually had developed an avoidance pattern to which he resorted in unpleasant and stressful situations. When the college crisis arose he naturally (habitually) resorted to this pattern. Steve's problem was not mental illness, but guilt, shame, and fear.

As he spoke with the counselors, Steve recognized that they were asking him now to make the basic decision he had previously sought to avoid. Steve knew that now he must decide whether he was going to tell the truth to his parents and his friends and leave the mental institution, or whether he was going to continue the bluff. When we left, on the fifth week, Steve was still working on that decision. He was actually posing the question himself in these words: "Would it be better to continue the rest of my life this way, or to go home and face the music?"

In the process of working with Steve, it became clear that the more others treated Steve as if he were ill, the more guilty he felt. This was so because Steve knew that he was lying. It is important for counselors to remember that whenever clients camouflage, whenever they hide to avoid detection, whenever they purport to be ill when they are not, sick treatment only makes them worse. To act as if they may be excused for their condition is the most unkind thing one can do. Such an approach only compounds the problem.

When Steve was approached by those who held him responsible, he responded. For the first time since his commitment he gained some self-respect. Under those circumstances he began to talk about his condition. Contrary to much contemporary thought, it is not merciful to be nonjudgmental. To consider such counselees victims rather than violators of their conscience, to consider their behavior as neutral, or as not blameworthy only enlarges their lie and increases the load of guilt. Such treatment, Steve explained, had been for him sheer cruelty because of the compounded mental anguish and distress it engendered. Nothing hurt more, he said, than when his parents visited him and treated him kindly, like an innocent victim of circumstances.

Mary, during the first interview, tried to camouflage herself in order to avoid detection, just as Steve had done. But the techniques that Mary had developed over the years were quite different. Mary had been diagnosed by psychiatrists as a manic-depressive. Instead of shutting up, withdrawing, rearing a wall and challenging the world to batter it down as Steve did, Mary's ploy was, "I'll drown you out so that you'll stop bothering me." As soon as the counselors began to put their finger on the real issue in Mary's life (which turned out to be adultery with her next-door neighbor), Mary began to howl and cry and scream at the top of her lungs. Besides inarticulate sobbing, she cried, "Leave me alone; leave me alone!" In the past Mary had successfully warded off all attempts by her parents and others to discover the reasons for her distress by driving them away. Mary was now using her tried-and-true ruse with the counselors, but they were not abashed at such responses. Instead, they looked Mary squarely in the eye and said:

O be quiet! Unless you stop this kind of nonsense and get down to business, we simply can't help you, Mary. Surely a young girl like you doesn't want to spend the rest of her life in this institution. We know that you have real problems, and we know that there is something wrong in your life. Now let's start talking turkey.

Instead of showing her sympathy, instead of responding to her tears, instead of being taken in by Mary's tactics, the counselors brushed aside the camouflage and pursued a straight course directly to the heart of the matter. At this, Mary turned off her antics almost as automatically as if she had pushed a button. She told the story, a miserable story, which had been so hard to tell she had never told it to another person before.

Mary was helped only because her counselors were not shaken by Mary's screams and tears. They dealt appropriately with her feelings and demanded more content. They insisted on working with data.[1] They called a spade a spade. Mary needed to learn that her habitual response pattern was faulty and that she would have to abandon it if she really wanted help. Agreeing, Mary found help in confession and change.

Often persons come for counseling prepared to perform their little acts, to go through their patterns. Women come with their purses stuffed full of Kleenexes. Men come with their tempers on edge ready to flare out. But the Christian counselor considers such acting out behavior an opportunity to help. He calls attention to the present behavior and confronts the counselee not only about his other problems, but also about the very way in which he is handling the counseling situation itself.

When confronting someone concerning such avoidance patterns, counselors must seek to correct such behavior for his benefit. They must point out the principles involved, give in-

---

[1] Rogerian theory is most defective at this point, concerning itself entirely with feeling. Cf. Chapter VI.

struction in biblical responses, and help him to understand how these very patterns of avoidance played a part in getting him into trouble. The counselor, then, does not simply seek information. It is true that he demands information. But he evaluates not only information, his evaluation also takes account of emotions and actions. All behavior is of concern to the counselor. When feelings are used as a cover up, the counselor tries to rectify this behavior as well as the problem behavior beneath the camouflage. The whole man, in every dimension of his problem, must be helped.

## Homosexuality Fits the Pattern

Homosexuality provides an additional example that fits this picture. Many cases of homosexuality show a similar pattern of development. The picture is somewhat as follows: Early in his life (usually during the pre-adolescent period), Frank became involved in homosexual activities. Before reaching his teens he began to engage in homosexuality with some regularity. Homosexual sin may first have begun out of curiosity or in order to act "smart." Frank's sin had a typical beginning when a group of young boys gathered together in a hideout on a vacant lot to form a club. All was innocent enough until someone got the idea that admission to membership in the club should be restricted to those who were willing to take off their clothes. However details of any particular story may go, homosexual sin does not appear to have been the result of genetic factors,[1] but is, as in Frank's case, a learned activity.

---

[1]In Romans 1:26 homosexuality is declared to be *para phusin* ("against nature"), and in vs. 27, it is called an "error." In all of Scripture there is only one God-given solution to the problem of sexual desire: "it is better to marry than to burn" (I Corinthians 7:9). Marriage is God's answer to immorality: "because of immoralities, let each man have his own wife, and let each woman have her own husband." The old sinful pattern must be broken and replaced by the new godly one. The basic goals, ways and means for counseling homosexuals are found in I Corinthians 7. Cf. also Gen. 19:1-10; Lev. 18:22; Judges 19:22-26; 20:13; I Cor. 6:9; I Tim. 1:10.

Before long a fixed pattern develops, and once having become a habit, homosexuality becomes a way of life. The habit may become so firmly established that homosexuality at first appears to be a genetic problem. But there is no reason for viewing homosexuality as a genetic condition in the light of the Scriptures which declare that the homosexual act is sin. Apart from the work of Christ in their lives, all sinful men will distort God's marvelous gift of sex in one way or another. The particular style of sin (whether homosexual or heterosexual in its orientation), however, is learned behavior. Homosexuality is the way in which some clients have attempted to solve the sexual difficulties of adolescence and later life.[1]

Usually one who commits homosexual sin develops a grossly distorted view of sex and other interpersonal relations. He finds, for instance, that he must lead a double life. So he carries a heavy load of fear and guilt. Part of the homosexual pattern is lying. Anyone leading a double life usually becomes an astute liar. It is very difficult to believe what he says, because he will make promises that he fails to keep. This is particularly frustrating to counselors who also must confront him about patterns of falsehood. The characteristics of homosexuals accord fully with what we know of other learned behavior. When patterns of anger and resentment are later discussed, these similarities will be noted further.

## Adrenachrome or Schizophrenia?

The view espoused in this book is that psychiatry has no exclusive province that it may call its own.[2] Phillips and Wie-

---

[1] It is possible that in some instances homosexual solutions to the problems occasioned by adolescent sexual drives may have been sought as "safe" solutions that alleviate the fears of pregnancy which accompany illicit heterosexual activity.

[2] Cf. John S. Werry's revealing article, "The Psychiatrist and Society," *Dis-Coverer* (Vol. 5, No. 3, August 1968), in which the psychiatrist's special training is said to equip him "no better . . . than any other hu-

ner are correct when they conclude: "The psychotherapist is only one of many behavior changers, and psychotherapy is only one of many methods for behavior change."[1] Freud himself was unwilling to say that psychoanalysis had to be performed by a physician.[2] If Christians who do counseling as a full-time calling prefer to use the word psychiatrist to describe themselves, that is a matter of no great moment (though perhaps unwise) so long as they do not claim a territory exclusive of the pastor or physician.[3] The pastor, or other Christian counselor, works back to back with the physician. The latter will help him immensely in sorting out cases in which thyroid deficiency, myxedema, or some other similar condition is at the root of a disorder. There is, of course, a gray area between, where it is uncertain to both whether a problem stems basically from organic or non-organic sources. The following material illustrates this problem.

There is a possibility that some of the bizarre behavior which one meets in so-called schizophrenic persons, stems from organic roots. For example, Osmond and Hoffer have

---

man being of similar age and similar experience of working directly with disturbed people," p. 8. Werry sees psychiatric training as largely irrelevant to the work he must pursue. Cf. also Harry Stack Sullivan, "Therapy and Education in Psychiatry," in *Interpersonal Relations* (Patrick Mullahy, ed., New York: Science House, 1967), pp. 204, 205. Bernard Steinzor wrote: "I will at a number of points bring into question whether the special technical knowledge the doctor presumably has, is significant in effecting a change in the patient's life."

[1] E. L. Phillips and D. N. Wiener, *Short-term Psychotherapy* (New York: McGraw-Hill Book Company, 1968), p. 9.

[2] Freud wrote: "Whether such a person is a qualified physician or not does not seem important to me." Freud, *The Problem of Lay Analysis* (Bretano, 1927). The Medical Model, and the exclusive territory concepts must be eliminated.

[3] The pastor is not *directly* concerned with gall stones or appendicitis, but helps even in such cases, as he ministers God's Word to those who face operations, to those who must endure prolonged illnesses, etc.

proposed a theory based on the idea that perception is distorted in some persons by a chemical malfunction.[1] When adrenachrome is formed in the body, it normally breaks down immediately into other chemicals. According to Osmond and Hoffer, in some people adrenachrome retains its integrity too long before breaking down, and this causes perceptual difficulties. In other people, although adrenachrome breaks down at the normal rate, the adrenachrome breaks down into abnormal chemical forms which also can become the cause of perceptual difficulties. For both of these reasons, some persons experience chemical abnormalities which result in perceptual distortions, which in turn lead to behavior which others interpret as bizarre.

According to the Osmond-Hoffer theory, the root of the problem does not lie in the person's mind or emotions, nor does the problem arise from sinful behavior, but involves faulty perception (i.e., chemically distorted perception). Many of the same effects that are experienced by people with adrenachrome problems are also reported by those who use LSD, mescaline, and other hallucinagenic drugs. Perception may be distorted in varying ways: colors may become exceedingly bright or dull. Words on a page may begin to bounce. Books lying flat on the table may seem to fly off. Depth perception may be lost. Foods which normally do not, may taste exceedingly bitter. Hearing may be so acute at times that the client is able to hear sounds from two or three rooms away. So when a client speaks of hearing voices, psychiatrists call these hallucinations; yet they are not hallucinations at all but actual voices. The only problem is that the client doesn't realize that he is able to hear voices at such a distance. When books seem to fly off tables he may raise his arms defensively and draw

---

[1]Cf. Abraham Hoffer and Humphry Osmond, *How to Live With Schizophrenia* (New York: University Books, 1966). Unfortunately, Hoffer and Osmond retain the confusing name "schizophrenia" for the adrenachrome syndrome.

back quickly. But when others see him do this, they call such behavior bizarre.

If the Osmond-Hoffer theory has any credence at all (and the final evidence is not yet in), a number of those who currently are labeled "schizophrenics" could no longer be considered "mentally ill" (as if their judgment were impaired), but would have to be reclassified as "perceptually ill."[1] If perception is the problem, there is nothing wrong with the mental responses to what is perceived. If a book seems to be flying toward you (as your senses wrongly tell you it is), the right thing for the mind to do is to send signals to the arms to protect the head. Seemingly bizarre gestures, therefore, make sense when they are rightly interpreted as a protective response. If faulty depth perception wrongly tells you that someone is about to bump into you, then for you to jog to the side suddenly is the correct thing to do. In other words, the counselee's mind is not sick; he is only seeing things wrongly and is, therefore, reacting in a proper way mentally to what he perceives wrongly. In our opinion, the Osmond-Hoffer view needs further investigation, but is an excellent example of the sort of explanation that may eventually be discovered to be at the root of some problems.

The H. O. D., or Hoffer-Osmond Diagnostic Test, is a card sort test (now in the form of questions) by which Hoffer and Osmond claim to be able to distinguish those "schizophrenics" whose problem is chemically based from those whose problem is not. If this theory is confirmed, the diagnostic test should be a valuable tool in helping the counselor to determine who needs the physician's help and who needs the counselor's help.[2] Hoffer and Osmond have developed a urine

---

[1] Of course, perception involves mental processes and must not be distinguished too sharply from them. The judgment has not been impaired, however; the problem is that a good judgment has been made on the basis of false data.

[2] I do not wish to make a complete disjunction here. If habit patterns

analysis test in which they claim that a mauve spot appears in the majority of the cases in which there are adrenachrome failures. Hoffer and Osmond also claim that a niacinamide treatment in massive doses has a very high incidence of success in curing biochemical adrenachrome problems.

So, whether the problem is chemical or moral, the answer to the question which heads this chapter (What's wrong with the "mentally ill"?) seems clear: there may be several things wrong with the so-called "mentally ill," but the one cause which must be excluded in most cases is mental illness itself.[1]

---

have developed through faulty perception (such as withdrawal from society, suspicion of others, etc.), there may be a great need for counseling in addition to medical treatment.

[1] I.e., with the exception of organically-based problems such as brain damage, toxic problems, hardening of the arteries, and insanity by gene transmission, which may affect the brain directly. In each case, as well as in adrenachrome deficiencies, to the extent that it is possible to do so, the patient is still responsible to handle his handicap in accordance with the revealed will of God.

*Chapter IV*

# WHAT IS NOUTHETIC COUNSELING?

Jesus Christ is at the center of all true Christian counseling. Any counseling which moves Christ from that position of centrality has to the extent that it has done so ceased to be Christian. We know of Christ and his will in his Word. Let us turn to Scripture, therefore, to discover what directions Christ, the King and Head of the Church, has given concerning the counseling of people with personal problems. The Scriptures have much to say concerning the matter. Perhaps the best place to begin is with a discussion of what I have called "nouthetic confrontation."

The words *nouthesis* and *noutheteo* are the noun and verb forms in the New Testament from which the term "nouthetic" comes. A consideration of most of the passages in which these forms occur will lead inductively to an understanding of the meaning of nouthesis.

## Nouthetic Confrontation: By the Whole Church

First, whatever nouthetic activity may be, it is clear that the New Testament assumes that all Christians, not simply ministers of the Gospel, should engage in it. In Colossians 3:16 Paul urged:

> Let the word of Christ richly dwell within you, with all wisdom teaching and [for the moment we shall simply transliterate the next word] *confronting one another nouthetically.*

According to Paul, all Christians must teach and confront one another in a *nouthetic fashion.* In support of this proposition Paul also wrote (Romans 15:14):

> Concerning you, my brethren, I myself also am convinced that you are full of goodness, filled with all knowledge and able also to *confront* one another *nouthetically.*

In both Colossians and Romans, then, Paul pictured Christians meeting in nouthetic confrontation as normal every-day activity. He was sure the Christians in Rome were able to do so because they were filled with knowledge and goodness. These qualities equipped them to confront one another nouthetically. So the first fact is plain: nouthetic activity is a work in which all of God's people may participate.[1]

## Peculiarly the Work of the Ministry

But while all Christians ought to engage in such confrontation, nouthetic activity particularly characterizes the work of the ministry. Paul considered nouthetic confrontation a vital part of his own ministry. Incidental remarks in several passages indicate clearly that such activity was central. In Colossians 1:28, for instance, Paul declared:

> We proclaim him *confronting* every man *nouthetically,* and teaching every man with all wisdom in order that we may present every man complete in Christ.

Paul's proclamation of Christ involved confronting every man nouthetically. Certainly public confrontation in preaching was a part of Paul's nouthetic activity, but he was engaged also in the nouthetic confrontation of individuals. Colossians 1:28 does not refer primarily to Paul's public ministry, but principally to his private ministry to individuals. This is apparent when he speaks of "nouthetically confronting *every man.*" Paul confronted people nouthetically in the day-by-day contacts of pastoral work. The fullest biblical account of Paul's private nouthetic activity occurs in his farewell address to the Ephesian elders in Acts 20. This is a moving scene; they would see one another no more. In his remarks, Paul reviewed his

---

[1]The priesthood of all believers, a biblical doctrine revived in the Reformation, led to calling the minister *pastor pastorum* (shepherd of shepherds). All believers have a ministry to all others, which Paul says involves counseling, or nouthetic confrontation.

three-year ministry at Ephesus, recalling the past, looking into the future, and describing the present. He warned about problems likely to arise, described the kind of activity in which he engaged while he was with them, and urged them to continue this same work among their people. Verse 31 is an informative statement that most fully describes nouthetic confrontation. His words give us a deep insight into the ministry of Paul in the place where he ministered (as far as we know) longer than any other. In Ephesus Paul carried on not merely an evangelistic but also a pastoral ministry. He ministered to the Ephesian congregation for three years. What did Paul do during that time? He says:

> Be on the alert [i.e., as I was], remembering that night and day for a period of three years I did not cease to confront each one nouthetically with tears.   *Acts 20:31*

It is important to notice first that nouthetic confrontation took up a fair share of Paul's time if he engaged in it *night and day* for three years *without ceasing*. Paul continually confronted people nouthetically. We seldom think about Paul involved in pastoral work. His basic image is that of the missionary, crossing vast territories, sailing across the sea. We think of his remarkable ministry which spread the Christian faith through the *oikoumene*.[1] Of course he was that, but wherever he stayed for any length of time, Paul engaged in the solid pastoral work that is necessary to build up individuals in their faith. He says that nouthetic activity was a prominent part of that work. That is one reason why his letters are studded with the names of specific individuals with whom he became involved very intimately. Paul not only preached in the market places, but he dealt with people as individuals, as groups and as families; and he confronted them *nouthetically*.

---

[1] The civilized Greek-Roman Mediterranean world.

### Three Elements in Nouthetic Confrontation

It is important to define nouthetic confrontation precisely. What does the word *nouthesis* mean? The term contains more than one fundamental element. That is one reason why it is difficult to translate. Traditional translations have vacillated between the words "admonish," "warn," and "teach." A. T. Robertson (in his exposition of Colossians 1:28) rendered it "put sense into." A few of the newer versions (e.g., the *New English Bible* and *Williams' Version*) sometimes translate it "counsel." Yet no one English word quite conveys the full meaning of *nouthesis*. Since it is a rich term with no exact English equivalent, the word has been transliterated in this book. It is probably important to continue to transliterate *nouthesis*. Since the word has no exact English equivalent, the concepts inherent in the term probably do not exist widely in the English-speaking world. An attempt to bring the Greek term over into English perhaps ought to be made as the first step in endeavoring to establish *nouthesis* both as a concept and as a practice.

### I

Nouthetic confrontation consists of at least three basic elements.[1] The word is used frequently in conjunction with *didasko* (which means "to teach"). But in Colossians 3:16 and elsewhere it is distinguished from that word. Nouthetic confrontation always implies a problem, and presupposes an obstacle that must be overcome; something is wrong in the life of the one who is confronted. Cremer says, "Some degree of opposition has been encountered, and one wishes to subdue or remove it, not by punishment, but by influencing the

---

[1]For a good discussion of the term, see Behm in Kittel's *Theological Dictionary of the New Testament,* Volume IV (Grand Rapids: William B. Eerdmans, 1967), pp. 1019-1022. Also Hermann Cremer, *Biblio-Theological Lexicon of New Testament Greek* (Edinburgh: T. and T. Clark, 1895), pp. 441, 442.

*nous.*"[1] *Didasko* does not imply any problem. *Didasko* simply suggests the communication of data (teaching); making information known, clear, understandable and memorable. The word *didasko* implies nothing about the listener, but refers exclusively to the activity of the instructor. The person taught may or may not be anxious to receive instruction. He may pay great sums of money or travel long distances at great personal sacrifice to be taught, or his may be the typical response of the recalcitrant schoolboy, but the word *didasko* says nothing (one way or the other) about this. On the other hand, the word *nouthesis* focuses on both confronter and the one confronted. *Nouthesis* specifically presupposes the need for a change in the person confronted, who may or may not put up some resistance. In either case there is a problem in his life that needs to be solved. Nouthetic confrontation, then, necessarily suggests first of all that there is something wrong with the person who is to be confronted nouthetically. The idea of something wrong, some sin, some obstruction, some problem, some difficulty, some need that has to be acknowledged and dealt with, is central. In short, nouthetic confrontation arises out of a condition in the counselee that God wants changed. The fundamental purpose of nouthetic confrontation, then, is *to effect personality and behavioral change.*

## II

The second element inherent in the concept of nouthetic confrontation is that problems are solved nouthetically by verbal means. Trench says:

> It is training by word—by the word of encouragement, when this is sufficient, but also by that of remonstrance, of reproof, of blame, where these may be required; as set over against the training by act and by discipline which is *paideia.* . . . The distinctive feature of *nouthesia* is the training by word of mouth.

---

[1]Cremer, p. 441 (*nous* means "mind").

Trench quoted as evidence, Plutarch's use of *nouthetikoi logoi* (nouthetic words) and continued: "*Nouthetein* had continually, if not always, the sense of admonishing *with blame*," and finally says that the idea of rebuke is affirmed by the derivation "from *nous* and *tithemi*" which indicate that "whatever is needed to cause the monition to be taken home, to be *laid to heart*, is involved in the word."[1] So to the concept of *nouthesis* must be added the additional dimension of person-to-person verbal confrontation. *Nouthesis* presupposes a counseling type confrontation in which the object is to effect a characterological and behavioral change in the counselee. In itself, the word neither implies nor excludes a formal counseling situation but is broad enough to encompass both formal and informal confrontation. Nouthetic confrontation, in its biblical usage, aims at straightening out the individual by changing his patterns of behavior to conform to biblical standards.[2]

Specific biblical instances of such nouthetic activity may be seen in Nathan's confronting David after his sin with Uriah and Bathsheba, or Christ's restoring Peter after His resurrection. The failure to confront nouthetically may be seen in the blameworthy behavior of Eli recorded in I Samuel 3:13:

> You tell him that I will execute justice over his family forever, because he knew that his sons were bringing a curse upon themselves, and he failed to *discipline* them (Berkeley Translation).

In the Septuagint (the Greek version of the Old Testament) the word "discipline" is the verbal form *enouthetei*. Eli's sin

---

[1] R. C. Trench, *Synonyms of the New Testament* (Grand Rapids: W. B. Eerdmans, 1948), pp. 112-114.

[2] Personality change in Scripture involves confession, repentance, and the development of new biblical patterns. None of this is viewed legalistically, but rather, all must be understood as the work of the Holy Spirit. Nouthetic confrontation involves the verbal ministry of the Word. All such ministry is made effectual by the power of the Spirit alone.

was failure to confront his sons nouthetically. He failed to speak soon enough, strictly enough, and seriously enough, to effect genuine changes in them. In I Samuel 2:22 ff. there is, to be sure, the record of one feeble, futile, final attempt made much too late:

> Now Eli was very old, and when he heard everything his sons were doing to all Israel; and how they cohabited with the women who served at the entrance of the meeting tent, he said to them, Why do you behave this way? I hear all the people talk about your misconduct. . . . This will not do, my sons; for what I hear is not a good report. You lead the Lord's people to transgress. When one person sins against another, the judges will do him justice; but when a person sins against the Lord, who will intercede for him? But they would not listen to their father's warning;[1] so the Lord was inclined to slay them.

The word "discipline" (I Samuel 3:13) in the Berkeley (Amplified and R. S. V. have "restrain") is not as good a translation as, perhaps, a transliteration of the Septuagint, *enouthetei,* by "nouthetically confront" or "counsel in a nouthetic fashion" would be. The Hebrew means, "to weaken" and seems to have the idea of subduing the sinful activities of another.

It is most interesting to note that in I Samuel 2:23 Eli said, "I hear all the people talk about your misconduct." He described his sons' behavior as "misconduct," i.e., literally, "sinful things" (deeds). Something was wrong if Eli had to discover his sons' misconduct from others. Indeed Eli himself should have been among the first to know and confront his sons nouthetically about these deeds. It is of even greater interest to note that when Eli did finally speak to his sons, he began with the fatal word, "Why":

---

[1] There is no word for "warning"; the original reads, "They did not listen to the voice of their father."

*Why* do you behave this way? I hear all the people talk about your misconduct. This will not do, my sons; for what I hear is not a good report.

Eli's stress upon "why" may indicate one of his failures as a father. It was not his business to speculate about the causes of his sons' wicked deeds beyond the fact that he already knew—that they were sinners. It was his task to stop them. Too great an emphasis upon "why" may indicate an attempt to find extenuating reasons for excusing conduct which otherwise must be described as sinful. Did Eli fail to confront his sons nouthetically in the past because he was always engaged in finding excuses for their bad behavior?[1] Eli would have done better to have emphasized the word "what" instead. If he had compared the behavior itself to God's standards, he might have been able to help his boys.

Usual counseling methods recommend frequent long excursions back into the intricacies of the whys and wherefores of behavior. Instead, nouthetic counseling is largely committed to a discussion of the what. All the why that a counselee needs to know can be clearly demonstrated in the what. *What* was done? *What* must be done to rectify it? *What* should future responses be? In nouthetic counseling the stress falls upon the "what" rather than the "why" because the "why" is already known before counseling begins. The reason why people get into trouble in their relationships to God and others is because of their sinful natures. Men are born sinners.

Much time is wasted by asking why.[2] The question "Why"

---

[1] Perhaps the word "why" is used only rhetorically in this passage, as it is in other places where information is not actually sought (cf. Genesis 4:6). But in any case, the point is that Christians do not have to ask the question; they already know why fallen human nature acts sinfully. God has revealed clearly *why* sinful acts take place. Such knowledge justifies nouthetic confrontation.

[2] This is one reason why nouthetic counseling may be spoken of in terms of weeks rather than months or years (as most psychiatrists are compelled to speak).

may lead to speculation and blame-shifting; "What" leads to solutions to problems. "What have you been doing?" is a very significant question to ask. Having answered that question, counselors may then ask: "What can be done about this situation? What does God say must be done?" Because nouthetic counseling seeks to correct sinful behavior patterns by personal confrontation and repentance, the stress is upon "What"— what is wrong? and what needs to be done about it? People never understand the why more clearly than when the focus is upon the what. The second element in nouthetic contact, therefore, is personal conference and discussion (counseling) directed toward bringing about change in the direction of greater conformity to biblical principles and practices. Any biblically legitimate verbal means may be employed.

## III

The third element in the word *nouthesis* has in view the purpose or motive behind nouthetic activity. The thought is always that the verbal correction is intended to benefit the counselee. This beneficent motive seems never to be lost, and often is quite prominent. For example, in I Corinthians 4:14, Paul uses the verbal form of the word in this fashion:

I did not write these things to shame you but to confront you nouthetically as my beloved children.

The antithesis in that sentence brings out the tender concern inherent in the term. Because of this element, the term appropriately describes the concern of the parent for his child, and is used frequently in familial contexts. The Septuagint translators evidenced their preference for the word in the relationship of Eli as a father to his sons. The parent-child relationship also appears in Ephesians 6:4. There Paul spoke about bringing up children "in the nurture and the nouthetic confrontation of the Lord." In the parallel passage in Colossians 3:21, Paul warned parents not to "exasperate" their children. In Ephesians he urged, "Do not provoke them to wrath." Even in the most serious circumstances, an unruly Christian is to be "confronted nouthetically *as a brother*" (II Thessalonians 3:15).

So then, the third element in nouthetic confrontation implies changing that in his life which hurts the counselee. The goal must be to meet obstacles head on and overcome them verbally, not in order to punish but to help him. Cremer wrote, "Its fundamental idea is the well-intentioned seriousness with which one would influence the mind and disposition of another by advice, admonition, warning, putting right according to circumstances."[1] The thought of punishment, even the idea of disciplinary punishment, is not contemplated in the concept of nouthetic confrontation.[2] *Nouthesis* is motivated by love and deep concern, in which clients are counseled and corrected by verbal means for their good, ultimately, of course, that God may be glorified.[3] As Paul wrote in Colossians 1:28, every man must be confronted nouthetically in order that every man may be presented to Christ mature and complete. These, then, are the three basic concepts in the word *nouthesis*.

## Nouthesis and the Purpose of Scripture

*Nouthesis* accords quite fully with what Paul says elsewhere about the purpose and use of Scripture. In II Timothy 3:16,

---

[1]*Op. cit.,* p. 442.

[2]Of course disciplinary punishment is taught elsewhere in Scripture; cf. Trench, *op. cit.,* on *paideia.* He says that Christians, who had learned the lessons of the book of Proverbs, added an idea to the Greek word *paideia* ("education"), so that it came to mean in the New Testament, education which "includes and implies chastening," pp. 111, 112. Discipline is also viewed as beneficial in Scripture. In Ephesians 6:4 fathers are urged not to provoke their children to anger (*parorgizete,* the word used here, also occurs in 4:26), but to nurture them in the *paideia* and *nouthesia* of the Lord (both words occur together).

[3]Cf. esp. I Thessalonians 2:7, 8 for a fuller explanation of Paul's view of loving parental involvement. The love of a parent, by which she gives herself to her child is prominent.

he wrote:

> All Scripture is given by inspiration of God and is useful for teaching, for reproving, for correcting, for training in righteousness.

Here, the same nouthetic goals that Paul had previously stated in Colossians 1:28 seem to be in view. There he spoke about confronting every man nouthetically in order that every man might be presented perfect in Christ. One might say that the Scriptures themselves are nouthetically oriented. In II Timothy Paul indicated that the Scriptures are useful to perfect the man of God, by what might be called nouthetic means (teaching, reproving, correcting and training).

The Scriptures then, are useful for the nouthetic purposes of reproving, teaching, correcting and training men in righteousness. Because this is the classic passage concerning inspiration, its primary purpose often has been overlooked. Paul was concerned to discuss not only inspiration but primarily the purpose of the Scriptures. He argued that because they were God-breathed, the Scriptures are useful for nouthetic purposes.

In the fourth chapter Paul continued this discussion. Based on his conclusions in chapter 3, Paul urged Timothy to use the Scriptures concretely in accordance with their nouthetic purposes. He wrote:

> Preach the word; be ready in season and out of season; reprove, rebuke, exhort with great patience and instruction (II Timothy 4:2).

Timothy could fulfil that mandate only by using the Scriptures nouthetically. So nouthetic confrontation must be scriptural confrontation. Nouthetic confrontation is, in short, confrontation with the principles and practices of the Scriptures. Paul's words in Colossians and II Timothy pertain to the same matter. In both passages Paul thought of bringing God's Word to bear upon people's lives in order to expose sinful patterns, to correct what is wrong, and to establish new ways of life of

52

which God approves. Since it embraces all of these ideas, the term "nouthetic" seems to be an appropriate modifier for "counseling."[1]

## Nouthetic Involvement

Turning again to the 20th chapter of Acts, notice Paul's comment about nouthetic pastoring "with tears." Today counselors seldom cry in counseling sessions, though from time to time nouthetic counselors find that it is impossible not to shed tears. But probably there is no need to cry as Paul did. Modern American culture is different. Paul lived in a society that encouraged people to express their emotions freely. Until very recently, our culture has considered free emotional expression taboo.[2] A Hebrew was likely to tear his shirt in half and throw ashes on his head when he became upset.[3] To modern Americans this is "losing one's cool." Most Americans simply do not "weep and wail and gnash their teeth" even when deeply grieved. Whether this stifling of emotion is good or bad is another issue. But Paul's tears plainly reveal one fact—that he became deeply involved in the problems of his people. Involvement may differ not only in intensity, but also in kind. Tears show that Paul's involvement was a total

---

[1]I have no great zeal for the label "nouthetic" beyond its obvious advantages. However, since every school of thought eventually must be identified by an adjective, I should prefer to choose that adjective for myself. The importance of the word, however, as describing a regulative central activity involved in the ministry of the Word should not be missed.

[2]A change may be taking place. The popularity of the word "demonstrate" itself (and of course, the activities it is used to describe) signals what seems to be a radical change of viewpoint. The next generation is likely to be a good bit more "demonstrative" than past generations have been. It remains to be seen whether the outward demonstration is truly an expression of deep inner emotion ("soul" it would be called at present) or whether it is merely a passing fad.

[3]Cf. Lamentations 2:10.

involvement both of intensity and of kind. To the Corinthians Paul wrote:

Who is weak without my being weak; who is led into sin
without my intense concern (II Corinthians 11:29)?

In his third letter, John too showed evidence of nouthetic involvement:

I have no greater joy than this, to hear that my own children walk in the truth (vs. 4). [1]

Nouthetic counseling, then, necessarily embodies involvement
of the deepest sort.

There is a prevalent view of counseling which says, "Don't
become involved too deeply with your counselee." The image
of the ideal counselor according to this view is that of a pro-
fessional who is stoically clinical, and who maintains a sterile
white-coated manner.[2] Like the physician's bedside manner,
the counselor is sometimes thought to need a couch-side manner. Even though he may feel strongly empathetic inside,
ideally he should not respond in any way which might reveal
his true feelings. He must never appear shocked. He always
must maintain a neutral non-judgmental posture regardless of
whether what the counselee reveals is good or bad. His stance
is neutral. He must never express his own feelings or his own
viewpoint on the subject. While the counselee is to be wholly

---

[1] Cf. also I Thessalonians 2:7, 8, *supra;* Galatians 4:19; Philippians
1:7, 8.

[2] Frieda Fromm-Reichmann wrote: "Freud taught that, ideally, the
analyst, as nearly as it is possible, must be a blank to the patient." Cf.
"Advances in Analytic-Therapy," *Interpersonal Relations,* Patrick Mullahy, ed., (New York: Science House, 1967), p. 125. Laurence Le Shan
agreed: "One cornerstone of therapy has been that the therapist's personality must come into the picture as little as possible. This view held
he should be a 'faceless mirror,' essentially 'silent' as a human being"
*op. cit.,* pp. 454-463.

open, the counselor must never be known in his total personality. There is a double standard.

Any idea that such neutrality is possible must be dispelled. We shall attend to this matter later. Perhaps it is sufficient to note here that biblical counseling frequently gets so exciting that nouthetic counselors might get up and walk around the room, shout, laugh uproariously and on occasion even shed tears.

## Love Is the Goal

What are the goals of nouthetic counseling? In I Timothy 1:5 Paul put it this way:

> But the goal of our instruction is love from a pure heart, and a good conscience, and a sincere faith.

The word "authoritative" might be added to that translation: "The goal of our authoritative instruction is love." The original word *(parangelia)* is more than simply instruction; it is instruction imposed authoritatively. The authority of God is presupposed. The purpose of preaching and counseling is to foster the love toward God and love toward one's neighbor which God commands. Jesus summed up the keeping of the whole law as love. Any notion of authority as antithetical to love is inconsistent with Scripture.

Love is precisely man's problem, however. How can sinful man love? Since the fall, in which Adam's sin led to a guilty conscience, hypocrisy, and doubt, it has been impossible for natural men to keep their hearts pure, their consciences good, or their faith unhypocritical. All are born with a warped sinful nature that vitiates any such possibility. And yet love depends upon these very qualities. That is why Paul conditioned love upon the solution to these problems (note: "love from," i.e., "which issues from"). God's authoritative instruction through the ministry of his Word, spoken publicly (from the pulpit) or privately (in counseling), is the Holy Spirit's means of producing love in the believer.

The overarching purpose of preaching and counseling is

God's glory. But the underneath side of that splendid rainbow is love. A simple biblical definition of love is: The fulfillment of God's commandments. Love is a responsible relationship to God and to man. Love is a relationship conditioned upon responsibility, that is, responsible observance of the commandments of God. The work of preaching and counseling, when blessed by the Holy Spirit, enables men through the gospel and God's sanctifying Word to become pure in heart, to have peaceful consciences, and to trust God sincerely. Thus the goal of nouthetic counseling is set forth plainly in the Scriptures: to bring men into loving conformity to the law of God.

## Authoritative Counseling

But notice that Christian counseling involves the use of authoritative instruction. "Authoritative instruction" requires the use of directive, nouthetic techniques. Technique, and all methodology, must grow out of and be appropriate to purpose and content. The end does not justify the means; rather, it regulates the means. Love will blossom as counselors focus their attention upon purification of the heart, the clearing of the conscience, and the building of genuine trust. Counseling will seek to reverse those sinful patterns which began in the Garden of Eden. When he disobeyed God, his conscience was awakened, and out of fear, sinful man fled, covered himself and tried to hide from God. When confronted by God, finding that he could not successfully avoid him, he resorted to blameshifting and excuses. In antithesis to running and hiding, nouthetic counseling stresses turning to God in repentance. Instead of excuse-making or blameshifting, nouthetic counseling advocates the assumption of responsibility and blame, the admission of guilt, the confession of sin, and the seeking of forgiveness in Christ. In his dealings with Adam and Eve, God literally did not allow them to get away with what they had done. Adam tried to make a getaway into the woods. But God confronted him nouthetically, in order to change him by words. The relationship between God and Adam had been established on the basis of God's Word, broken by Satan's challenge to that Word, and had to be reestablished by God's Word. God elicited a confession from him. He probed until he got satisfactory answers. God gave hope and promised salvation in Christ.

The same nouthetic methods were used when God, through Nathan, confronted David and when God, in Christ, confronted Peter after his denial. Christ did not hide in the garden or run from the cross but, open and naked he exposed himself to direct encounter with a God of wrath. He pled for no mercy in that hour, and made no excuses. He did not attempt to cover or protect himself, but rather bore the full brunt of the fury of God in the stead of guilty sinners. Nouthetic counseling rests upon the dynamics of redemption, and reflects this fact at every point. Therefore, its power (as well as its fearful responsibility) stems from the fact that nouthetic confrontation necessarily utilizes the full authority of God.

## Failure in Nouthetic Confrontation

A genuine question is, "Do you ever fail?" Yes, nouthetic counselors fail. However, since the beginning of nouthetic counseling, failures have been relatively infrequent. Failure is often complex and therefore difficult to analyze. When a counselor fails to do his job adequately (as, for instance, when he fails to uncover some of the factors involved in the counselee's problem) other elements of failure also may be present so that it may become difficult to know precisely in what way a failure has occurred.

When failures take place, counselors must first ask, "Who failed?" Counseling was a failure, that is evident, but who failed—the counselor, or the counselee? In Luke 18:18-30, the story of a counseling failure is recorded, but clearly that failure was a counselee failure, not a counselor failure, for the counselor was Christ. The rich young ruler failed. He failed when Jesus confronted him nouthetically and put his finger on the sore spot in his life. Christ suggested action that would give evidence that his desire to serve and love God was sincere. But the ruler's response demonstrated that his boasted adherence to the commandments was shallow. The Scriptures say that "he went away sorrowing" because he had many riches. The failure in that instance, like the failure of the crowds who forsook Christ and walked no longer with him, was a counselee failure. Nouthetic counselors must recognize that failure may not be their fault.

Sometimes counselees will interpret failures as successes. Sometimes, for instance, they want to settle for something less than a total reorientation of their lives. They often settle for solutions to the immediate problem. They are willing to seek help in solving the incapacitating or performance problem rather than digging down and rooting out the preconditioning problem, of which the performance problem was but one instance.[1] Such premature terminations of counseling must be considered failures, even if counselees do not think so.

And so the question of failure becomes a difficult matter. Failure has to be looked at from various viewpoints. Counselors expect to fail because they are sinners and because the persons they are working with also are sinners. Failure is a recognized part of counseling and every counselor who works with others will fail. The incidence of failure, however, need not be anything like the failure that is represented by counseling or psychotherapy which is sustained over long months or years of time with no change or a worsening condition. Nouthetic counselors claim high-level success by comparison.

The question of failure necessarily implies a discussion of success. What is nouthetic success? In its fullest meaning, success is the attainment of the biblical change desired, together with an understanding by the counselee of how this change was effected, how to avoid falling into similar sinful patterns in the future, and what to do if, indeed, he should do so. At-

---

[1] These terms will be discussed, *infra*, pp. 148 ff.

tainment of only part of these goals must be considered by the counselor as only a partial success.

## Some Reasons for Failure

When nouthetic counseling fails, what are some of the reasons? First, consider failures by counselors. Probably the chief reason why nouthetic counselors fail is because they sometimes become too sympathetic to the complaints and excuses of the counselee. Frequently when a counselee tells a very pitiful tale, there is the temptation for a counselor to decide that this indeed is a special case. If the counselor agrees that under the circumstances the counselee was not responsible for his action, there is little more that the counselor can do. The counselor has placed himself in an impossible position. He has, in effect, denied the promises and the assurances of God in I Corinthians 10:13 which will be discussed fully elsewhere.[1] There is only one thing for him to do if the counselor comes to his senses in time: admit his mistake to the counselee[2] and continue properly from there.

Counselors fail when they become too sympathetic toward excuses and do not hold counselees responsible for their behavior, but they can never fail when they become truly sympathetic toward them. Perhaps the first attitude may be called sympathy and the latter empathy.[3] When counselors simply become softhearted, they are most unmerciful toward their counselees. The most kindly (empathetic) stance is to tell the truth, help the counselee to face up to his own sin, and encourage him to make the changes necessary to rectify the situation.

Counselors also fail by coming to conclusions too quickly.

---

[1]*Infra,* pp. 131 ff.

[2]A biblical and, therefore, nouthetic approach rarely encountered in other counseling.

[3]The terms are unimportant, and merely help to distinguish true from false sympathy.

It is possible to hear too little of a story or only one side of
the story and jump to conclusions. When counselors fail to
dig down to the underlying patterns and only handle performance problems, they also fail. Counselors may fail by becoming too involved emotionally. They can never become too involved in the proper sense, but they may get too involved in
the sense that they may allow their own emotions to cloud
their judgment. When this happens, counselors have been
caught by the same snare as their counselees, who are so emotionally involved in their problems that they no longer think
straight, but instead allow feelings to govern actions.

Nouthetic counselors always face the temptation to become overbearing in the use of authority, using authority for
its own sake, or failing to keep God's authority and one's own
opinions discrete. When this happens the nouthetic element
of concern for the counselee's welfare disappears. The coun-
selor-dilettante who may read this book in a casual manner,
missing the true goal of love to the glory of God, might well
misinterpret and misuse the system to his own detriment and
that of his counselees. That is why it is important to consider
the qualifications of a counselor in the next section.

To shorten what otherwise might become a long list of possible points of failure, it is sufficient to say that counselors
may fail in exactly the same ways that their counselees have
failed. Consequently, it is important for counselors to exam-
ine their own lives and their counseling practices in the light
of every failure they detect in others. Counselees become
strong reminders of human error and sin and, in that sense,
are among the counselor's most valuable teachers.

## Qualifications for Counseling

What are the qualifications for counseling? In deciding the
question of competence, it is important for Christians to determine the biblical qualifications for counselors. In Romans
15:14, Paul wrote:

And concerning you, my brethren, I myself also am convinced that you yourselves are full of goodness, filled with all knowledge, and able to admonish (nouthetically confront) one another.

Paul set forth goodness and knowledge as qualifications for good counselors. These qualities are essential; nothing less makes one "competent to counsel" (Williams). Paul recognized that any Christian may engage in nouthetic counseling, so long as he possesses the qualities of goodness and knowledge. We have seen, however, that this is *par excellence* the work of the Christian minister. In Colossians 3:16, a parallel passage, where Paul also regarded nouthetic confrontation as part of the normal activity of the members of a Christian congregation, he conditioned nouthetic confrontation upon a "rich" knowledge of God's Word, skillfully applied *in "wisdom."*

Knowledge and goodness, information and attitude, truth and the desire to help another, are equally important qualities. Under ordinary circumstances, Paul admitted, there would have been no need for him to write to the Roman church, since he was convinced that they fully possessed these qualities and, therefore, were "competent to counsel (i.e., nouthetically confront) one another." But, he says:

I have written very boldly to you on some points so as to remind you again, because of the grace that was given me from God, to be a minister of Christ Jesus to the Gentiles (Romans 15:15).

Two things are apparent. First, as Paul boldly reminded them of some truth, he was in effect nouthetically confronting them by mail. The letter to Rome (particularly in its latter half) is a good example of nouthetic confrontation. As a matter of fact most of Paul's letters are nouthetic in tone. To understand what nouthetic confrontation means in concrete instances, one needs but to turn to the epistles in which again and again Paul handled difficulties in local congregations. And that is what Paul had been doing in Romans. He had been reminding them very boldly about some matters, in spite of the fact that they were capable of nouthetically solving such problems on their own. Nevertheless, Paul felt that because of the special grace that had been given to him, because of the way God had used him in preaching the Gospel with great power, there was something he could do to help.

Paul also notes that nouthetic ability involves goodness and knowledge in large measure (fulness). Preeminently, a nouthetic counselor must be conversant with the Scriptures. This is one reason why properly equipped ministers may make excellent counselors. A good seminary education rather than medical school or a degree in clinical psychology, is the most fitting background for a counselor. Real counseling involves the imparting of information. Counseling means, among other things, giving advice. The Holy Spirit uses counselors to right wrongs by the application of God's Word to human problems. Knowledge of Scripture does not mean merely the memorizing and cataloging of facts. One in whom the "word of Christ dwells richly" (Colossians 3:16), is one who knows the meaning of Scripture for his own life. Because he is capable of solving his own problems scripturally, he is qualified to help others do so. Knowledge and goodness combine for this purpose, since one must have the welfare of the other person at heart to motivate him to spot wrong courses of behavior and endeavor to correct them. Goodness embraces both the involvement and empathetic concern about which something already has been said.[1] It also comprises an enthusiasm of life in which Christ is apparent, and which thereby communicates hope to the counselee.

---

[1]Freud would have failed at this point. His own approach is a good example of the cold, disinterested or even negative attitude which is antithetical to the loving concern and good will required of a counselor. He wrote to Pfister: "I have found little that is 'good' about human beings on the whole. In my experience most of them are trash" *op. cit.,* p. 61.

Two essential qualifications for nouthetic counselors are goodness and knowledge, but there is also a third: wisdom (cf. Colossians 3:16). An examination of Proverbs 1:1-7 shows that words of three sorts were used to explain what God means by wisdom. These words involve: (1) learning and knowledge; (2) practical skill in the application of general principles to concrete situations; (3) behavior with a covenantal-moral orientation. In short, wisdom is the skillful use of divine truth for God's glory. Knowledge and concern must be buttressed by skill in personal relations. Counselors who wish to counsel nouthetically must seek to grow most fully in these three elements.

## Pastoral Applications

Most of the clientele with which the writer works come by referral from former counselees. Some come also as the result of speaking in churches or over the radio about nouthetic counseling principles. But mainly, people who have been helped by counseling tell relatives and friends who also have problems. "The satisfied customer is the very best advertisement" applies to nouthetic counseling. Pastors will discover that as soon as they become successful counselors the word will get around both in the congregation and in the community. Before long such a pastor may have more counseling than he can handle. Fortunately, nouthetic counseling principles will not only make him a more successful counselor, but will enable him to help larger numbers of people over shorter periods of time with the result that he may carry on an expanded and wider ranging ministry.

Nouthetic counseling principles affect a man's entire ministry. The pastor who is nouthetically oriented will tend to become lovingly frank with his people. Counseling principles carry over into every area of the pastoral ministry. A pastor who takes nouthetic interest in his people seeks their benefit for God's glory. Therefore, he will not mince words or spar around with people. Rather, he will be specific about personal problems and straightforwardly attempt to correct them. His people will discover that he is interested in the real issues, not secondary ones. They will count him to be a man of courage. Because he will not settle for the status quo, some people will be offended, but the majority will be helped greatly and nearly all (whether they agree with him or not) will respect him. A man with the loving involvement of which Paul spoke will have a unique ministry in his community. The conservative ministry desperately needs a nouthetic orientation.

Harold, a pastor who went through nouthetic training[1] was faced with a problem of his own. A man who had been attending another conservative church in the community now began visiting his church. But Phil, the pastor of the former church, had commented to Harold that this man was about to join his church. The pastoral trainee was perplexed to know whether he should call on the visitor and whether he ought to encourage him to continue attending Phil's church. He did not want to become involved in sheepstealing. A counselor suggested that perhaps an open, frank nouthetic confrontation was in order. He suggested that he might confront both the pastor and the man directly with the problem. "If you don't know what else to say," he continued, "why not introduce the subject by saying, 'I've got a problem. . . .' and then, just spell it out. If you have a problem, and don't know any other way to begin, you can always start with that." Harold did. As he talked to the other pastor, the latter said, "If he is visiting your church, go right ahead and encourage him." What else could he say? Then, in turn, Harold called on the visitor. Again, he began by saying, "I've got a problem. . . ." The visitor said,

> I'm interested in the way that you've presented this issue straightforwardly to me. I'm going to be straightforward with you in return. The other minister may have thought

---

[1] The writer has been offering training in actual counseling sessions both for seminary students and for ordained ministers during the last three years.

that I was about to join his church, but I never intended to do so. I want you to know that I'm interested in your church, and one of the things that has interested me most is the fact that you have been able to talk to me straight-forwardly about a problem of this sort.

Subsequently the visitor joined the trainee's church and has become a valuable member. The pastor who brings a man into his congregation on those terms can feel free to talk to him at any time in the future about any matter without hesitancy. His relationships to both the other pastor and the prospective member are open and clear, and his conscience is at peace. Many false charges of sheepstealing might be avoided by a clear nouthetic approach.

## Chapter V

# THE PASTOR AS A NOUTHETIC COUNSELOR

### What Is a Pastor?

The Bible calls the minister a *pastor*. This is a rich word which is found in no other religion. Psalm 23 vividly describes the shepherd's relationship to his sheep. The Psalm begins, "The Lord is my shepherd." This might be translated, "The Lord is my pastor," for the word "pastor" means "shepherd." This first verse of Psalm 23 is an enthymeme. An enthymeme is a syllogism with one term missing. The tripartite syllogism is familiar to all: "All men are mortal; Socrates is a man; therefore Socrates is mortal." There are only two statements (or terms) in this first sentence: "The Lord is my shepherd; I shall not want" (or, "shall not lack"). One term is missing, the middle term, which would read, "Shepherds in caring for all of the needs of their sheep see that they lack nothing." Try reading it as a syllogism: "The Lord is my shepherd; shepherds in caring for all of the needs of their sheep see that they lack nothing;[1] therefore as one of his sheep I shall not lack."

Notice the description of the shepherd's work in the second and third verses. The sheep are made to lie down in green pastures (literally, pastures of tender green grass) and the sheep are led beside restful waters. The shepherd then revives them. ("Soul" in Hebrew poetry is used frequently as a synonym for "me" or "myself." Here it provides another way of saying

---

[1] It is important to distinguish between "need" and "desire" (or drive). The word "need" has been used too frequently (even by Christians, cf. *Baker's Dictionary, op. cit.,* p. 234) as a synonym for "desire" or "drive." All true needs are to be met, but frequently it will be the pastoral counselor's duty to help the counselee to learn to control the desires or drives. His true need frequently is not the satisfaction of the drive, but rather the need to learn self-control or patience. Cf., for example, Proverbs 16:32; 15:28 with the supposed need for catharsis.

"revives *me*.") The shepherd leads them in the paths of right-eousness for the sake of God's name, and though they walk through the valley of the shadow of death, they have no fear of harm, for the shepherd is with them. He carries in his hand a rod and a staff. His staff keeps them from falling over the edge of a precipice; his rod, perhaps with spikes protruding from a ball on the end of a mace-like object, was used to beat off any animals that might attack the sheep. The rod and the staff comfort the sheep even in the shadowy valleys where wild animals lurk ready to attack.

This picture embraces the idea of the shepherd's taking care of tired, weary, worn sheep. They also may be discouraged. A large part of pastoral work consists of reviving sheep. Pastors must know how to take tired, discouraged sheep to restful waters and green pastures. They also must protect their sheep from dangers.[1]

The good Shepherd, the Lord Jesus Christ, demonstrated what a shepherd really is in the fullest sense of the word. He is one who will not flee like a hired hand when the wolf comes, but instead gives his life, if necessary, for the sheep. He loves his sheep; he knows them so well that he can call them by name, they know his voice and they will not follow another (John 10). The biblical picture of intimacy and love between the shepherd and the sheep is foreign to us. The oriental shepherd lived with his sheep. He slept with them out on the hillsides at night, as David must have done. He went out seeking the hundredth sheep, not satisfied with only ninety-nine in the fold.

All this pictures the responsibility that a pastor carries for his people. The reviving of the soul, rest, peace of heart and mind, are still basic needs of God's sheep. And pastors, as un-dershepherds, cannot shirk their responsibility to provide for these needs. They cannot delegate this responsibility to a psy-

---

[1]Including overt or covert attacks upon Christian values by unbeliev-ing psychiatrists.

chiatrist. A minister, therefore, must consider nouthetic confrontation as an essential part of his pastoral responsibility. By definition, a pastor (i.e., shepherd) cares for worn, weary, discouraged sheep. He sees to it that they find rest. The pastor, then, must take up his ministry to men in misery.

## Evangelism and Counseling

So far, our discussion has been limited to the pastoral counseling of professing Christians. But what may be said of counseling directed toward unbelievers? Any such counseling that claims to be Christian surely must be evangelistic. Counseling is redemptive. What God has done for sinful man in Christ conditions what the counselor does. Counseling should follow and reflect God's order in redemption: grace, then faith; gospel, then sanctification. Counseling must be redemptive. The way Paul proceeded in the book of Romans, for instance, affords clear direction. He showed all (Gentile and Jew) that they have sinned. Next he refuted false ideas of redemption through attempted law keeping, and established the truth of justification by faith alone; finally he exhorted to personal holiness.

What Paul did is what counselors must do. Nouthetic confrontation requires the deepest involvement; deep enough to take people seriously when they mention their sin, even when they fail to identify it as sin. Sin cannot be minimized or glossed over. God took sin so seriously that he sent his Son to die for sinners. God's great involvement with his people is evident in Christ's death. Matters such as law and love, irresponsibility and responsibility, relationship and alienation, guilt and forgiveness, hell and heaven make up the content of counseling. Counselors must be careful not to represent Christ as the member of a first-aid squad who offers bandaids to clients. Redemptive counseling is radical surgery. Because of the radical nature of man's problem, radical measures are required. The diagnosis leading to radical surgery must be open, frank honest and to the point—man has sinned and needs a Savior.[1] Nothing less than death to the past and resurrection to a brand new way of life can really solve one's problems (cf. Romans 6). Consequently, a proper concept of nouthetic counseling must have deeply embedded in it the premise that man cannot be helped in any fundamental sense apart from the gospel of Jesus Christ.

Actually, counseling becomes truly nouthetic only when the counselee is a Christian. Otherwise, it is always something less. When the Holy Spirit effects regeneration in a soul, that person becomes "a new creature in Christ; old things have passed away and all things become new." The Holy Spirit takes up his residence in the life, begins to change that life, and empowers the individual to live according to the promises and commands of Scripture.[2] Unsaved counselees are neither capable of understanding God's revealed will (cf. I Corinthians 2) nor capable of doing it (Romans 8:7, 8). The Holy Spirit is the one who must motivate both counselor and client. Motivation not generated by the Spirit is humanistic and cannot honor God (cf. Paul's words on the ministry of the Spirit in Romans 8). To ignore this transforming change in counseling, to attempt to effect changes apart from God's power, is a colossal mistake.

Much counseling nevertheless avoids the issue of evangelism and yet claims to be Christian. Some object to evangelism in counseling because they say that counselors must not impose their standards and values upon another. But that, of course, is precisely what evangelism is all about. Evangelism imposes new standards and new values. Evangelism means confronting

---

[1]Much contemporary talk about frankness, honesty and openness fails in that the essential fact of redemption through Jesus Christ is missing. Sensitivity training is one current rage that suffers especially from this fault. The movement seems to encompass many diverse approaches and is therefore difficult, if not impossible, to define.

[2]Not automatically, nor perfectly, for redeemed men are still sinners who do not yield entirely to the Spirit's will (cf. Galatians 5:17).

men with the gospel and commanding them to repent and believe. Repentance is a change of mind leading to a new outlook in which faith in Christ brings about a change of purpose and a change of direction. The answer to the objection to evangelism in counseling is simply that the counselor does not impose his own standards upon the counselee, but that he seeks to impose God's standards. Of course, he must be careful not to confuse the two. No man is free to ignore God's standards. No one has the right to choose not to serve God, for God has made man to serve him and has commanded "all men everywhere to repent" (Acts 17:30). He has called them to turn from idols to the true and living God, to serve him and to wait for his Son from heaven.

Not all men, however, obey that command. Sin has cosmic dimensions. The entire universe has been brought into a state of misery. The whole creation groans like a woman in labor. Man is included as a part of that groaning creation, and his misery which is due to the very existence of sin, is part of the problem in counseling. Counselors must take note of this underlying dimension of guilt, for man is born guilty (culpable) before God. He sinned in Adam. He became estranged from God and man by Adam's sin. The feeling of estrangement is always present on that level. Man is not only guilty in the sense that he has sinned in Adam as his federal or representative head, but man is also corrupt by his relationship to Adam. Man's corruption leads to actual transgressions on the part of each individual as well. These actual transgressions bring further misery to his soul. Thus there is a double layer of misery and guilt in men before they are forgiven in Christ.[1]

But the man whose sins have been forgiven is happy (Psalm 32:1, 2). To be true to God's commission and thus offer an adequate solution to man's need, evangelism is absolutely essential to counseling. Counselors consciously must avoid every

---

[1] "Guilt" may mean culpability before God or the feelings triggered by a bad conscience (misery). The two are related as cause and effect.

attempt to preempt the work of the Holy Spirit. They must recognize that the salvation of the soul is God's task, not theirs. Their work is to confront unsaved men with the universal offer of the gospel. This offer is genuinely made to every man, but only God can bring life to dead souls to enable them to believe. He does this when and where and how he pleases by his Spirit, who regenerates, or gives life leading to faith. But counselors, as Christians, are obligated to present the claims of Christ. They must present the good news that Christ Jesus died on the cross in the place of his own, that he bore the guilt and suffered the penalty for their sins. He died that all whom the Father had given to him might come unto him and have life everlasting. As a reformed Christian, the writer believes that counselors must not tell any unsaved counselee that Christ died for him, for they cannot say that. No man knows except Christ himself who are his elect for whom he died. But the counselor's task is to explain the gospel and to say very plainly that God commands all men to repent of their sin and believe in Jesus Christ.

### Nouthetic Evangelism

How can evangelism be carried on in counseling?[1] There may be many legitimate answers to this question. But one point of beginning is with the evangelistic ministry of Jesus Christ. As a nouthetic counselor who confronted men daily, he showed us how the healing of the body and the solution to human difficulties and problems may be conjoined with evangelism. "Rise, take up thy bed and walk," and "thy sins be

---

[1]John Bettler, my colleague in counseling at the Hatboro center, notes the impossibility of evangelism in a consistently Rogerian context. Even if the client led the counselor to the subject, it would be the counselor's task to focus only on feeling, and not on the gospel. Moreover, the counselor could only reflect the gospel whenever the client first correctly outlined it, or he would be "guilty" of imposing his own beliefs upon the client.

forgiven thee" are two concepts which stand side by side in the gospel record. Nouthetic counselors attempt to replicate this in their counseling. Counselors present biblical answers to man's physical, social, intellectual and psychological needs. But at the same time they affirm that only redeemed men can live in a manner pleasing to God.

It is true, of course, that a counselor's first utterance to an unsaved person usually is not "believe the gospel." Many clients are not immediately ready to listen to the gospel. When a person is on the run, he has to be stopped first before you can talk to him. Men are on the run from God. Moreover, the gospel at first was not preached to Adam in terms of forgiveness. God first stressed the sin of breaking his law. He emphasized Adam's problem and need. His need for a savior was clearly pointed up as God confronted him, exposed his sin, and disclosed to him the penalty for his sin. Only after having proclaimed the bad news of the broken law with its penalty and sanctions, did God give the glorious promise of redemption in Christ. Nouthetic counselors also appropriately talk about needs. They speak about sin and its consequences. They explain that estrangement has resulted from sinful behavior. They show how failure to follow Scripture, ignoring God, and sinful life patterns have brought misery. Then, in this context, they present the gospel.

While it may take several sessions to reach an appropriate point to present the gospel, nevertheless all counseling should be done from within a Christian milieu. At the outset counselees should know that the orientation is biblical.[1] God is mentioned frequently. Counselees are shown how all of life is religious (i.e., related to God). Prayer is offered at appropriate junctures. And the Scriptures are used as the authoritative

---

[1] Obviously, Christian pastors have an advantage from the outset. Rather than considering their office a liability (as some seem to), they should look on their position as a distinct advantage.

standard, throughout. Counselors usually do not argue about the authority of the Scriptures, but simply tell their counselees that the Bible is the basis upon which counseling is conducted. Solutions are reached in a Christian context. Thus counselors *envelop* all from the beginning with the Christian faith, but allow the gospel confrontation itself to *develop* at an appropriate point.

In chapter 16, section 7, the Westminster Confession of Faith says:

> Works done by unregenerate men, although for the matter of them they may be things which God commands; and of good use both to themselves and others: yet, because they proceed not from an heart purified by faith; nor are done in a right manner, according to the Word; nor to a right end, the glory of God, they are therefore sinful, and cannot please God, or make a man meet to receive grace from God: and yet, their neglect of them is more sinful and displeasing unto God.

This is a well balanced statement derived from the Scriptures, that helps explain the counselor's viewpoint. First of all, it clearly says that works done by unregenerate men, even though they be acts that God commands, are of no value in making them fit to receive grace from God, nor are they of any merit before God. The Confession states that such works proceed from hearts that have not been purified by faith; neither are they done in a right manner nor for the right purpose (to glorify God). Therefore, these works are sinful. Any idea of salvation by merit or of preparation for grace is excluded.

Nevertheless the Confession says such works are "of good use both to themselves and others," and that "their neglect of them is more sinful and displeasing unto God." It would seem then that according to the Confession, it is right to help unregenerate men to conform (even though it be such an outward conformity) to scriptural standards. Since he does good works from the wrong motives, an unregenerate man cannot please

God (Romans 8:8). Yet the Confession rightly observes that for the unbeliever to neglect doing the right thing would be more displeasing unto God. So that to help unbelievers solve their problems, to help them to change habit patterns from less correct to more correct patterns, to get them to do formally what the Word of God says about certain aspects of their lives, is to honor God and to do that which is of good use, both to the unbeliever and to others. And so there is a warrant, in conjunction with evangelism, to help unbelievers (all the while evangelizing) though evangelism be unsuccessful. Jesus cleansed ten lepers, but only one returned to give him thanks. Counselors too may sometimes ask, "Where are the nine?"

It must be said, however, that in our counseling sessions normally we have a large proportion of Christians. The name which we have used, just like the pastor who counsels nouthetically, largely draws Christians and tends to screen out others. And so a large proportion, perhaps three-fourths, of our clients are Christians. Yet that other fourth affords the opportunity for using a problem-oriented approach to evangelism,[1] which looks at the counselee's problem in the light of God's explanation of why the problem exists (rebellion against his holy law), and finds its solution in faith in Christ and sanctifying conformity to God's Word. This is the divine pattern for evangelism in counseling.

## Sanctification and Counseling

Nouthetic counseling in its fullest sense, then, is simply *an application of the means of sanctification.* The prerequisite for sanctification is the Holy Spirit's presence in the life of a regenerate person. In Colossians 2 and Ephesians 4, Paul stressed this in his discussion of the new man and the renewal

---

[1] I must express thanks to Alan Moak for the wording used here. Mr. Moak's paper for a seminary course was entitled "Problem-centered Evangelism."

of God's image. This image was ruined at the fall. The goal of counseling is the renewal of that image. Concretely this means likeness to Christ, who perfectly imaged God as man. The attainment of that goal is achieved as a client changes from his former sinful life patterns and grows into the stature of Christ (Ephesians 4:13). This is begun when the Holy Spirit reestablishes communication with God. (I Corinthians 2 shows that no communication with God exists apart from regeneration.) By his power the Spirit then enables the client to begin to put off the old man with its old patterns of life, and to put on the new man with its new biblical patterns. Day by day the Christian should grow in grace, by "trying to learn what is pleasing to the Lord" (Ephesians 5:10).

## Sanctification Means Change

Sanctification means more than learning what the Bible teaches. It involves personal change.[1] Sometimes when counselees are cornered and forced to acknowledge that their behavior is irresponsible, they attempt to dodge the issue by replying: "Well, I guess that's just the way I am." They say this in a resigned manner and expect to leave the whole matter right there. They speak as though there were no possibility for genuine personality change. Such a view of man is decidedly unscriptural. Human beings in one way might be described more accurately as human becomings. Personality can be changed. God, throughout history, has turned Jacobs into Israels, Simons into Peters and Sauls into Pauls. Today's personality is based on yesterday. What one is today is but the composite of his past. At birth, God gave to each of us a basic

---

[1] Here we must differ radically with Christians who think that the pastor's aim in counseling "is not . . . to induce any major personality change." Why leave such major change in the hands of psychiatrists whose beliefs and methods are antithetical to Scripture? Cf. *Baker's Dictionary, op. cit.,* p. 209. The work of the Holy Spirit is precisely the work of personality change, and the Christian counselor must become involved in this work as an agent whom the Spirit may use.

deposit of inherited stuff which Scripture calls *phusis* (nature). This is a matter of gene makeup.[1] But that is not personality. How one uses the *phusis* in responding to life's problems and life's challenges determines the personality. Those response patterns may become deeply etched over a period of time. At length, they may seem to be, as we say, "second nature," i.e., almost as "given" as the original *phusis*. Though habit patterns are hard to change, change is not impossible. Nouthetic counselors regularly see patterns of 30-40 years' duration altered. What was learned can be unlearned. An old dog can learn new tricks.

Sometimes people also think that past decisions must be maintained as firmly as the laws of the Medes and Persians. Such people should reread the biblical account which shows the consequences of those foolish laws. Counselees must realize that past decisions were based upon yesterday's data and judgments. The former might have been insufficient and the latter poor. If new data have come to light, if one finds his judgment clearer today, he should attempt to rectify yesterday's bad decisions. God's Word changes people, changes their thinking, changes their decisions, and changes their behavior. Change is an important matter to nouthetic counselors. The Scriptures everywhere anticipate change. The Holy Spirit is

---

[1] Depending upon whether one is a creationist (God creates each new soul afresh at birth) or a traducianist (the soul is *transmitted from one's parents*) he may wish to include or exclude the human spirit from the inherited *phusis*. I do not wish to discuss this issue here, but it is fair to say that a more-or-less traducianist position has been presupposed. At least, *phusis* has been thought to include the genetic and any other element received at birth. When Christ says "out of the heart" proceeds evil of every description (Luke 6:45; 15:19), he refers to what emanates from man's inherited nature (*phusis*), not what is learned. Man does not learn his responses as a passive, neutral being. Rather, he is an active, committed organism with a nature disposed toward sin because he is at enmity toward God. Sinful response patterns are inevitable, but the particular patterns developed, the particular styles of sinful expression, are not; they are learned.

the Spirit of change. His activity is everywhere represented as the dynamic and power behind the personality changes in God's people. Wherever the Holy Spirit's activity is demonstrated, people are changed. God says, "Grow in grace and in the knowledge of our Lord Jesus Christ." Static living, static decisions, static personality is inconsistent with the biblical picture of the new life. Where there is life there is growth,[1] and growth means change. Growth means maturation; it means refining of ideas and ways of doing things. So a Christian counselee must not be allowed to plead that he is what he is and nothing can be done about it.

Change for some people is difficult to accept. Change is difficult because change means doing something new, something unusual, something not done before. It usually means exchanging old habit patterns for new ones. Such change is a threat. They are afraid of the unknown, and therefore unwilling to launch out into new adventures. But to a Christian, change should be thrilling rather than threatening. The Christian life is an adventure into God's newness. Newness need not make the Christian feel insecure because the future is new only in that he has not yet experienced it; it is not unknown to God. Christ is the pioneer of the Christian's faith. He is its author and finisher. He knows all about our lives. Christ himself has experienced the worst this life has to offer, all that death holds, and now stands victorious on the other side of both in eternal glory. So for the Christian the providence of God is a vital reality. The Savior has blazed a trail before him.[2]

---

[1] All living organisms grow. Growth may sometimes take place in large spurts, and at other times may occur more slowly. In all Christians the potential for growth is significant.

[2] Gibson Winter was one of the first to sound the note that the modern family is uprooted. He wrote: "We are like gypsies on the move" (*Love and Conflict,* Garden City: Doubleday and Company, 1958, p 16). Granberg echoes the cry that ours is a rootless society and also see: this as the source of many problems. Cf. *Baker's Dictionary, op. cit.*

A Christian sins if he becomes a static, sedentary person who fears positive biblical change and frantically clings to the past, either in his personality growth, in his life decisions, or in his manner of living. To resist sanctifying change is to resist and grieve the Holy Spirit. The scriptural doctrine of sanctification necessarily involves growth in holiness. Christians must change in order to become more like Christ. Growth means changing into the fulness of the stature of Christ. In principle it is true that believers have been declared perfect in Christ, but now they must grow more like Christ in practice. New truths discovered in the study of the Scriptures must become new practices woven into the fabric of one's daily life. Fundamentally, then, pastoral counseling is helping Christians to become sanctified. Counseling involves helping people to put off old patterns which grew out of rebellion toward God, and helping them to put on new practices which grow out of obedience to God. This is the shepherd's challenge, opportunity and duty.

---

p. 194. It must be granted that rootlessness that is due to modern mobility offers many temptations, but Christians may not blame this rootlessness for their problems. Although the problem takes on modern dimensions, it is not a new one. Abraham's life, like ours, was that of a "pilgrim and stranger." Christ spoke of leaving houses and brothers and sisters and father and mother and children and farms for his sake (Matthew 19:29). Such mobility and rootlessness actually affords great opportunity for demonstrating to others that "the world is not our home," and that "we seek a heavenly country" (see Hebrews 11:8-10; 13-16; I Peter 1:1; 2:11). The vital importance of the covenant family and the larger covenant community (the Church) is only emphasized by the rootlessness of modern society. One's taproot in God finds nourishment and life through these.

## Chapter VI

## NOUTHETIC AND ROGERIAN COUNSELING

It is astonishing how often a conservative pastor blatantly denies his theology by his practices in counseling. It seems that the presuppositions of counseling rarely have been discussed by Evangelicals. Consequently, the pulpit and the study often have become quite disjunctive. An eloquent (or at least authoritative) preacher standing behind the pulpit proclaims God's message with power. Yet he abruptly dons another hat and closes his mouth as he shuts the study door. He uneasily slips into the uncomfortable role of a listener, nondirectively guiding a counselee. It is an uncomfortable role because it violates his convictions, his conscience, and his calling. He acts as if God had nothing to say to the counselee. "The counselor," wrote fundamentalist Stanley E. Anderson, "should listen, show no authority, give no advice, not argue, talk only to aid or relieve or praise or guide the client and to clarify his problem."[1] Julian Hartt sums it up this way:

> The more recent alumni of theological schools are very reluctant to be directive in the office of pastoral counselor. The good pastor in this office is not judgmental, he is not directive; and as we have ourselves insisted throughout, he is not moralistic. So when someone puts this kind of question to him, "What ought I to do?" he knows that he must not answer it, whatever else he does or does not do. He is permitted to ask, "Well, what do *you* think you ought to do?"[2]

---

[1]Stanley E. Anderson, *Every Pastor a Counselor* (Wheaton: Van Kampen Press, 1949), p. 55. Anderson's intention is clear, although his sentence seems self-contradictory, for "guidance" involves what he rejects.

[2]Julian Hartt, *A Christian Critique of American Culture* (New York: Harper and Rowe, 1967), p. 338.

Rollo May follows the same line. In his book, *The Art of Counseling,* a client says to his counselor, "I think you're right. Now what steps shall I take to do this?" Rollo May interjects,

This is a crucial point. The counselee asks for advice. If the counselor succumbs to the temptation with its implicit flattery and gives advice or even specific instructions, he short-circuits the process and thwarts the real personality readjustment of the counselee . . . Rather, he must seize this request for advice as a means of making the counselee accept more responsibility for himself.[1]

Then May's counselor responds,

You wish rules on the matter. You want these rules to compel you from the outside and you follow them with the same strain and tension which you manifest now. That will make your problem all the worse. Your desire for rules, you see, rises out of that same basic mistrust of life.[2]

Here, of course, is a denial of the authority of God, of God's commandments, and of the Scriptures. May explains, "In the first place *personality is not transformed by advice.* This misconception we must destroy once and for all; true counseling and the giving of advice are distinctly different functions." He continues, showing the link between Freud and Rogers:

The psychotherapists do not mince words in their rejection of the position of advisor. Many quotations could be cited of the same tenor as the following one from Freud:

---

[1]Rollo May, *The Art of Counseling* (New York: Abingdon Press, 1939), p. 139. One cannot help but wonder why it is flattery to ask a minister of the gospel how God wants him to go about changing his life. May considers such advice flattery because he assumes that there is no written objective revelation from God, and that the counselor must reply from his own resources alone. Why should Christians who accept the revelation of Scripture act like May?

[2]*Ibid.*

80

"Moreover, I assure you that you are misinformed if you assume that advice and guidance in the affairs of life is an integral part of the analytic influence. On the contrary, we reject this role of the mentor as far as possible. Above all, we wish to attain independent decisions on the part of the patient."[1]

May continues in the next paragraph:

Advice-giving is not an adequate counseling function because it violates the *autonomy of personality* [emphasis mine]. It has been agreed that personality must be free and autonomous; how, then, can one person justifiably pass ready-made decisions down to another. Ethically one cannot do it; and practically one cannot—for advice from above can never effect any real change in the other's personality. The idea never becomes part of him, and he will cast it off at the earliest convenience.[2]

Adaptations of Carl Rogers' so-called "client-centered coun-

---

[1]*Ibid.*, p. 151. Salter cites the case of Carney Landis, the principal research psychologist of New York State Psychiatric Institute, who underwent a "complete psychoanalysis," paid for by the Rockefeller foundation. Landis reported that in 221 hours of analysis, his analyst spent two per cent of the time in discussing the material that he brought forth, which "averages down to a little over *one minute of discussion by the analyst in every analytic hour."* Andrew Salter, *The Case Against Psychoanalysis* (New York: The Citadel Press, 1963), p. 140.

[2]*Ibid.* On the face of it this is absurd. But of more importance, God says, "Listen to advice and accept instruction that you may gain wisdom for the future" (Proverbs 19:20, R.S.V.). When one considers the effect of scriptural advice, coupled with the illuminating, convicting and energizing power of the Holy Spirit, the utter foolishness of his man-centered viewpoint becomes apparent. This emphasis upon autonomy is widespread among Rogerian existentialists. Cf. Carroll Wise: "To the extent that a person has failed to develop autonomy or has lost it, he is sick" (*The Meaning of Pastoral Care,* New York: Harper and Row, 1966, p. 51).

seling"[1] dominate the field of pastoral counseling and form the basis of most liberal and much conservative counseling. Hulme wrote:

Some of the leaders in pastoral counseling consider the client-centered therapy of Rogers extreme and have modified it to fit into their particular concept of the pastoral role, while others have taken it as it is and given it a religious setting.[2]

Modified or intact, Rogers is the foundation of much pastoral counseling. J. Lyn Elder says that Rogers' early principles "are still central in most counseling."[3]

## Rogers' Basic Presupposition

The fundamental presupposition of the Rogerian system is perfectly consistent with liberal and humanistic thought, namely, that the solution to man's problems lies in the man himself. Man is thought to possess adequate resources which can be tapped by the use of non-directive techniques. "The non-directive viewpoint," says Rogers, "places high value on the right of every individual to be psychologically independent."[4] Man is autonomous. Consistent with this presupposi-

---

[1] I say "so-called" because the word "client" etymologically indicates "one who is dependent upon another" and has as its root the Greek *kluo,* "to listen." This means that a "client," strictly speaking, is one who is dependent upon the information imparted by the counselor. A word with a more unfortunate etymology hardly could have been found by Rogers for his so-called "client-centered" counseling. When nouthetic counselors refer to the counselee as the client, they always do so in its etymological sense.

[2] William E. Hulme, *Counseling and Theology* (Philadelphia: Fortress Press, 1956), p. 4.

[3] J. Lyn Elder, *Pastoral Care, an Introductory Outline* (Mimeographed: Mill Valley, 1968), Appendix 2.

[4] Carl Rogers, *Counseling and Psychotherapy* (Boston: Houghton Mifflin Company, 1942), p. 127. This whole viewpoint is theologically

tion, in non-directive (or reflective) counseling, the counselor becomes a wall upon which the client bounces his questions. As he verbalizes in the presence of a counselor, the counselor replies reflectively, repeating the client's words in a more sharply focused form. Eventually, by this process, the client gains insight into his problem and gradually devises a solution. James Dittes describes this technique vividly. The pastor speaks:

> If I thought I could answer your questions helpfully, Fred, I would. But I know from my experience that I can be of more help to you in another way. I am convinced that you have everything in you—good judgment and a good sense of what all the implications are and what the situation is really like—to make a good decision, really better than I can. But what I can do is provide some guidance in thinking through these complicated questions and be a kind of sounding-board.[1]

The Rogerian system confirms sinful man's belief that he is autonomous and has no need of God. Conservatives must reject Rogerian counseling on the basis of its humanistic presuppositions alone. It begins with man and it ends with man. Man is his own solution to his problems.

Rogerian techniques based upon this presupposition are so

---

grounded in Rogers' fundamental denial of man's sinful nature. He wrote: "One of the most revolutionary concepts to grow out of our clinical experience is the growing recognition that the innermost core of man's nature, the deepest levels of his personality, the base of his 'animal nature' is positive in character—is basically socialized, forward-moving, rational and realistic," in LeShan, *op. cit.,* pp. 454-463. Anyone who knows anything of Christian Science might think that this unscriptural statement was a quotation from *Science and Health* by Mary Baker Eddy.

[1] James Dittes, *The Church In the Way* (New York: Charles Scribner's Sons, 1967), pp. 279-280.

unsatisfying to many conservatives[1] because they clash with scriptural principles. According to Rogers, men in sin must be "accepted," not admonished: "The counselor accepts, recognizes, and clarifies these negative feelings."[2] The nouthetic element in all such counseling is conspicuously absent, for genuine responsibility is undermined by the idea of acceptance.

## Responsibility is Respondability

What is responsibility? Responsibility is the ability to respond as God says man should respond to every life situation, in spite of difficulties. It is the ability to do good to those who despitefully use you. It is the ability to feed one's enemy when he is hungry. It is the ability to give him a drink if he is thirsty. It is the ability to overcome evil with good (compare Romans 12:9-21 and also Matthew 5:43-48). Responsibility is respond-ability: the God-given ability to respond to any situation of life in accordance with his commandments. It is the ability to respond biblically to whatever God or man does or says. It is the ability, as Romans 15:1-3 says, to bear the weaknesses of those without strength and not just please ourselves. It is the ability to please one's neighbor for his good to his edification. It is the ability to emulate Christ who did not please himself, "but, as it is written, the reproaches of those who reproached thee fell upon me."

Responsibility is the ability to "accept one another, just as Christ also accepted us to the glory of God." This does not

---

[1] The writer, at one time, had an administrative post in a small conservative denomination which required him to visit nearly every congregation in that church. Often, he had occasions to speak at length with pastors, who nearly always welcomed the opportunity to discuss their work with an outsider. He found that many ministers were concerned about counseling. He discovered uneasy consciences among them. Man after man expressed dissatisfaction with both the theory and the results of the counseling usually recommended in the books.

[2] Carl Rogers, *Counseling and Psychotherapy,* p. 37.

mean accepting Christian brethren because they are wonderful or because the counselor is neutral, but rather it means accepting them in Christ who died for their sin. His acceptance of us cost him his life. Christians are accepted by God "in the beloved one," who bore their guilt and accepts them because their sins are forgiven. God himself does not accept them in their sin. As Christians we accept one another only because we are brethren in Christ. In all such acceptance, judgments about sin are made. Rogerian permissive "acceptance" bears no resemblance to Christian acceptance in Christ. It is therefore irresponsible acceptance.

## No Neutrality

Think of the sorry picture the conservative Christian minister makes as he sits behind his desk grunting non-judgmentally. The Christian pastor is called to be a paraclete, not a parakeet.[1] He ought always to act like a Christian—even when counseling.

Rollo May clearly believes in man's autonomy. Moral neutrality stems from that belief. May tries to justify his view scripturally:

> This brings us to the matter of moral judgments in counseling. It is clear, first from a Christian point of view, that no one has a right to judge another human being; the command, judge not, is an incontrovertible, particularly since it

---

[1] *Paracletos* means "one who is called to another's side to aid him by his counsel." The word comes to mean "counselor" in exactly the same sense as when we speak of a counselor-at-law (cf. I John 2:1). It is possible that in all of John's references the word has the meaning of advocate or lawyer. In no instance in biblical usage does the word convey the idea of neutrality or non-directive counseling; rather, Christ and the Holy Spirit are denominated "paraclete" by virtue of *what they do for us.* When Paul speaks of the *paraclesis* (help or counsel) which God gives by the Scriptures (Romans 15:4, 5), it is obvious that he speaks of a Book conceived of as an authoritative directive aid to our perseverence and hope.

was given a dynamic by Jesus' own life. And psychotherapeutically in the second place, judging is unpermissible; "and above all," as Adler says, "let us never allow ourselves to make any *moral* judgments, judgments concerning the moral worth of a human being."[1]

May's interpretation of Matthew 7:1-5 is false. Not only are there situations of all sorts in which judging is essential, but the Scriptures specifically command believers to make judgments (cf. John 7:24). The passage only condemns illegitimate judging. Christ assumed that Christians would find it necessary to judge others, and in Matthew 7 was therefore specifically directing them how to do so. The passage in question condemns judging in a hasty manner, without evidence. Judging others before straightening up one's own life is also forbidden. Judging intended to denounce another in order to raise one's own ego is condemned. But judgments of moral value in counseling are precisely what the Scriptures everywhere commend.[2] There can be no morally neutral stance in counseling.

How can the Christian pastor "accept" sinful behavior? He is pledged to give a proper Christian response to such behavior. How can he fail to offer known biblical solutions to problems? He is pledged to declare and minister God's word. Shall he sit back non-committally watching the client struggle with a problem to which he can only bring his own hopeless, sinful response, when in the closed Bible on his desk he knows lies the answer that God has given to the problem? In short, how

---

[1] Rollo May, *op. cit.,* p. 176. Carroll Wise agrees with May: "We can say frankly that we see no place in pastoral care for the passing of judgment in terms of condemnation or name calling, or of moralistic preachments" *op. cit.,* p. 80.

[2] Moral judgment is the essence of counsel in the book of Proverbs. The unique element in the wisdom of that counsel is its moral orientation. These are commands for the covenant people which enable them to live in proper covenant relationship to God. Cf. p. 61.

can he forget that he is a Christian and attempt to become neutral or disengaged? Such neutrality is impossible. The pastor cannot set aside his convictions—even temporarily. Even if he could, he would be wrong in doing so. His Christian presuppositions *must* at all times control the interview.[1] To "accept" sinful behavior in the eyes of the client is to condone it. Rather, Christian counselors must become nouthetically involved in the lives of their counselees. They must respond as whole persons, like Paul who declared:

> Out of much affliction and anguish of heart I wrote to you with many tears (II Corinthians 2:4).

In that passage Paul refers to his own counseling, in which he had responded Christianly in the first letter, offering judgment and advice.[2]

---

[1] Hulme wrote: "The client-centered approach breaks with set patterns of thought and practice. It compels the pastor to set aside, at least for the time being, his own value judgments as he acknowledges the sentiments of the counselee." Hulme then attempts to "reassure" the reader with a statement even more devastating in its implications: "There is no attempt to rid the pastor of his convictions, but only to prevent these convictions from controlling the interview" *op. cit.,* p. 5.

[2] Jay Rochelle, in a review of Carroll Wise's recent book, *The Meaning of Pastoral Care,* describes Wise's system well as teaching that "Pastoral care can only happen in a relationship which is completely open, free, and non-judgmental" *The Pittsburgh Perspective,* June 1967, p. 63. But those are contradictory terms. A non-judgmental relationship would require the counselor to be closed rather than open. It would demand rigid restrictions upon him rather than a free exercise of his whole personality. It would destroy genuine empathy (or at least its expression) and at best could develop only a superficial relationship; more likely a non-relationship would ensue. Lowell G. Colston correctly stresses the inevitability of judgment and counters the false view of Wise, *et al,* who naively seek neutrality. But Colston's own basic Rogerianism militates against his cry for judgment, leading him to redefine judgment in "reflexive" terms which amount ultimately to self judgment rather than judgment by God according to his objective written Word.

## What About Listening?

Can the Rogerian non-directive method be used without compromise? Hasn't Rogers at least taught us something about listening? Must we reject everything? Can't we listen to people? Of course we should listen. The Bible taught the importance of careful listening long before Rogers said anything about it. In fact, Proverbs 18:13 makes the crucial remark on this point.[1] But listening, which so often is equated wrongly with Rogers' non-directive method, is not Rogerian methodology, for Rogerian counselors do not listen.[2] That is precisely what they do not do. A good listener is interested in what another has to say. But they consider content to be unimportant. They care only about emotional emissions and refuse to address themselves to data. Rogers wrote:

> The counselor . . . must be prepared to respond not to the intellectual content of what the person is saying, but to the feeling which underlies it.[3]

He clarifies:

> Objective facts are quite unimportant. The only facts

---

[1] Proverbs 18:13—"If one gives answer before he hears, it is his folly and shame."

[2] A typical instance of such misunderstanding occurs in Shrader: "She began, 'Every day I live, I live a lie. You must tell me what to do.' This, of course, is precisely what a counselor is supposed not to do. His role is that of listener" (Wesley Shrader, *Of Men and Angels,* New York: Holt, Rinehart and Winston, 1957, p. 64). Fortunately Shrader found himself compelled to disregard the dictum.

[3] Rogers, *op. cit.,* p. 37. Carroll Wise echoes this view when he says that the pastor "must listen below the level of the manifest content of speech" (*op. cit.,* p. 76).

which have significance for therapy are the feelings which the client is able to bring into the situation.[1]

Rogers himself calls attention to the differences between what he denominates client-centered and problem-centered counseling. He sets his view (supposedly a client-centered view) over against the problem-centered approach to counseling. But is this antithesis, thus stated, accurate? Are Rogerians interested in people, while nouthetic counselors are interested in problems? No, the nouthetic counselor is concerned about people with personal problems, i.e., nouthetic counselors draw no such distinctions. They are interested in problems for the sake of people. They refuse to recognize any such antithesis. Instead of opting for an either/or choice, the nouthetic counselor has his cake and eats it too. His is a truly client-centered approach in which, out of concern for him, the client's feelings and his problems are both taken seriously. It is precisely because he wishes to help the client that he becomes thoroughly involved in the latter's problems. That is why this book consistently speaks about counseling people with personal problems.

In the same volume, Rogers contrasts the techniques of directive and non-directive counseling.[2] Here are some of the differences as Rogers sees them: 1. the directive counselor asks *highly specific questions:* in contrast, the non-directive counselor recognizes *feelings or attitudes;* 2. the directive counselor explains, discusses, gives information; the non-directive counselor interprets feelings or attitudes; 3. the directive counselor marshals evidence and persuades clients to undertake proposed action; the non-directive counselor explains, discusses or gives information rarely; 4. the directive counselor points out a problem or condition needing correc-

---

[1]*Ibid.,* p. 244. It is surprising to see Grounds accept this viewpoint uncritically, in *Baker's Dictionary, op. cit.,* p. 208.

[2]Rogers, *op. cit.,* p. 123.

tion; the non-directive counselor defines the interview situation in terms of the client's responsibility for using it.[1] In some respects this analysis is substantially correct. Rogers is best, of course, in stating the limitations involved in his own methodology. Yet, even here, he fails to recognize the subtle directiveness that even his method must employ. Yet, no nouthetic counselor would consider his activity limited to the items Rogers describes as "directive." He does all those things which Rogers calls directive, but also does many of those things which Rogers calls non-directive. The fact is that the whole range of appropriate Christian responses is available to the nouthetic counselor. He does not force every case into one limited mold. Rather, in responding appropriately to each client and each problem, the entire gamut of possible Christian responses may be used in nouthetic counseling.

Seward Hiltner, who stands in the Rogerian tradition, writes:

> To focus our attention on externals is the opposite of concentrating on the basic thing—feeling or attitude—which the parishioner is trying to convey to us.

Few parishioners try to do anything of the sort. They are not vitally concerned about conveying feelings at all, even though they will certainly say a good bit about their feelings. To see nothing more basic is to take a shallow dip into the case. The client says so much about his feelings because he wants to impress the counselor with the gravity of his problem. His real concern thereby is to try to get help in solving the problems which cause such discomfort. Hiltner believes that counselors go astray and become involved in data because some interest or knowledge of theirs is touched by what the parishioner

---

[1]Perhaps the poverty of Rogerian techniques may be seen by trying to apply these four principles to a concrete situation. A potentially suicidal client on the other end of the telephone line asks for any last help. He declares, "You are my last hope. I have the gun at my temple." What will a Rogerian do?

says, "Instead of responding to him," he continues, "we respond to the idea which has touched the button in us. This diverts our attention from him as a person trying to communicate something."[1]

## Who is Really Client-Centered?

Notice that, despite all his claims, the Rogerian counselor's interest is not really in the client. The client has come with a problem to which he wants a solution. He recognizes that if his problem were solved, he'd feel better, but the Rogerian counselor will take interest in the client only as some vague, one-dimensional person; only as a carrier of feelings. What the client thinks is of no importance. The problem is incidental, and data must be spurned as diverting.

But the client is struggling with a problem, and when the Rogerian ignores the data (afraid to respond because something may "touch the button" in him), it is he who has become diverted from the client as a *thinking person.* He has reinterpreted personality as mere feeling. But when counselors nouthetically discuss the client's ideas as well as his feelings, they show genuine concern for him as a whole person who is "communicating something" to them, namely, the personal problem and his struggle with it.

Hiltner clearly set forth the truncated Rogerian view of man-as-feeling when he accused one counselor of

being caught up in the narrative rather than the character,

---

[1] Seward Hiltner, *The Counselor In Counseling* (New York: Abingdon Press, 1957), p. 27. Ideas often touch buttons in us because our problems are substantially those of our clients (I Corinthians 10:13a). Touched buttons can be helpful indices to the biblical solutions that we have found applicable to similar problems. A good counselor knows how to use his own experience to help another (cf. II Corinthians 1:4). To become really involved with another means not only to allow him to touch buttons, but also to be willing to share pertinent material for his benefit.

the facts rather than feelings. Chester's acts rather than Chester's views and conflicts.[1]

Rogers insists that it is wrong to advise clients, yet the biblical approach requires giving advice. Nouthetic counselors listen in order to gather the data about which to advise people. Hulme concedes, indeed, that

> although there may be a place for advice in the counseling process it is certainly on the periphery.[2]

Rogers insists that counselors should give no advice. Rollo May put it this way:

> *Personality is not transformed by advice.* This misconception we must destroy once and for all; true counseling and the giving of advice are distinctly different functions.[3]

Rogerians are not interested in gathering data. The client himself must come up with all of the answers.[4] The image of the wall is not the only image one may use to describe Rogerian counseling. The mirror might be just as descriptive. We all know the typical scene. The client begins the interview: "I'm really upset." The counselor focuses upon that word and reflects it back in different words: "I see that you're torn two ways." "That's right," says the client, "I'm very distressed." "I see," the counselor replies, "that you are quite troubled." "My difficulty is that I don't know what to do about a certain problem," says the client. "You are trying to find a solu-

---

[1]*Ibid.,* pp. 25, 26.

[2]Hulme, *op. cit.,* p. 23.

[3]May, *The Art of Counseling, op. cit.,* p. 150.

[4]Carroll Wise says: "We ministers do not solve anybody's problems. . . . We are simply a means by which a person is enabled to work out his own destiny." He is so opposed to advice giving that he said, "The kind of preaching which is exhortation . . . may do a lot of harm." Wise wants the non-directive method carried into the pulpit! (*A Clinical Approach to the Problems of Pastoral Care,* Western Interstate Commission for Higher Education: Boulder, 1964), p. 87.

tion," says the counselor. "Yes, that's right. I've had problems with homosexuality. Do you think homosexuality is wrong?" asks the client. And his counselor replies, "I see you are asking me whether homosexuality is ethically or religiously proper."

This is not listening. Listening means taking interest in what another says, and responding appropriately. Taking an interest in content is one essential element in taking an interest in the client. The Rogerian stance, on the contrary, avoids help, avoids advice, avoids value judgments, avoids applying divine declarations to personal problems: Rogerians substitute repetition of the client's questions for the application of biblical principles. It is not too much to say that the Scriptures say nothing of treating people in this way.

But Hiltner continued, saying:

> Action is no substitute for clarification. Even the scantiest kind of observation suggests to us that most counseling situations which begin with a wrestle over an action decision do not get far if they remain only at that level; if they fail to explore the feelings which lie beneath each possible action.[1]

Hiltner has raised a basic point of contention. Precisely here the issue is drawn. Nouthetic counseling assumes that the feelings are not the most profound level of human relationship with which one must be concerned in counseling. God speaks of love in attitudinal and behavioral forms when he defines it as keeping his commandments. Moreover, feelings cannot be

---

[1]Hiltner, op. cit., p. 15. One of the best ways for counselors to obtain accurate, firsthand information is to observe the patterns that emerge as clients respond to concrete problems. Wrestling over action decisions is a better indicator of the true nature of problems than mere talk. Valves are tested for flaws by applying pressure. To ignore action in favor of talk alone as the solution to problems is to violate the biblical principle to be "doers of the word" and "not hearers only." Cf. footnote 1, page 203. Nouthetic counselors follow the dictum—Do not merely talk about problems—talk them through to solutions.

altered directly in the same way that one can change behavior. Consequently, in accordance with Scripture, nouthetic counselors spend less time finding out how people feel. They are more interested in discovering how clients behave.[1] They have learned also that this approach much more successfully cuts through what Hiltner calls the "emotional underbrush."

## Feeling and Behavior

Since Rogers has stressed the primacy of feeling, it seems appropriate to discuss the relationship between feeling and behavior.

One very pertinent passage is found in Genesis 4:3-7. When God rejected Cain's offering (Abel in contrast to Cain had brought the firstlings and fat, i.e., the best), Cain became angry and upset, "and his face fell" (vs. 5). God then rhetorically asked Cain, "Why are you depressed?" and pointed the way toward overcoming it: "If you do right, will it [your face] not be lifted up?" Here, God sets forth the important principle that behavior determines feelings.

Sometimes instead of speaking of mental illness, people talk about "emotional problems." But this language is as confusing as the former. When a client feels depressed or high, or anxious, or hostile, there really is no problem with his emotions. His emotions are working only too well. It is true that his emotions are not pleasant, but the real problem is not emotional, it is behavioral. Solutions aimed at relieving the emotions directly (as, e.g., chemical methods like pills or alcohol), therefore, must be considered to be nothing more than the relief of symptoms.

People feel bad because of bad behavior; feelings flow from actions. This relationship between feelings and behavior is set forth very clearly in Scripture. For example, Peter often point-

---

[1] Of course, voluntary changes in behavior depend upon intelligent decisions and affect the emotions as a result, thus reaching the *whole* man.

ed out that good living produces good feelings. In his first letter (3:10), he quoted Psalm 34:12, 13:

Let him who means to love life, and see good days, refrain his tongue from evil, and his lips from speaking guile: and let him turn away from evil, and do good; let him seek peace, and pursue it.

So to have good days, one must do good deeds. This is not to say, of course, that good deeds save anyone, or that supposed "good deeds" apart from the energizing power of the Holy Spirit are good in God's eyes, but good deeds (in the full biblical sense of the term) lead to good days. All legalism must be rejected as unbiblical. Good deeds are the result of God's work in us, as Paul clearly says in Ephesians 2:10: "created in Christ Jesus unto good works."

Peter speaks of the value of maintaining a good conscience,

. . . so that in the thing which you are slandered, those who revile your good behavior in Christ may be put to shame (I Peter 3:16).

A good conscience, according to Peter, depends upon good behavior. Good lives come from good deeds; good consciences come from good behavior. Conscience, which is man's ability to evaluate his own actions, activates unpleasant visceral and other bodily warning devices when he sins. "When he fails he feels it."[1] These responses serve to alert him to the need for correction of the wrong behavior which the conscience would not tolerate. Bad feelings are the red light on the dashboard flashing out at us, the siren screaming at high pitch, the flag waving in front of our faces. Visceral discomfort is a God-structured means of telling human beings that they have violated their standards. Vernon Grounds is correct when he says that "psychic pain is inflicted by the Holy Spirit as He creates

---

[1] Ronald McKenzie, in a counseling session, 1969.

the conviction of sin, a conviction which testifies that God's law has been broken."[1]

What must one do to set his conscience at rest? The same thing he does to extinguish the red light on the dashboard. He doesn't take a hammer and smash the red light. Instead, he gets out and lifts the hood to see what is wrong. His problem is not with the light on the dashboard. He is thankful for the light; it has warned him early enough to do something about the real problem. Likewise, one's problem is not with his conscience. It is his friend, warning him that there is something wrong with his behavior. There is no emotional problem. One should not try to smash his conscience then. He will not want to put it to sleep by pills or any means that would anesthetize it. In I Timothy 4:2, Paul referred to those who are "seared (cauterized) in their own conscience as with a branding iron." The word "seared" does not speak of the act of branding, but of the result of branding. It refers to the condition of flesh which has been seared with a branding iron and as a result is no longer sensitive to pain. Paul seems to refer to the same phenomenon in Ephesians 4:19 where he speaks of those who are "past feeling" or "callous" (the word indicates inability to feel pain). If the red light were inactivated the driver might be likely to forget about the problem under the hood, which will grow steadily worse until there is a breakdown. The same is true of the man with an inactivated conscience. Such cauterizing of the conscience comes by ignoring its message or by anesthetizing it over a period of time.

The only satisfactory way to deal with conscience is to set it to rest by lifting the hood on the faulty behavior that activated the warning device. Conscience is a "good conscience" when it gives approval to one's behavior. When conscience has

---

[1] Vernon Grounds, "When and Why the Psychiatrist Can't Help You," *Seminary Study Series* (Denver: Conservative Baptist Theological Seminary, n. d.), p. 3.

been set to rest with respect to past problems by seeking forgiveness, making restitution, affecting reconciliation, or whatever a specific case requires, one's coping level rises. Cyclical
movement begins in a positive direction. A downward destructive cyclical movement is reversed. Hopefully now this
movement will gain momentum and snowball in the direction
of good feelings. More must be said later on about positive
and negative cyclical movements (or snowballing). A new
sense of satisfaction comes through responsible (biblical) living patterns.[1] This humble confidence enables one to attack
more difficult problems and to undertake new endeavors for
the future. One physician recently wrote:

> Equally important is the belief that the patient can do
> something about his behavior and not merely talk about it.
> We've made life hard for ourselves and our patients by pos-
> tulating that only a change in attitude or motivation will
> change behavior, overlooking the alternate possibility that
> changed behavior can change attitudes.

She concluded: "Our psychology of introspection has too often neglected the psychology of doing."[2]

## The Nervous System Corresponds to the Nouthetic Approach

Something might be said about the human nervous system
with respect to behavior and feeling in counseling. There are
basically two sides to this system. One side is emotional and
involuntary. The other side, associated with problem-solving
and voluntary action has to do with behavior. The importance
of this fact is that it is in the client's behavior that changes
can be made directly, because behavior, in contrast to emo-

---

[1] Incidentally, this is why when visiting aged persons it is wiser not to
ask, "How are you doing?" (i.e., how do you feel?), but instead, "What
are you doing?" If they have become inactive, they usually feel useless.

[2] Marianne Eckardt, "Roundtable: Female Orgasm," *Medical Aspects of Human Sexuality* (April 1968), Vol. 2, No. 1, p. 46.

tion, is controlled by the voluntary, not the involuntary side of man. Emotional states flow secondarily from the behavioral or the voluntary system. The former involves the involuntary control of visceral and vascular emotional responses, whereas the latter involves action responses by the skeletal musculature. Communication between both nervous systems must be supplied by sensory pathways of the central system. There is a close relationship or a connection between the two so that they can't really be divided as precisely as one might on paper. While there is no direct voluntary access to the emotions, the emotions can be reached indirectly through the voluntary system, because extensive fiber overlappings in the cortex allow unified correlation of the two systems. Thus actions affect emotions. Voluntary behavioral alterations will lead to involuntary emotional changes. It is important to understand, therefore, that feelings flow from actions.

All this may be seen in good preaching. One of the causes of lifeless preaching is that content is often devoid of its proper emotional counterpart in the preacher. When, however, a preacher "relives" the event he is describing rather than merely "reporting" it, he will feel emotionally something of what Peter, or David, or Abraham felt. Good preachers have learned to use intellectual content to elicit and control the emotional state of the body. They imagine themselves as participants and the mind stimulates the emotions appropriate to their simulated experience. The fact that the preacher himself only relives the event in his mind shows that emotions are controlled not only by behavior, but also by behavior consciously contemplated and evaluated.

## Proverbs: A Book of Directive Counseling

Nouthetic counselors frequently hand out individual portions of the Book of Proverbs. One reason why they have found the Book of Proverbs so useful in counseling is that essentially it is a book of good counsel given to covenant youth. Proverbs was written primarily to promote divine wisdom among God's covenant people. It anticipates the pitfalls and problems of life and directs the reader to make biblical responses to them. Proverbs capsulizes segments of life as God expects his children to live it in a sinful world. The book contrasts the way redeemed and unredeemed sinners behave.

In essence, a proverb (the word means a comparison or likeness) is a crisply stated principle of living. The book consists of capsulized statements concerning patterns of problem solving in various areas of life and the consequences to which these lead. These patterns and consequences are succinctly stated by the Hebrew poetical device of comparison or contrast (proverbs that compare usually contain the word "and" and proverbs that contrast often contain the word "but"). Some proverbs, however, take the form of more lengthy vignettes.

There are many interesting parallels in the introductory chapters among the words used to describe the purpose of the book. For example, the words "counsel" and "reproof" occur in Hebrew parallelism of a comparative rather than contrasting sort, indicating that reproof is considered synonymous with or similar to counsel: "And you have ignored all my counsel, and would have none of my reproof" (1:25). Notice also the same parallelism in verse 30, "You would have none of my counsel and have despised all my reproof." In chapter 3, verse 11, and 12, similar comparisons adding another term are apparent:

> My son, do not despise the Lord's discipline or be weary of his reproof: for the Lord reproves him whom he loves; as a father the son in whom he delights.

Plainly the reproof that is spoken of is the kind of discipline that a father gives to his son for the son's own benefit. So that "counsel," "reproof" and "discipline" are all used in Proverbs in similar ways, if not as synonyms. Notice also the terms that are used for teaching or instruction. A father urges his son: "Do not forget my teaching; let your heart keep my commandments" (3:1), and "I give you good precepts, do not forsake my teaching" (4:2). The ideas of discipline, advice, reproof, teaching, instruction, precept and commandment all converge in Proverbs. Together they constitute the idea of wise counsel.

The same emphasis rings out in every part of Proverbs. Following an exhortation to listen to his father, a disobedient son is told:

> At the end of your life, if you do not listen to me, you groan when your flesh and body are consumed and you say "How I hated discipline and my heart despised reproof! I did not listen to the voice of my teachers or incline my ear to my instructors. I was at the point of utter ruin in the assembled congregation" (5:11, 12).

Counseling in Proverbs is anything but non-directive. In nouthetic counseling the Book of Proverbs plays a very significant part because these proverbs give instruction; they offer directive counsel and advice. Such counsel involves corrective reproof ("The commandment is a lamp; and the teaching is a light; and the reproofs of discipline are the way of life" 6:23). The "reproofs of discipline" are, according to the Hebrew, "reproofs whose aim is correction." The system of counseling advocated in the Book of Proverbs is plainly nouthetic. Proverbs assumes the need for divine wisdom imparted (as in nouthetic counseling) by verbal means: by instruction, by reproof, by rebuke, by correction, and by applying God's commandments in order to change behavior for one's benefit.

Throughout Proverbs anti-Rogerian thought appears. For instance, wisdom is personified and made to say: "I have counsel and sound wisdom," and "I have insight; I have strength" (8:14). Wisdom (as the ideal counselor) gives advice; tells people what to do. As a matter of fact, the Book of Proverbs exhorts the young man to listen to others rather than depend upon his own ideas: "Do not rely on your own insight" (3:5). Words could hardly be more anti-Rogerian.

100

The young man is assured, "He who listens to me will dwell secure, and will be at ease without dread of evil" (1:33), and promised:

> My son, if you receive my words and treasure my commandments with you, making your ear attentive for wisdom and inclining your heart to understanding; yes, if you cry out for insight and raise your voice for understanding, then you will understand the fear of the Lord and find the knowledge of God, for the Lord is wisdom, from his mouth cometh knowledge and understanding (2:1-6).

So it is clear that an outside source imposed upon the counselee from above in an authoritative fashion by means of precepts, commandments, instruction, words, reproof, discipline, and correction, is what a young man (or any client seeking counseling) needs. Rather than encouraging clients to do all of the talking, counselors frequently ought to urge clients to listen to words of advice. The counselee needs to learn to listen to words of counsel, reproof, commandment and instruction. That he has not done so in the past, may be one major cause of his present distress.[1]

## Methodology Grows out of Presuppositions

The sort of eclecticism by which one assumes that he can adopt techniques that grow out of non-biblical principles that rest upon non-Christian presuppositions has done much damage to Christian counseling. We have seen that non-directive techniques grow out of and are consistent with Rogers' principle of autonomy, and that listening to feelings alone must be rejected because it is of a piece with Rogers' faulty view of man. The other side of the coin is also true: all techniques and methodology must grow out of and be appropriate to the

---

[1]Many other passages refer to directive counseling. Cf. especially Isaiah 40:13,14 for the biblical description of the functions of a counselor.

biblical presupposition that underlying the surface problem is a sinful life style.

Consider another example, the use of transference. By "transference" Rogerians and other Freudians mean that clients frequently redirect their feelings (often negative) for one person to another (in this case to the counselor). Hatred for a father may be transferred to the counselor. Transference is encouraged by many as a useful technique in counseling. But is transference a technique that Christians may use? No. When counselors encourage or allow clients to transfer feelings of hatred and resentment to themselves, they thereby encourage clients to perpetuate and multiply their sin and guilt.[1] In contrast, nouthetic techniques call for the loving rebuke of sinful attitudes and actions, even when directed toward the counselor. Instead of adopting reflective methods which encourage transference, the nouthetic counselor considers incidents of transference a nouthetic opportunity to put an end to such transference. He will therefore employ methods appropriate to bringing about repentance and reconciliation rather than the acceptance of sinful feelings. He points out to the client that his negative transference is one evidence that he has been using wrong methods of handling his problems. Whenever a client transfers strong feelings of antipathy toward his counselor, for instance, the counselor should seize upon this opportunity to observe that such behavior may be one instance of underlying patterns which in the past have gotten the client into difficulty. The nouthetic counselor will probably say something like this:

> Jim, so far as I can see, this attitude toward me is totally unwarranted. If I've wronged you, tell me how, and I'll rec-

---

[1] Positive transference seems to be no better, for it is but a kind of fantasizing in which the client is allowed to "use" the counselor in an unrealistic relationship. Transference is simply one more faulty pattern which clients develop instead of squarely facing the actual people involved in their problems.

tify the situation; if I haven't, you'd better take note of this pattern. In either case, you have failed to handle the problem biblically, and this is precisely the sort of thing which has been getting you into trouble.

The counselor, by capitalizing upon this instance of the client's sinful behavior, already has begun to help him by not allowing sin to go unchallenged. Because he handles sin at this level, he is able to show concretely how sinful behavior brings difficulty into the counselee's life on many other levels, as well.

It is impossible to destroy the foundation and preserve the superstructure. Because non-biblical systems rest upon non-biblical presuppositions, it is impossible to reject the presuppositions and adopt the techniques which grow out of and are appropriate to those presuppositions. Rogerian "acceptance" and Freudian "transference" techniques fail because of the fallacies of the Rogerian philosophy of autonomy and the Freudian ethic of irresponsibility upon which they rest.

One specific objection to the use of transference as a tool in counseling is that such usage encourages clients to sin against another and, thus, adds to their guilt. Corollaries to that basic objection are: first, that counselors become a party to the client's sin, so that counselor and counselee both sin in employing such transference. Secondly, sin is condoned. Even if a counselor simply sits back in an accepting manner without making nouthetic responses to sinful attitudes or statements about sin, he has become a party in condoning that sin, in the eyes of many clients. Acceptance of sin is sin. Thirdly, to agree to use transference is to agree that the ends justify the means.

Of course, one might also ask, does transference really help? The answer again is, no.[1] Sinful attitudes and behavior are

_____

[1]Cf. especially Phillips and Wiener, *Short-Term Psycho-therapy and Structured Behavior Change* (New York: McGraw-Hill Book Company, 1966), pp. 209-212. In this book, the authors have gathered an aston-

never helpful, for they violate God's law. And it is a fundamental Christian assumption that any practice which is contrary to God's law will harm clients. Thus Christians must look upon the use of transference and all other such eclectic borrowings as counterproductive.

Rogerianism, therefore, must be rejected *in toto.* Every remnant of this humanistic system exalting man as autonomous must be eradicated. The basic premises lead to the methodology. Reject the one and you reject the other.

To illustrate factitiously the differences between the various systems, consider the following parable. Picture a poor fellow sitting on a tack suffering from severe pain. A counselor approaches him who holds the somatic or chemical viewpoint. Hearing the client's complaints, he immediately prescribes tranquilizers or pain killers. The solution is to anesthetize him. Or perhaps the client is a do-it-yourselfer who does not have any pills in the medicine closet. He may resort to his own chemical solution by anesthetizing his brain with alcohol. If a surgical specialist is on hand he may suggest that the nerves which are activated may be severed. This will knock out the symptoms and give the client relief. Smash the red light on the dashboard! Then, of course, there's the Freudian analyst who looks over the situation and says:

> These pains are located near the sexual area. I think we'd better go back into the patient's childhood experiences and learn about some of his early sexual experiences. Then, perhaps we'll be able to alleviate his pain, though of course no assurance can be given. We recognize that he has been

---

ishing amount of evidence which runs counter to the institutionalized views. Cf. also S. I. McMillen, *None of These Diseases* (Westwood: Spire Books, Fleming H. Revell Co., 1963), Chapters 10, 11. Transference of hostility in the end turns out to be nothing less than one more repetition of a sinful pre-conditioned response (cf. ch. VII, *infra*). As one instance of such a preconditioned pattern, it must be opposed rather than accepted or encouraged.

wrongly socialized and his superego is a cruel tyrant. If he can be resocialized he will possibly get better.

Next, a disciple of Rogers appears. When the sufferer asks him what he must do to get relief, the therapist replies:

> I'm not going to advise anything. I'm sure that you have all the resources within yourself to solve the difficulty. I'll reflect your questions back to you and help you clarify and gain insight. Now, sir, you say you are torn two ways? . . .

Finally a nouthetic counselor comes upon the scene. He looks around and finds a tack under the client. He says, "Get off that tack. Now that you're up, sit down on a chair over here and we'll talk about how you can avoid sitting on tacks in the future."

## Chapter VII

## CONFESS YOUR SINS

The thesis of this chapter is set forth succinctly in Proverbs 28:13.

He who conceals his transgressions will not prosper: but he who confesses and forsakes them will obtain mercy.

Those words are straightforward and simple. There is nothing obtuse about them; they say exactly what they mean and mean precisely what they say. God's remedy for man's problems is confession. The concealing of transgressions brings misery, defeat and ruin, but the confession and forsaking of sin will bring merciful pardon and relief.

### James 5:14

James 5:14 was referred to in an earlier chapter. There can be no doubt that James taught that there is a possibility that sickness may stem from sin. James directed Christians who become sick to "call for the elders of the church." This scriptural provision puts the organized church of Jesus Christ squarely in the business of working with those who are sick because of sin. The work of the officers of the church cannot be handed over to psychiatrists on the basis that such persons are "mentally ill." Psychiatry has no means for curing *hamartiagenic* sickness.[1] The church must not cower before the threats of psychiatrists who have usurped her territory and now declare that she may not repossess it.[2]

---

[1]*Hamartiagenic* sickness is literally "sin-engendered" sickness. While all sickness stems ultimately from Adam's sin, and in that indirect sense is *hamartiagenic,* some sicknesses are the direct result of particular sins. The word is used in the latter sense here.

[2]Freud went beyond healing, declaring that psychoanalysis is "the study of the soul of man," and involved instruction in "the art of liv-

James directed the elders to pray for the patient, anointing him with oil. He explained that the prayer of faith will make the sick member well, and if he has committed any sins they will be forgiven him. James further exhorted the sick to confess their sins one to another, "that they may be healed." James seems to have seen a high correlation between sickness and sin. He assumed that much sickness is the result of sin. The "if" clause allows for the possibility of sickness from disease, injury, or other innocent causes. James clearly recognized two sources for sickness; one organic, one non-organic (cf. p. 29). But if the cause is otherwise unknown (and perhaps even in the case of some known causes) James directed that when the patient discusses his sickness with the elders and prayer is made, the possibility of sickness as the result of sin ought to be discussed. If sin is found in the background of the problem, it must be confessed.

When James referred to confessing sickness-causing sin, he meant primarily confession to God. But he spoke also of confessing sins "to one another." The sick person is directed to reveal and confess his sins to the parties against whom he has sinned. Whether he should confess to the elders as well is problematical. Probably, they are considered as counselors in this matter, for the passage says that after they pray together, healing takes place. The best understanding of the passage seems to be that the sick believer did confess his sins to the elders. This would seem to be the force of the *oun* ("therefore") with which verse 16 in the Greek begins. The generalization of verse 16 ("therefore keep on confessing your sins to one another and praying for one another so that you may be healed") seems to grow out of the experience described in verses 14 and 15 which would presuppose that confession had been made to the elders. The word *exomologeo* ("confess") used in James 5:16 means literally, "to speak out the same

---

ing." Cf. Erich Fromm, *Psychoanalysis and Religion* (New Haven: Yale University Press, 1950), p. 7.

thing." The idea contained in it is to publicly (or at least outwardly) say to another that you agree with his adverse judgment about your behavior. It means to admit to someone else that you have sinned against him. The Westminster Confession of Faith put it this way:

> As every man is bound to make private confession of his sins to God, praying for the pardon thereof; upon which, and the forsaking of them, he shall find mercy; so he that scandalizeth his brother, or the church of Christ, ought to be willing, by a private or publick confession and sorrow for his sin, to declare his repentance to those that are offended; who are thereupon to be reconciled to him, and in love to receive him (XV:VI).

### What about Oil?

Someone may wonder about the directions for anointing with oil. Whether James thought of the anointing as simultaneous with or antecedent to the prayer is uncertain and probably unimportant. Olive oil was considered medicinal. In fact, in biblical times oil was used as the universal medicine. For instance, note Mark 6:13 and Luke 10:34 (where the Good Samaritan treated the man who fell among thieves by pouring oil into his wounds). Isaiah lamented the condition of God's people whom he described by the figure of an injured person whose wounds have not been softened with oil (1:6).

James contemplated no magic, therefore, when he mentioned the use of oil. Neither did he refer to the Roman Catholic sacrament of extreme unction. As a matter of fact, James did not write about ceremonial anointing at all. The Greek word "anoint" (aleipho), which James used, does not mean ceremonial anointing. The ordinary word for a ceremonial anointing was chrio (a cognate of christos [Christ] the "anointed One"). The word James used (aleipho), in contrast to the word chrio ("to anoint"), usually means "to rub" or simply "apply." The word aleipho was used to describe the personal application of salves, lotions, and perfumes, which usually had an oil base. The word is allied to *lipos,* "grease." It was even used to speak of plastering walls. The cognate, *exaleipho,* intensifies the concept of rubbing or applying oil, and conveys the idea of smearing, wiping, blotting, erasing, etc. An *aleiptes* was a "trainer" who rubbed down athletes in a gymnastic school. *Aleipho* was used frequently in medical treatises.[1] And so it turns out that what James required by the use of oil was the use of the best medical means of the day. James simply said to rub oil (often used as a base for mixtures of various medicinal herbs) on the body, and pray. What James advocated was the use of consecrated, dedicated medicine. In this passage he urged the treating of sickness by medical means accompanied by prayer. The two are to be used together; neither to the exclusion of the other. So instead of teaching faith healing apart from the use of medicine, the passage teaches just the opposite. But when medicine is used, it must be used in conjunction with prayer. That is why James said that the prayer of faith makes the sick well.

But James did not consider the use of medicine and prayer alone to be effective if the patient has committed sins. In such cases, prayer specifically must include the confession of sins. Sin is at the root of some illnesses and may at least be a contributing factor to some complications of other illness. And James further explained that confession must not only be made to God, but that sins must be confessed "to one another." Of course, confession is not an end in itself. Repentance and confession are but a means to reconciliation, which is the ultimate goal.[2]

### Not all Sickness Related to Particular Sins

It is plain that the Scriptures never represent all sickness as the result of immediate sin or even sinful patterns of life. The

---

[1]Cf. Trench, *Synonyms of the New Testament, op. cit.*
[2]Cf. Matthew 5:24; 18:15.

book of Job protests against any such notion.[1] The Bible teaches that the existence of all sickness, however, goes back to Adam's sin, and in that sense all sickness may be said to be the result of sin; but only in that sense. Yet the Bible does acknowledge an immediate relationship between sin and sickness in many instances. For example, in John 5:14, Jesus says to one man whom he healed:

> Behold, you have become well: do not sin any more, so that nothing worse may befall you.

The implication seems to be that his original sickness came from sin, and that if he, indeed, continued in such sin, even worse judgments might possibly come upon him. I Corinthians 11:30 is even more explicit. In the church at Corinth the Lord's Supper was being abused. Christians were eating and drinking judgment upon themselves by failing to discern the Lord's body in the bread and wine. For this reason, Paul says that many among them were weak or sick and a number slept (i.e., died). Thus Paul, like James, taught that God in the ordering and disciplining of his church frequently uses sickness as a rod of chastisement. James, therefore, urged Christians to make it a practice to pray for one another concerning this problem. James used the present imperative in verse 16 which means *"keep on praying* for one another in order that ye may be healed."

## Nouthetically Confronting the Sick

The New Testament teaches that sickness may stem from sin, and James therefore urged the need for nouthetic confrontation by the elders of the church. Pastors always ought to be aware of their obligation in this matter when visiting the sick. It would seem that as a regular practice pastors should inquire into the possibility of sin as the root of the sickness. The need to distinguish between sin-engendered sick-

---

[1]See also John 9:1-3.

ness and disease-engendered sickness has been emphasized so strongly in our time that modern conservative pastors rarely raise the issue with the sick.[1] Of course it also takes courage to do so. One wonders how many illnesses (or at least complications of illnesses) might have been cured by careful attention to and application of James' words. Counselors must learn to take James seriously.

## Confessing to Others

Sin first must be confessed to God. Much in Christian literature has been said about this, but very little has been said about confession to one's brother. How does one go about confessing his sin to another? One way to answer that question is to say something about the value of rehearsal prior to making confession of sins. Christ represented the Prodigal Son as engaging in a kind of rehearsal. He tried to imagine what would happen when he went back home, and rehearsed what he would say to his father. In the far country, when he "came to himself" during the famine, he grew so hungry that he wished he could eat the pods that the swine were eating. He said to himself:

> I will get up and go to my father and will say to him, Father, I have sinned against heaven and in your sight. I am no longer worthy to be called your son; make me as one of your hired men (Luke 15:17-19).

Everyone knows the outcome. The father received him with compassion and love. He ran to meet him, embraced him and kissed him. Then the son began to make his speech:

> Father, I have sinned against heaven and in your sight. I am no longer worthy to be called your son.

---

[1] That healing cults (as well as the psychiatric cult) have flourished ever since the church has abdicated her legitimate role in healing, strongly suggests a causal relationship.

He had rehearsed what he was going to say ahead of time. Clearly, he didn't need to use it, for the father had greater plans growing out of grace and mercy. Nevertheless, we might consider well how the Lord Jesus pictured the prodigal preparing for the encounter with his father. He "came to his senses," Christ says. A man in his right mind then will do several things: (1) he will make a wise decision and follow it with the appropriate action; (2) he will acknowledge his sin against God and man; (3) he will seek to right all wrongs, even at his own expense; (4) he will confront the one whom he has wronged; (5) he will prepare for that confrontation, and one means of preparation might well be to determine and rehearse what one wishes to say beforehand.

Often when people find it necessary to confess sin to another, or to deal with some problem of interpersonal relationship, it is very difficult for them to do so, since for them it is usually a new and unfamiliar experience. As a result, some people may make mistakes that could further complicate an already bad relationship. The pressure and stress of the occasion itself, in addition to the basic lack of familiarity with this kind of situation, stack up together against the client. Sometimes a role-playing rehearsal helps. In the counseling session prior to the stress situation the client may rehearse what he is to say and do. One of the counselors plays the part of the person to whom the client must speak. If there is another counselor he may act as the director. There is danger, of course, that the client may simply parrot what the counselor has suggested. So prior to any role play, prior to sending anyone to confess to another, the counselor tries to make sure that the client's expressed desire to bring about reconciliation is genuine. Surely one basic index to this is a good confession to God. The whole matter must be handled in the spirit of repentance as a fruit fitting or appropriate to repentance (cf. Matthew 3:8). Unless every step is taken asking the Holy Spirit to bless, the result is no more than staging.

In addition to aiding clients in making confession, role play often shows whether the client understands what he is to do. Sometimes role play helps the counselor to discover errors in the client's understanding of the situation that need to be corrected. Moreover, role play may uncover problems that otherwise might have passed unnoticed or that the client had not recognized were so serious.

## Allow No Minimizing

During the rehearsal or role play, it is particularly useful to anticipate some of the possibilities of what might happen. The way that a client approaches and sets up the nouthetic situation is important, but how he responds to feedback is equally as important. Often when a client asks for forgiveness, the other person tries to minimize his problem. A husband, for instance, says to his wife, "Honey, I'm sorry that I stormed out of the house the other day." She replies, "Oh, John, don't think any more about it; forget it; I don't care about it." When she begins to minimize in that fashion, there is a great temptation for the client to allow her to do so and close the matter. Instead, he must be careful to say something like—

No, I really mean this. I've sinned against God and I've injured you. I don't want you to look lightly upon what I've done. I really want your forgiveness and I need your help to be a different person in the future.

And so he presses for a genuine decision for at least two important reasons.

First of all, sin should never be minimized. Sin is an important matter. Sin can't be handled lightly, because it is primarily against God. Sin is a violation of the commandments of God. In their relation to God, all sins are equally heinous, even though their social effects may differ widely. And so, when the client continues to press, he presses for a real decision on the part of the other person about a serious matter.

Secondly, minimizing may be a way in which the other person seeks to avoid making a definite decision. Minimizing may be an attempt to avoid facing the possibility of extending genuine forgiveness and thereby rejecting reconciliation. Only by pressing for an answer to the question, "Will you forgive me?" can the client be sure that the issue has been joined and settled. When the client settles a matter with another in this manner, he may go away with peace in his heart, for the matter has been set to rest one way or another. Only then can the client hold the other party to the fact that he has sought, by asking forgiveness, to reach a full decision on the matter so that the question might be closed. This is why others often will try to avoid saying decisively, "Yes, I forgive you," or "No, I won't."

When Jane came for counseling, she expected her counselors to respond to her complaints and self-pity in the same way that others did. Her friends had assured her that her resentment against her mother was justified and that probably she had done all she could do about the bad relations between them. She would have to learn to live with her problem. Her counselors, however, stressed the importance of righting the wrongs she had done, beginning with the confession of her resentment and the hateful acts this had led to. They then suggested that she and her mother work on a program in which her mother could rightly become involved with her and her children. When Jane got around to squaring things off with mother, the latter sighed with relief and said she too knew that as Christians they should have become reconciled long before. Together, they worked out a new relationship because Jane not only asked forgiveness, but also requested help. Requesting help lets the other party know immediately that one means business.

## Securing Help

In role play the client not only is taught how to ask for forgiveness, but whenever possible how to ask for help. He needs help in breaking old patterns and establishing new biblical ones. He needs help in working out a new relationship with his brother now that reconciliation has been effected. Otherwise, he and the others may slip back into old sinful patterns once more. This not only provides help for the client, but gives the client and his friend an opportunity to establish a better future relationship by encouraging them to consider not only the problems in the immediate situation, but also the underlying patterns in their relationship. Discussion and action on this level alone will bring about the desired relationship. Only then can they truly ask God's blessing on their renewed friendship.

Sometimes instead of playing the role of a minimizer, the counselor may respond negatively to see how the client will handle hostility. He will be interested, for example, in discovering whether the client has learned how to face anger in a Christian manner. Many other possibilities, varying according to the individual cases, may be imagined. Role play is very useful in these ways, and possibly can be useful in other ways as well.

### Psychosomatic Illness

Nothing that Paul (I Corinthians 11) or James said indicates whether the sin-connected illnesses of which they wrote were psychosomatic, directly inflicted judgments or providential judgments involving the use of disease or accident. There are, however, portions of Scripture which particularly discuss the psychosomatic effects of unconfessed sin.

In Psalm 32 David affirmed that happiness comes through confession and forgiveness. This proposition is stated in verses 1 and 2:

> Blessed is he whose transgression is forgiven, whose sin is covered. Blessed is the man unto whom the Lord does not charge iniquity and in whose spirit there is no guile.

The Psalm begins with a description of the unhappy state of hidden sin causing distress of soul and body (verses 3, 4). As evidence, he shared his own experience: "When I kept silence" (that is, before I confessed my sin) "my bones became old through my roaring all the day long." David's remarks show how severe the psychosomatic effects of sin may be. The misery of this condition made him feel as if the bones in his body were growing old and ready to crack. His body suffered so that he groaned loudly all day long.

Use of the figure of suffering bones elsewhere helps in understanding its meaning here. Proverbs 14:30 says: "A relaxed mind makes for physical health: but passion is rottenness to the bones" (Berkeley Translation). The psychosomatic effects of a mind that is at peace (relaxed), free from the stress and tension of guilt, are evident. Note the antithetical elements in this verse: mind over against body; relaxation over against passion; physical health over against rottenness of bones. Physical health contrasted with rottenness of bones shows that the latter expression refers to the psychosomatic effects of inner turmoil upon the body. The idea of psychosomatic problems is not new. The Bible has a great deal to say about this matter.

Psalm 38:3 is also instructive:

There is no soundness in my body in the presence of thy anger; there is no peace in my bones in the presence of my sin (Berkeley Translation).

The parallelism in verse 3 also helps one to understand the meaning of David's references to difficulty with his bones. In the first half of the verse he wrote: "There is no soundness in my body," which explains the meaning of its synonymous parallel in the second half of that verse, "there is no peace in my bones." The second parallel in the verse also shows the identity of meaning: "In the presence of thy anger," "in the presence of my sin." David mentions the result and its cause, the anger of God over the sin of David. The pairs of words, "body" and "bones," and "soundness" and "peace" indicate a synonymous use of terms. When he spoke of rot in the bones, bones wasting away, bones aching, or bones feeling as if they had been broken, it seems evident that David was speaking generally of the whole body. This is natural since the body is framed upon the bones. The bones are the most essential structural element of the body. By an easy synecdoche (taking a part to represent the whole), David pictured the whole body aching, the whole body affected by sin. The exact parallel of "body" to "bones" in verse 3 of Psalm 38 makes this conclusion probable.[1]

The psychosomatic effects of sin are more readily seen in the Berkeley Translation of Psalm 38. David said that he felt as if his loins were charged with inflammation, he felt as though he were benumbed and thoroughly bruised (verse 8). He wrote: "I groan because of my heart murmurings," and,

> Lord, all my longing is known to thee; and my sighing is not hidden from thee. My heart beats fast, my strength fails me (verse 9).

These symptoms all can be the effects of anxiety upon the body. A rapidly beating heart is a fear reaction. He is generally depressed. He feels as if a load is crushing him down and he finds no peace in his body, that is the body feels as if it is in constant distress.

### Depression

"Day and night thy hand was heavy upon me" (32:4), David cried. The hand of God pressed hard upon him. He literally felt depressed (pressed down). It was as if God's hand were crushing him. He believed depression was from God and considered it the merciful punishment of God warning him and leading him to repentance. The sense of guilt crushed him.

---

[1]Cf. also J. A. Sanders, *The Dead Sea Psalms* (Ithaca: Cornell University Press, 1967), p. 71: "Near death was I for my sins, and my iniquities had sold me to the grave" . . . "let not Satan rule over *me,* nor an unclean spirit; neither let pain nor the evil inclination take possession of *my bones.*"

"My sap, my moisture," he says, "is turned into the drought of summer." The effects of this anxiety upon his body were evident. The saliva in his mouth dried up (a natural response in an anxiety state).

The 51st Psalm parallels Psalm 32 in many respects. The two Psalms may refer to the same event. In Psalm 51 David wrote about his sin against Uriah and Bathsheba. The Psalm is the record of his repentance after Nathan accused him of adultery and murder. In verse 3 he described the anxiety state caused by his guilty conscience prior to repentance. He wrote: "My sin is ever before me."[1] Conscience was at work contin-

---

[1] Counseling experience underscores the biblical idea that most people know why they are in trouble, even when at first they deny it. Whenever counselors operate on the assumption that this is so, they find most people drop their defenses and tell it like it is. Counselors who presuppose that clients do not know the problems in their lives tend to ignore or reinterpret genuine expressions of guilt and thereby discourage and confuse clients about the causes of their difficulties. It is a serious question whether a Christian whose conscience judges him according to the explicit standards of Scripture can ever become seriously depressed over the guilt of sin committed without that sin being "ever before him." Cf. also Job 6:30. Some people who otherwise might be aware of their sin, because they have been taught that sin has no relationship to depression, need to be shown that feelings flow from actions. Of course there are persons "past feeling" whose conscience has been "seared with a branding iron." To the best of my knowledge, the Bible does not seem to speak about the so-called sociopath (psychopath), who is supposed to have little or no conscience. The matter needs further study.

Proverbs 28:1 vividly pictures the effects of a haunting guilty conscience: "The wicked flee when no one pursues: but the righteous are bold as a lion." A guilty conscience leads to fear, and a good conscience leads to boldness. The wicked flee in many ways. Henry was burdened with a guilty conscience. Walking down the street one day, he saw Ron coming his way. Henry knew he had wronged Ron in a business deal. Seeing Ron, Henry was suddenly afraid and felt as if he had to avoid him at all costs. He turned a corner as quickly as he could and escaped. He felt as if he would do almost anything to avoid meeting Ron. Because Henry had wronged him, Ron had become a stressor to Henry.

118

ually accusing him of his sin. Constantly, day and night, it haunted him. He cried out,

> Make me to hear joy and gladness that the bones which thou hast broken may rejoice (verse 8).

The condition which before he had likened to aching old (rotting) bones that caused him to groan all day long, at length seemed so sharply painful that it approximated the pain of broken bones. The same sort of discussion may be found in Psalm 38. In Psalm 38:1 David again related his experience. He described how the Lord rebuked him in wrath and chastened him in fury. He pictured himself as a wounded soldier staggering about with God's arrows sticking fast in him. Again he pictured God's hand pressing heavily upon him. In verses 3 and 4 he enlarged upon the effects of guilt upon the body. In words which show no difficulty in connecting sin and its adverse bodily effects, David complained:

> There is no soundness in my flesh because of thy anger, nor is there any rest in my bones because of my sin, for my iniquities have gone over my head. Like a heavy burden they are too heavy for me.

The pressure of the feeling of guilt was overbearing. David loathed his condition. It was so distasteful he could only cry out: "My wounds stink and are rotten because of my foolishness" (verse 5). He moaned, "I am greatly troubled, I am bowed down greatly, I go mourning all the day long." No one figure of speech was adequate to describe his misery. David

---

Unforgiven sinners are vulnerable people. They often become intensely self conscious. Even innocent words frequently are interpreted as personal attacks. They interpret as personal affronts acts that have no direct relationship to them. A guilty person may claim that a sermon was a personal attack, or lacking the courage to do so, will object to some incidental feature of the sermon, or some supposed slight of the minister. To call such a person paranoid is to misinterpret the dynamics of his problem. On the other hand, a man at peace with God and with other men is invulnerable and can be bold as a lion.

described himself as a wounded soldier lying helpless on the battlefield with putrifying wounds. Such agony of soul was as if he were being crushed under a load heavier than he could carry. It was as though he mourned over the death of a loved one. He says, "My loins are filled with a burning. There is no soundness in my flesh." Pain wracked his body. He declared: "I am feeble and painfully broken. I have roared because of the groaning of my heart," and he prayed,

Lord, all of my desire is before thee, and my groaning is not hidden from thee. My heart pants, my strength fails me.

David came to the end of his rope; he was in despair. He felt he could endure the pain no longer. He was about to give up. At that point, he recalled the cause of these sufferings, and resolved to adopt the only solution to the problem:

I am ready to fall, and my pain is always before me. I will declare my iniquity. I will be sorry for my sin (verses 17, 18).

These passages in Psalms 51 and 38 are parallel to Psalm 32. All three Psalms speak of the same kind of anxiety, the same sort of depression, the same type of physical distress, and the same class of emotional visceral responses. All three describe the anxiety of a man who is guilty over his sin and who is crushed by that anxiety. To summarize then, David's first contention was: hiding sin causes distress both of soul and of body (Psalm 32:3, 4).[1]

## Happiness Through Confession

The second fact to be noted in the 32nd Psalm is that confession of sin brings relief and happiness. David expressed this in verses 5 through 7:

---

[1]Counseling experience amply illustrates the human dynamics of depression caused by guilt. There is probably no more frequent problem met by nouthetic counselors. God was good in providing such an explicit paradigm in the life of David—for dealing with depression.

I confessed my sin unto thee, and my iniquity I have not hidden. I said I will confess my sins unto the Lord, and thou didst forgive the iniquity of my sin.

Confession is an acknowledgement and an admission that one has sinned. "I confessed my sin unto thee; my iniquity I have not hidden." Confession involves a rejection of the pattern that was first established in the Garden of Eden. There, Adam and Eve refused to acknowledge their sin, but instead shifted the responsibility to someone else. But David acknowledged that he had sinned, that he had violated God's law. He was sorry for his sin. He poured out his heart before God and asked him for cleansing, forgiveness and the restoration of joy. The New Testament word for "confession" means to "admit or acknowledge," or literally, "to say the same thing." Confession comes about when one views himself as God views him. Confession is saying the same thing that God says about one's sin. It is to plead guilty to the charges made by conscience. This concept of confession is crucial to biblical counseling. By confession of sin alone may Christians stand right before God. Confession and forgiveness through Christ relieve the pressures which bring about psychosomatic effects of sin. But confession must not simply be a means to relieve misery; first and foremost it must be the attempt to tell God that he is right and we are wrong. Confession, therefore, is absolutely essential to counseling.

According to Psalm 51:4, 5, David confessed:

Against thee, and thee only, have I sinned and done this evil in thy sight that thou mightest be justified when thou speakest and be clear when thou judgest. Behold I was brought forth in iniquity and in sin did my mother conceive me.

David's words must not be misunderstood. The Westminster Confession of Faith is correct when it says that an erring Christian "ought to be willing, by a private or public confession, and sorrow for his sin, to declare his repentance to those that are offended" (XV:VI). Now when David spoke in this manner, he did not mean to imply that his wrongs against Uriah and against Bathsheba could be confessed to God only. Surely David, like the prodigal son, would have been willing to confess: "I have sinned against Heaven and in your sight" (Luke 15:18). His words do not contradict James 5:16. David, of course, recognized that he had done a terrible evil against both Bathsheba and Uriah. David's statement does not ignore the social or horizontal effects of sin. But what he was saying when he wrote:

Against thee, and thee only have I sinned and done this evil in thy sight that thou mightest be justified when thou speakest and be clear when thou judgest (verse 4)

is something like this:

Lord, I recognize and acknowledge that I have violated *your* law, not simply man's law. Against thee—that is, by your standards alone, God—do I judge myself; for against your standards have I sinned. I have violated your holy law. I confess that I am truly a vile sinner, for my sin is a direct affront to you. What I have done is heinous, for I have violated divine, not human, law. And so, when you pronounced a verdict against me through Nathan your prophet, I acknowledged that your verdict was true and I agree with it. I confess my sin to you.

True confession always involves repentance before God. It can never be but a technique by which one may obtain relief from his misery, or "make up" with another.

Confession nevertheless brings joy from knowing that one's sins have been forgiven. David summed this up in memorable words:

Blessed is he whose transgression is forgiven. Blessed is the man unto whom the Lord does not charge iniquity (Psalm 32:1, 2).

Large among the elements of such forgiveness is the joy of relief, the blessing of having the whole matter set to rest once and for all: "Thou shalt circle me with songs of deliverance" (Psalm 32:7). David says that the joy of forgiveness is like rings of people around him shouting and singing the praises of God. He feels so joyful and so happy that it is as if he were part of a crowd singing God's praise. Elsewhere he put it this way: "Deliver me from the guilt of shedding blood, O God" (Psalm 51:14), that is, from the consequences of the murder of Uriah. He cried, forgive me, relieve my soul of the burden of this guilt,

> And my tongue shall sing aloud of thy righteousness. O Lord, open thou my lips and my mouth shall show forth thy praise.

When forgiveness came, David was so happy that he sang aloud. Such joy—joy that makes one sing—is precisely what people who come for counseling seek. David pointed the way.

Many cases can be cited which show exactly the same pattern. Clients who through nouthetic counseling have confessed hidden sin, have entered into happiness such as they had not known for a long time. One woman said her daughter's girl friend told her that her daughter had said, "Mom and Dad are acting like newlyweds." Another said, "In all our thirteen years of marriage we have never known such happiness."[1]

## Proverbs

The beneficial effects of righteous living are consistently noted in the Scriptures. References abound in the book of Proverbs. Proverbs 3:1,2 reads:

> My son, do not forget my teaching; let your heart keep

---

[1]The reversal of feeling from depression and despair to joy and singing can be sudden and rapid. In one instance a woman who had been trying to escape her responsibility during a difficult problem, when faced with these facts snapped back dramatically after the second session. Two weeks before, a psychiatrist had prescribed shock therapy.

my commandments; for length of days and years of life, full of peace, will they add to you (Berkeley Translation).

The proverb says that long life and peace of mind come through keeping God's commandments. This principle is constantly reiterated throughout the book. For instance, Proverbs says that departing from evil and revering the Lord bring "healing to your body and nourishment to your bones" (3:8). Proverbs 3:16 describes wisdom as holding "Length of days in her right hand, riches and honor in her left." The writer urged: "Hear, my son, accept what I say, and the years of your life will be many" (4:10). He explained:

Listen to my words, incline your ear to my sayings. Let them not depart from your eyes; keep them in the midst of your heart, for they are life to those finding them and healing to all their flesh (4:20-22, Berkeley Translation).

The Bible teaches that a peace of mind which leads to longer, happier living comes from keeping God's commandments. A guilty conscience is a body-breaking load. A good conscience is one significant factor which leads to longevity and physical health. And so, in a measure, one's somatic (bodily) welfare stems from the welfare of his soul. A close psychosomatic connection between one's behavior before God and his physical condition is an established biblical principle.

### Counseling Others

Finally, in the latter part of the 32nd Psalm David said that he wished to share the experience of the joy of such forgiveness and longed to use his experience to counsel others. In verses 8 and 9, he explained this desire:

I will instruct you and teach you in the way that you shall go . . . I will guide you with my eye.

And he exhorted the reader,

Be not like the horse or like the mule which have no understanding, whose mouth must be held in with bit and bridle so that they do not come near to you.

Some think that God (rather than David) is the speaker in verses 8 and 9, but there is good evidence that this is not so. Note especially the exact parallel in Psalm 51:13. There, after forgiveness is granted, David likewise says: "I will teach transgressors thy way, and sinners shall be converted unto thee." The natural response of forgiveness is to help others by sharing one's own experience and specifically by counseling others in trouble.

## Parents Counseling Children

Incidentally, one of the reasons why parents fail in their attempts to counsel their children is because parents seldom share their failures with them. Rather, they tend to talk about how successful they were in school, how good they were as children, and so on. In doing so, they set up ideals which usually are not true to the facts as they actually occurred, but only as they like to remember them. Not only that, even if these stories were true, they wouldn't help greatly. The sinning child needs to learn the consequences of failure in concrete ways, the problems failure brings, what to do to avoid failure, and how to deal with failure when it does occur. Mythical legends of parental success do not teach these principles. David strikes an entirely different note, a genuine counseling note. Out of his own sinful failure, David exhorts others to successful obedience. This is painful, as one can readily see in David's poetic narrative, yet nouthetic concern will move a counselor to share even painful personal experiences whenever such sharing will help another.

Notice also the directive nature of David's counseling. First of all, the verbs "instruct" and "teach" are themselves directive words. They mean "instruct" and "train" or "drill" one in the way in which he is to go. The idea of restructuring another's life is plainly evident. Rogerians can only shudder with horror at such a thought. But David went beyond this, saying, "Not only will I teach and drill you, but I will guide you as well." The training and instruction will be under David's supervision. He will follow the results and make sure that his instructions are being carried out: "I will keep my eye on you." Such counseling methods are appropriate only to nouthetic presuppositions. More will be said presently about restructuring through training.

The Psalm concludes (verse 9) with a strong exhortation to confess.

> Don't be like the stubborn horse or the foolish mule which has no sense or understanding, who must be dragged by a bit and bridle.

David pleads, "Don't wait for God to 'pull' a confession out of you, as he did from me" Probably verse 9 does not mean that the mule has to be held back so that he won't come near, but rather he has to be dragged by the bit and bridle. In other words,

> Don't be like I was, stubborn and foolish in failing to confess my sin to God. Instead, willingly come to God. Don't wait to be dragged to confession. I foolishly hid my sin and confessed it only after the hand of God pressed heavily upon me, only after my body was terribly affected by my guilt, only after my soul was in grief, and only after I was confronted by Nathan in that embarrassing encounter. Instead, come willingly. Then you, too, will be like all those who, having found the blessing of sins forgiven, are glad in the Lord and rejoice and shout for joy (verse 11).

Thus, nouthetic counselors adhere closely to the principle enunciated in Proverbs 28:13:

> He who conceals his transgressions will not prosper, but he who confesses and forsakes them will receive mercy (Berkeley).

and confidently assure their clients that in this way they may

126

find mercy from God. This methodology is biblical methodology; it is therefore certain and sure. It is fitting to and grows out of the fundamental nouthetic principle that man's problems stem from sin. Depressed persons whose symptoms fail to show any sign of a biochemical root should be counseled on the assumption that they are depressed by guilt.

Sometimes the following diagram is used in counseling. Clients are asked to consider everything they can think of that may be loading them with guilt (matters seemingly large or small).

Write along the arrows any unforgiven sins in your life that are adding to your load of guilt and thereby depressing you. Each matter that is dealt with lightens the load, makes you stand taller and enables you to handle other problems more readily.

The diagram is not always useful or necessary. Many clients with no more than the usual initial inquiries get right to the heart of their problem. Yet it does give the client the framework for an important homework assignment if he does not readily produce adequate data.[1] The format enables him to reflect upon the relationship between his depression and its cause. Sometimes clients will return after the assignment with a list of sins, some of which are erased or crossed out because, they disclose, "As a result of this assignment I have already settled that matter."

---

[1] The question of homework assignments must be discussed, *infra*, p. 195.

## Chapter VIII

## SOLVING PROBLEMS NOUTHETICALLY

### Man's Basic Problem

When God created man he gave him a commission to "subdue" the world and "have dominion" over it (Genesis 1:28). Man alone was created in the image of God. One aspect of that image, as the passage shows, was authority and rule. Man was to reflect God's rule by a kingly rule over the earth. Of course, man's was a derived dominion; God's is natural to him as the Creator of all things. When Adam sinned, man lost that dominion, and to this day he has not fully regained it. The writer of Hebrews notes that all things have not yet been placed in subjection to man. Only in Christ has that human rule truly been perfected (Hebrews 2:8, 9). Christ became man, rose from the dead and was exalted to the throne of the heavenly kingdom of God. But even redeemed man is still subject to the difficulties and the effects of sin.

Sin brought the reversal of man's rule over the earth, so that the earth gained dominion over man. The earth began to fight back; it brought forth thorns. Man's task no longer was to trim and dress the garden, but now, in the sweat of his face, he found it necessary to toil against the earth in order to eke out an existence. Whenever man fails to do so, the impact of the reversal becomes evident. Naturally enough, the problem in counseling is that, contrary to God's mandate, clients have allowed the environment to control them.[1] The client who whines, "I can't; I'm helpless" is simply submitting to the rule of sin in a warped universe set against him. No Christian has a right to act that way. The Christian's task is to "subdue." God's command is still in force; the Christian is called

---

[1]"Naturally enough," because of the sinful orientation of the "natural man" (cf. I Corinthians 2).

to master his environment. By God's grace he can. In this way he may once again reflect the image of God by subduing and ruling the world about him. The picture of a man crippled by and in subjection to his environment, cowering before it, crying out that he is helpless under its pressure is, of course, a pitiful distortion of the picture of God's all-powerful rule. This distortion of God's image is so gross that it vitiates the very concept of the rule of God. Christians, whose basic orientation has been reversed so that they now seek to glorify God, must learn to take the initiative, subdue and rule. To do nothing is to do something. To fail to bring biblical solutions to bear upon problems is to allow sinful conditions to continue. To accept them and adapt to them is contrary to God's mandate. The concept of adaptation to sin is non-biblical.

Four methods of meeting problems are set forth in the following chart:

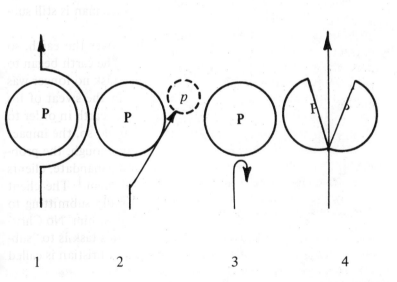

The *first* represents man going around, the *second*, man going aside, the *third*, man going back, and the *fourth*, man going through. The first response is expressed in the words, "It does not matter; it's unimportant; I'll just simply avoid it." The second response may be verbalized in words like "It isn't what I wanted anyway; this isn't the course I wanted to take," and so man allows the problem to deflect him from his course. A false problem *(p)* may be manufactured as camouflage. "Look, I'm dealing with the real problem" is the usual explanation in such a case. The third response amounts to saying, "It simply can't be done; it's impossible; it's hopeless; I give up." The fourth response is Christian: "It can be solved through Christ." Notice that the first three responses leave the problem intact and as a result the person and his course of activity is changed. Man adapts to the problem; man is subdued by the problem; whereas in the fourth situation, the problem is dealt with. The problem is sliced in two. In nouthetic counseling, clients are taught to solve problems rather than adapt to them. There is a biblical solution to every problem.[1]

Problems that are left unresolved by side-stepping them in one way or another tend to grow larger as time goes on. They grow in two ways. They become more complex, like the un-extracted tooth that abscesses, and the stress of the problem makes the problem grow in the mind of the client. For these reasons, the question which keeps popping up in one form or another is: "Will the proposed solution resolve the problem? Is it really a solution, or will the proposal only postpone the day of reckoning?"

---

[1] Circumstances cannot always be altered, of course, but the problems they present can be solved. One is in control of circumstances and thereby solves his problems when he has done what God requires him to do about them. The client must get a handle on the problem rather than sprout handles himself. Every situation in which one finds himself can be changed because one element in the situation is the client himself, who, by the grace of God, can be changed. In any case he will be changed; the only question is whether he allows the problem to change him or whether he changes according to Scripture by the power the Spirit gives to meet the problem differently.

## You Can't Say Can't

One of the words which is taboo in nouthetic counseling with Christian clients is the word "can't." A catchword of nouthetic counselors is, "You can't say can't." In I Corinthians 10:13, Paul makes that point quite vividly. He says that there is no test[1] which has overtaken you but such as is common to others. God allows no Christian to plead that his case is unique or special. There are, of course, unique features about everyone's problems. No two cases are exactly the same. But the basic elements of the problem are not significantly different from those which others have faced. Christ faced the same problems of hunger, sleeplessness, misunderstanding, hatred, discouragement and pain that Christians today must experience. Countless other Christians, in following him, also have faced these problems successfully. Knowledge of this fact brings encouragement and hope.

If the doctor says an operation is needed, it is very encouraging to know that others have successfully undergone a similar operation. Clients need such encouragement in the hour of trial. That is why Paul declares that no test is unique. But such encouragement also removes any possibility of excusing one's self on the grounds that "my case is an exception to the rule." I Corinthians 10:13 allows for no such exceptions. Christians can't say "can't" because God says they *can.* They can cope with their problems just as Christ did, and as thousands of other Christians have done.

---

[1]The word used here may be translated "trial" or "temptation" as well. The term itself is colorless and depends upon the context for its specific hue. In one sense every trial (or test) is also a temptation for it affords the opportunity to fail. Viewed from one perspective, a problem is a test which, if solved biblically, strengthens and helps one grow in grace (cf. James 1:2-4). Looked at from a different perspective, the same problem may be used by Satan as a temptation for sin. The book of Job shows the two-sidedness of every trial.

132

Secondly, Paul says that Christians can't say "can't," because even though the basic designs are not unique, temptations and tests are tailor-made to each individual; and God is the Tailor.[1] He will not allow the Devil to tempt them above that which they are able to withstand. The book of Job stands as a sturdy witness to this promise. At any given period in his life, what a Christian is able to withstand may differ from his previous ability or from that which God will enable him to endure at a future time. But whatever the test may be at any moment, it is not beyond his ability to withstand in Christ. Given the grace (help) of God, given his knowledge of God's Word, given the sanctification that is his to that point, given the resources of the Holy Spirit, no test is beyond his ability to withstand. It may be that it is only in stepping out to do God's will that the strength will come. God does not promise dying grace before it is time to die.

That this is an important promise to which to refer in counseling, is evident in counseling. Most Christians who come for counseling use speech studded with the word "can't." A client's language not only indicates what he thinks,[2] but also influences the way he acts and reacts. If Christians continually say, in effect, "I can't do all that Christ asks me to do," instead of saying, "I can do all things that Christ requires me to do," they soon begin to believe their own rebellious lie. The lie is so flagrantly rebellious because of the nature of the promise; it is based upon the faithfulness of God. Paul introduces the promise with the words, "God is faithful . . ." The promise that God will not allow Christians to be tested beyond their capacity is as certain as God's nature itself. To deny it is to call God unfaithful, and a liar. So in nouthetic counseling the very use of certain words sometimes must be

---

[1] "God is faithful who will not allow you to be tested beyond what you are able to bear."

[2] Cf. Luke 6:45 on this important point.

counteracted, because words are not only indicative of but also influence thinking, attitudes and behavior.

Counselors often come down hard on the word "can't" when they find Christians using it in counseling sessions, and they say, "You can't say 'can't.'" For so long some Christians have excused themselves with the idea that their case is unique or that they have some overwhelming "cross to bear" (a misinterpretation of the phrase[1]) that when someone for the first time confronts them with the promise in I Corinthians 10:13, they are astonished. They sometimes protest and say, "But, you see, it's different with me." And yet Paul was very careful to note that no matter how difficult, their problem is not significantly different. Eventually, after an evasive attempt or two, most Christians agree that they have been living according to a false notion of responsibility and reluctantly accept Paul's promise as referring to them. When they do, an important gain has been made; a reversal of attitude has occurred, and God's promise gives rise to a growing hope.

John was a Christian who was having difficulties with the problem of frequent masturbation and impure thoughts. John was compounding the problem largely by his attendance at pornographic movies. When John presented his problem, he said, "I just feel compelled to go into these movies; I can't resist the impulse. I don't understand it: I walk by and it's as if a magnet were drawing me in." The counselor asked John, "Do you have to walk by the movies in order to get to work?" "No," he replied. "To go home?" "No." "Well why, John, are you down there on the street where those so-called 'art films are shown?" John had no reply. The simple answer was that John walked down that street in order to be drawn in.

When clients think they are helpless, that some strange

---

[1] The cross was the instrument of crucifixion. "Bearing" it does not mean carrying a heavy burden (problem), but rather, crucifying one's self. "Take up your cross daily" and "deny self" means daily crucifixion of old sinful desires and practices (cf. Luke 9:23).

mysterious force is at work overpowering them, and they say that I Corinthians 10:13 does not apply to their case, the truth may be that they are not serious about wanting to do the Lord's will. They may be talking out of both sides of their mouths. They may deceive others or even themselves, in part, about the sincerity of their desire to obey God. They are struggling with the same internal problems Paul faced in Romans 7:15-25.[1] The old desires conflict with the new. Clearly in John's case the problem was exactly that. On the one hand, he wanted to get rid of the habit which was enflaming masturbation and causing a great sense of guilt, but on the other hand, because he enjoyed his sin his actions were counterproductive. To keep from falling over the edge of the precipice, one should move as far back from that edge as possible. This was John's problem. As a starter, he needed to stop frequenting the street where the movies were.[2]

Finally, Paul assures us that together with the test God will send a way of escape in order to help endure it. Jean said,

---

[1]In Romans 7 some wrongly see Paul refusing to assume responsibility for his sin (esp. note vss. 17, 20). But he *does* take full responsibility in other verses in the passage (vss. 15, 16, 19, 25). The distinction is between his inner (deepest) desire as a Christian (vs. 22), and the deeply ingrained habits of the past (programmed in the nervous system and manifested in the body, vss. 23, 24). There is no body-mind dualism here, but the new impulses of the Spirit are set over against the old impulses of a body patterned by the past.

[2]Some clients may protest inadequacy. One client spoke of having only "reservoirs of inadequacy." He was correct, because he had been living inadequately. His past provided little more than a record of inadequate solutions to fall back upon and draw upon. But the solution to his problem was to begin drawing upon God's reservoirs of grace. In this way alone could he begin to fill his own reservoirs with adequate living. Experiential backlogs are not essential; one may rely upon the promises of God. Action based upon faith was his need. As he began to live adequately (i.e., according to the commands and promises of God), he would begin to fill his own reservoirs with adequacy and a sense of humble confidence would grow.

"I *can't* go on; I *can't* take it any longer—I'm in a box and I *can't* get out." It is true that her problems were difficult ones. Jean was married to an irresponsible husband whose work brought very little money. She didn't have a car, a TV, a washer and dryer, or even a vacuum cleaner. But they were Christians and she knew she couldn't leave him. Jean took the only way she knew to get out of the box—she had tried to "cop out" by giving up; quitting. But letting down on her responsibilities as a mother and wife had only complicated the problem and proved no solution at all. Jean needed to understand that God provides "a way of escape" with every trial; Christians are *never* in a box. God can make the walls of the box fall flat like the walls of Jericho; he can open the lid and reach down with his mighty hand and support one through the test; or he can make the bottom fall out. Whatever way of escape God may provide—even the best issue of all (to take us to himself)—we may trust that the way out will come *as surely as the problem itself.* Knowing that there will be a way out, an end to the problem, is itself reassuring. One can endure anything (even this book) if he knows that it has an end. Thus, by a threefold cord, which is not easily broken, God assures us we *can* meet life's problems. We can't say "can't," when God says we can.

One important point ought to be made concerning the use of I Corinthians 10:13 in counseling. The passage is particularly useful to set the tone of counseling from the very beginning. Sometimes these principles must be asserted frequently in the first few sessions. When a client has begun to solve his problems, when he has turned the corner and has begun to establish new biblical life patterns, and is ready for debriefing, it is also good to remind him of I Corinthians 10:13. At this point, his reluctance is gone and he wholeheartedly concurs. Then he may be asked to turn to I Corinthians 10:12, which adds the other half of the picture. While it is true that in Christ he can solve every problem, he must be careful to solve them in *Christ.* Paul says, "I can do all things through Christ, who strengthens me": he does not say, "I can do all things in my own strength." So in the debriefing session, the client is warned, "Let him who thinketh he standeth take heed lest he fall" (I Corinthians 10:12). Clients who begin to establish Christian habit patterns and who find themselves quite successful in the application of these Christian patterns to their present difficulties, may get an early flush of joy and confidence which can turn easily into cocksureness. This must be discouraged.

Martha was a case in point. Martha had just solved some very difficult problems. She immediately offered to go to work for the Counseling Center. She said she would be willing to do any sort of work she might be asked to do. But she suggested specifically that she might go around to speak and represent the organization before women's groups. Her counselors said, "Martha, we appreciate your offer, but you've just come through some serious problems. You're not ready." She became quite upset over this. In fact, she was incensed. But the very fact that she became incensed when her offer was temporarily turned down only pointed up the fact that she had not yet solidified her gains. Her counselors pointed this out to her, seizing upon this exchange as a nouthetic opportunity. They noted that her response was clear evidence that she still had much to learn about controlling her temper. The experience jolted her. She got the point and she saw how appropriately I Corinthians 10:12 applied to her. That lesson itself moved her a long way ahead. She was helped so much by that nouthetic experience that even though no one told her so, after that session and the remarkable transformation that this made in her, it might have been possible to use her in a variety of ways. But Martha needed time to consolidate her gains by putting these principles into practice long enough to let the new patterns jell.

Because nouthetic counselors know that problems are not unique, that they are not beyond the client's ability to solve in Christ, and because they have God's promise that the probems will not continue indefinitely, they approach counseling with a sense of hope and assurance rather than a sense of doubt and despair. Because counselor attitudes are easily communicated to clients, this is of great significance in counseling. Paul's reassuring words help the client both directly and indirectly. Clients often comment about counselor attitudes. Most frequently they say something like Jim, who remarked at the conclusion of his sessions—"I couldn't understand why you had such hope when we began, but it really helped me through those early days."

Often, too, counselors on the basis of Paul's promise build hope by letting their clients know that they understand their problems. Since problems are not unique, they follow patterns of which counselors soon become aware. Moreover, a counselor knows that in his own sinful heart is the tendency to succumb to every failure which he observes in his clients. Counselors may let clients know that they understand by narrating an incident or giving an example which strikes a responsive note in the client.[1] In this way, they also may test whether their own conclusions about a particular pattern are on target by listening to client feedback. Nearly always clients who reverberate emotionally to such examples respond openly, since they welcome the knowledge that they are not really alone, that others have faced their problem before, and that their counselor understands. Such an understanding brings genuine hope, just exactly as intended in I Corinthians 10:13.

## Hope

One of the important factors in counseling is giving hope, as the discussion of I Corinthians 10:13 has shown. Man in misery needs hope. God gave hope to Adam. During the nouthetic confrontation which took place after Adam sinned, God raised all the issues connected with Adam's sin, including

---

[1] The parables of Christ were so devastatingly powerful in their effects upon his enemies and his followers alike for this very reason.

its punishment, but he also revealed that he would send the Lord Jesus Christ to destroy the Serpent and his work (Genesis 3:15). The nouthetic counselor must follow God's pattern. Christ confronted Peter, not passing over a single aspect of his sinful denial,[1] but also including words of restoration and a commission to future service. The consistent theme of nearly all of the prophets was judgment, but they also proclaimed a message of hope.

The Gospel, the good news that Christ triumphed over sin and all its effects, is the soil out of which hope grows; it is central to all hope. Colossians 1, for example, speaks of "the hope of the gospel." The Christian's hope brings him the assurance that because Christ died for his sins he shall have eternal life, and that at death his spirit shall be made perfect. But he also has hope that now he may overcome much of the misery into which sin has plunged him; especially misery resulting from personal sin. Christ not only offers pie-in-the-sky-when-you-die, but he says that Christians may begin slicing in this life.

---

[1] Note the charcoal fire, reminiscent of the fire at which Peter denied the Lord, the reference to the proud boast (John 21:15; cf. Mark 14:29), and the threefold question corresponding to the threefold denial. While it is true that Peter was empowered for his work by the coming of the Holy Spirit on the day of Pentecost, it is also true that it was a forgiven, changed, restored man upon whom the Holy Spirit came. There could have been no Pentecost for Peter apart from this restoration. Peter's sermons and letters reflect this encounter; note especially his emphasis upon proper shepherding of Christ's flock, e.g., I Peter 2:25; 5:1-4. It is here that Simon turned into Peter, the *rock*. It is also important to note that in the very completeness of the recreation of all the elements of Peter's sinful failure, lay both pain and mercy. Peter's painful grief is mentioned by John. But the pain passed quickly in the joy of *complete* restoration. Since all of the elements of his sin had been dealt with once and for all, Peter no longer had to be concerned about any of them. He could pursue the Lord's work with a good conscience, untroubled by depression which might otherwise crop up from time to time. The painful encounter was a most merciful one.

The Medical Model destroys hope. Discouragement and despair permeate the concept of "mental illness." Most people are aware that the mental institutions are not helping many people. They also know that psychiatrists characteristically say, "You must expect therapy to take a long time, and then we can promise you nothing."[1] So to inform a Christian client in an early interview, "Your problem seems basically to be the result of sin," does not discourage him, but rather gives him hope. Christians know that sin and its effects can be dealt with because God has said so in the Scriptures and Christ died to overcome sin. So when sin is mentioned, there is real hope.

To call homosexuality a sickness, for example, does not raise the client's hope. But to call homosexuality sin as the Bible does, is to offer hope.[2] Probably there is no more im-

---

[1] This attitude communicates despair which is the opposite of the hope built into the nouthetic approach. These opposite attitudes themselves may partially account for the significant differences in results.

[2] Cf. Romans 1:26-28; 32. In verse 26 Paul speaks of homosexuality as a "degrading passion," in verse 27, as an "indecent act" and "an error," in verse 28, the improper activity of a "depraved mind," and in verse 32, declares it is "worthy of death." One is not a homosexual constitutionally any more than one is an adulterer constitutionally. Homosexuality is not considered to be a condition, but an act. It is viewed as a sinful practice which can become a way of life. The homosexual act, like the act of adultery, is the reason for calling one a homosexual (of course one may commit homosexual sins of the heart, just as one may commit adultery in his heart. He may lust after a man in his heart as another may lust after a woman). But precisely because homosexuality, like adultery, is learned behavior into which men with sinful natures are prone to wander, homosexuality can be forgiven in Christ, and the pattern can be abandoned and in its place proper patterns can be reestablished by the Holy Spirit. Some homosexuals have lost hope because of the reluctance of Christian counselors to represent homosexuality as sin. For an excellent recent discussion of homosexuality see Hebden Taylor, *The New Legality* (Philadelphia: The Presbyterian and Reformed Publishing Company, 1967), pp. 36-49.

portant factor in the work of helping homosexual sinners. Hope is desperately needed by them as much as anything else. It is essential to counteract every aspect of the hope-destroying medical and/or genetic models of homosexuality.

One of the first things that clients need is hope. Since much despair stems from the general failure of counseling, many people come with little hope. Counselors, therefore, must learn to engender hope by taking people seriously about their sin. For example, if a client says (perhaps almost parenthetically), "I guess I haven't been much of a mother or wife," she probably expects the counselor to minimize her evaluation of herself. Most other people have failed to take her comments seriously in the past. They invariably say something like this: "Don't talk like that Susie; you know you haven't been that bad." Such responses destroy hope, because the client has not been taken seriously. Minimizing responses indicates to the client that the counselor is not going to deal with the problem at the level on which the client believes the problem exists. Hope of help from him is thereby largely diminished. Moreover, minimizing another's adverse evaluation of himself is really a backhanded compliment, because while it wrongly tends to excuse bad conduct which the client already recognizes to be bad, and about which he already feels guilty, minimizing further degrades him by telling him he doesn't even know what he is talking about. Minimize a man's estimate of himself and you minimize the man himself.

Nouthetic counselors try not to let the client's adverse evaluations of himself go by without comment, and try never to respond in ways which might minimize the client's bad opinion of himself.[1] Instead, any statement of that sort by a

---

[1]In suicidal cases, when a client has such a low opinion of himself that he thinks the world would be better off without him, it only hurts to deny that his low estimate is valid. Counselors should acknowledge that he is probably right about the present worthlessness of his life, and should attempt to discover how bad he has been. However, they should

client is promptly investigated. If a client says, "I haven't been a good mother," nouthetic counselors might reply, "That's a serious matter. Tell me about it. What have you been doing? How have you been failing as a mother?" If she says, "I have not been much of a wife," they might say, "Well now, that's a serious matter before God; how have you failed as a wife?"

When counselors take clients seriously, they usually respond quickly, pouring out problems, failures and sins. Others who minimize such comments frequently succeed only in pushing material back down inside the client again. Clients understandably do not want to reveal themselves to someone who won't take them seriously. Many clients receive some help almost immediately from the fact that someone at last has taken them seriously. Taking people seriously about their sins is an important way to give them hope.

Christ's consistent approach toward those who came to him was to take their sins into account. His characteristic phrase was, "Your sins have been forgiven you." Far from minimizing sins, he often raised the issue of sin with those who themselves failed to do so. Cf. the story of the Rich Young Ruler (Luke 18:18-23).

Millie was one such person. Millie, a Christian, had been in and out of mental institutions for thirteen years. No one seemed to be able to help her. She was lying around the house unable to do her housework, not caring for her children. Her husband was in complete despair and Millie, herself, was totally depressed. She was brought for counseling by friends from another state.

Millie's first visit made a remarkable change in her life. When a nouthetic counselor confronted her strongly on that first day about her lazy, undisciplined, irresponsible behavior and told her to go back to church, to get to work at home, to

take issue with his proposed solution, and instead point him to God's solution through repentance and holy living.

do her ironing and cleaning, everyone was shocked. That is, everyone but Millie, who responded with hope. Her husband was dumbfounded. Millie had been coddled by a psychiatrist for nearly a year. The psychiatrist listened to her sympathetically and sold her tranquilizers, yet there was no improvement. After her first week of nouthetic counseling, on her own Millie laid her pills aside.[1] She cleaned her house from stem to stern. When she returned the next week, she was driving the car herself, and she was a new woman. She had gone to church for the first time in years, to the amazement of the pastor and congregation. In just a few weeks, Millie was released from counseling. Several other problems, notably one with a son, were also solved during counseling. Counseling need not take long if one can lay his finger on the heart of the issue early, and if there is proper motivation on the part of the client. Taking clients seriously about their sin, is the first step.

Proverbs 25:20 is pertinent to the problem of minimizing:

He who sings songs to a heavy heart is like one who takes off a garment on a cold day and like vinegar on a wound.

Minimizing is precisely the wrong thing. Its effect is like tak-

---

[1] The excessive use of pills among psychiatrists and physicians is alarming. Sometimes personality is so distorted by mood-affecting drugs that it is difficult for the counselor to know whether he is talking to the person or to a pill. Whenever possible, the prescribing physician should be contacted to determine whether the pills could not be eliminated or dosage reduced during counseling. Pills may remove much motivation by lessening pain and depression. While not all medication is unnecessary, clearly much is. There may be cases in which the counselor must refuse to work with the client until the use of drugs has been moderated or eliminated. No nouthetic counselor advises clients about the use of drugs unless he is a physician, but whenever possible he should become acquainted with a physician whose judgment and advice can help him make his own judgments.

ng off a coat on a cold day, or like rubbing vinegar on a wound that already stings. Minimizing actually magnifies problems. Only one thing lifts the depressed spirit crushed by a load of sin: confession and forgiveness of sin. David's music therapy did not really help Saul; it soothed him temporarily, but did not change him. Saul's own attitudes and actions kept making his condition worse, as day by day he brooded with jealousy and resentment. Saul's pride and self-centeredness affected every aspect of his life. The Scriptures do not attribute Saul's madness to sickness. Nor is his sin "excused" because he is considered sick. Rather, his madness and his sin are linked directly (I Samuel 18:6-11). The idea of the futility of singing songs to a heavy heart needs to be qualified only to the extent that it should be noted that such treatment might temporarily calm the afflicted. Play therapy or work therapy may temporarily take a client's mind off his sin. Hard work will sometimes remove the pain of guilt and bring temporary relief, but it cannot effect a permanent cure. Proverbs speaks of the ultimate, if not immediate effects of such treatment.

In Scripture, physical illness is compared and contrasted with a spirit broken under the burden of a guilty heart. The comparison runs this way: "A man's spirit will endure sickness, but a broken spirit who can bear?" (Proverbs 18:14). The writer is saying that emotional trouble is far more serious than physical trouble. Painful emotions are more serious than the pain of a serious disease. The right spirit within enables one to bear physical pain, but what is there to sustain one with a broken spirit crushed in pain? Minimizing inner turmoil is cruel. The only way to relieve the pain is to begin by taking clients seriously.

Secondary issues sometimes may not be secondary at all. Sometimes the depression which arises from the failure to do one's work, that comes from not cleaning, not ironing, not assuming one's responsibilities, is really not a secondary effect but the primary cause of the problem. There are lazy people. The book of Proverbs frequently discusses the slothful, or lazy man. The sloth puts his hand into a dish and is too lazy to raise it to his mouth (Proverbs 19:24). A humorous picture is painted of the lazy man: "A little rest, a little folding of the hands" (Proverbs 24:30-34). See him leaning back in his chair; see his hands folded across his chest; see him looking up in the air and his eyelids slowly closing? It is time for work to be done, but he is lying down relaxing, taking it easy with his feet up. A lazy man gets his job done only in part or not at all because he doesn't start early enough. He indulges his body and fulfills every lazy wish. But finally, the guilt of neglect, the guilt of doing work with a lick and a promise, the guilt of facing others who have depended on him catches up with him. Once laden down with guilt, and because of the depression that accompanies it, he finds he can't do even the work he has been doing very effectively. So he slackens up still more. Thus he is caught in a cyclical downward whirlpool of depair. What is true of the lazy man is true generally of clients caught in the vortex of their sin and subsequent failure to deal with it properly.

## Cyclical Movement

Romans 6:19 is pertinent to the problem at hand. Paul, engaged in an exposition of the new life to which Christians have been called, urges them to abandon the sins of the past, for with Christ they have "died" to the old life. United to him, they are to consider themselves (as God does) dead to the past and resurrected to a new life. To reinforce this truth, Paul illustrated his point by the relation of a slave to his master. In the past, Paul said, Christians were sold to Sin (here personified as a slave master). They were willing slaves who offered every part of their bodies to obey Sin's desires. As Sin used their bodily organs they became tools (instruments) for obeying Sin's wishes (vss. 12, 13). Their willingness to have sin rule over them is clear from the fact that they "presented" or "offered" themselves freely to Sin for this purpose (vs. 13a). The inevitable result of such sin-directed activity was "impurity and lawlessness" (vs. 19). Now, with the same enthusiasm and willingness, they must offer their whole persons to God in obedience for the purpose of producing righteousness (vs. 19). While they lived the old life of obedience to Sin, one sinful act led to another (vs. 19, "impurity and lawlessness" resulted in "further lawlessness"). One lie had to be covered by a dozen more; wronging others made them stressors (people whose very presence creates stress for another), and attempts to avoid these stressors led to further irresponsible acts, etc. Now that they have become Christians, they must yield themselves as willingly to their new Master to work righteousness by all the parts of their bodies.

The downward cycle of sin moved from a problem to a faulty sinful response, thereby causing an additional complicating problem which was met by an additional sinful response, etc. That pattern needs to be reversed by beginning an upward cycle of righteousness resulting in further righteousness. Here the reverse pattern may be seen: a problem met by a biblical response leads to a solution which strengthens one's ability to solve new problems.

Proverbs plainly warns against the slavery of sinful habits:

> For directly before the eyes of the Lord are man's ways, and all his paths are well considered. His own iniquities seize the wicked, and he is held fast by the ropes of his own sin. He dies for lack of discipline (Proverbs 5:21, 22, Berkeley).

Sinful habits are hard to break, but if they are not broken they will bind the client ever more tightly. He is held fast by these ropes of his own sin. He finds that sin spirals in a downward cycle, pulling him along. He is captured and tied up by sin's ever-tightening cords. At length, he becomes sin's slave. Paul, we saw, uses the figure of slavery in the book of Romans (6:12-23). He pictures sin as the cruel master who rules over the sinner. Here, Proverbs says, "He dies," destroyed by his own sin. He "dies for lack of discipline," because he does

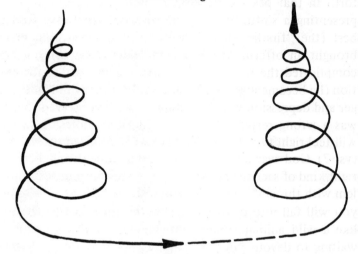

DOWNWARD SPIRAL
[enlarges problems]

UPWARD SPIRAL
[reduces problems]

(side view)

Good Feeling

Good Feeling

(top view)

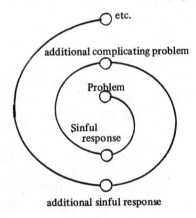

etc.

additional complicating problem

Problem

Sinful
response

additional sinful response

additional complicating problem

Original Problem

Solved by
biblical response

Solved by biblical response

not have the kind of structure that only God's command-ments provide.

Earlier, reference was made to Genesis 4:3-7, the story of Cain.[1] The dynamics of the downward cycle are plainly set forth in that passage by God himself. Cain began badly by presenting a sinful offering before God. Abel gave God the best (the "firstlings" and the "fat"), whereas Cain merely brought an offering.[2] When God rejected his offering Cain complicated the problem by responding wrongly to the rejec-tion (he became angry and depressed: his face "fell"). The an-ger and depression were noted by God who observed that this was a wrong response. Instead, God says, do right and you will feel right (vss. 6, 7—your face will be "lifted up"[3]). Then (vs. 7) God warned against failure to repent and offer the right kind of sacrifice. If you continue to complicate the prob-lem with this sinful response ("If you misbehave"—Berkeley), you will fall into deeper sin (into the clutches of sin, which like a wild animal is now crouching at your door anxiously waiting to devour you). Your only hope is to rule over sin by breaking out of the sinful pattern that is developing through repentance and a subsequent change of behavior.

Of course, the sequel to these words shows that Cain failed to heed God's warning and fell into deeper depths of sin just as God had said he would: the downward cycle led to the

---

[1] p. 93.

[2] This is the only distinction implied by the text itself. To read back into the passage distinctions between a bloody and unbloody sacrifice may be reading too much into the account. The reason for God's rejec-tion of Cain's offering, however, is unimportant to the point of our dis-cussion.

[3] The King James rendering of verse 7, "If thou doest well, shalt thou not be accepted?" obscures the true intent of the passage, which literal-ly reads: "If you do right, will there not be a lifting up [i.e., of Cain's face which had "fallen"]?"

murder of Abel. Nursing his grudge, self-pity, and anger were all elements of the depressed look on Cain's face about which God strongly warned him.

Sin leads to guilt and depression, sinful handling of sin further complicates matters leading to greater guilt and deeper depression, *ad infinitum*. In the downward cycling the depression certainly contributes to further failures as it often becomes the excuse for a faulty handling of the sin itself. But, in contrast to those who would speak of changing the feelings in order to change the behavior, God reverses the order: he declared, "do right" and "there will be a lifting up of your face."

### Three Dimensions of Problems

In the spiraling of sin, problems become more and more complex. Beyond the basic sinful nature itself, three levels of complexity may be distinguished and for convenience might be called:

1. *Presentation problems:* e.g., "I'm depressed" (often presented as a cause when really an effect)

2. *Performance problems:* e.g., "I haven't been much of a wife" (often presented as an effect when really a cause)

3. *Preconditioning problems:* e.g., "I avoid responsibility whenever the going gets tough" (often presented as an effect when really the underlying cause, the habitual response pattern, of which the performance problem is but one instance; the preconditioning problem generally does not come fully into focus until its relationship to the first two has been understood).[1]

In counseling, the three problems ought to be distinguished and frequently considered separately. First, it is wise to listen

---

[1]There is no great value in these particular terms. They seem appropriate to describe the various levels of a problem which may be discussed.

to the presentation problem—"I'm tired all the time." However, it is not wise to stop there. The next step is to take a performance inventory as soon as possible. The counselor must become specific in order to discover performance problems. He must probe specifically by asking the next logical question (e.g., "How much sleep do you get?"). If the answer was, "I got an average of six hours' sleep each night during the last two weeks," he will probably try next to discover a preconditioning problem. He may ask, "What have you been doing when you should be sleeping?" "I have been watching the late show nearly every night for several months."

Typical presentation problems sound something like this: "I'm depressed; I'm not making it with people; I'm afraid to . . . drive the auto at night, cross bridges, etc.; people are out to get me." What is important about the performance problem is the specific way in which there is a poor behavioral response to life's problems. Frequently, one can generalize from the performance problem to the preconditioning problem. Through the former, he can at least work his way back to the latter. While the performance, or debilitating, problem may be handled in and of itself, the failure of mere crisis intervention is that generally it deals with that problem only and does not get at the underlying roots of it. Often clients are willing to settle too readily for a solution to the performance problem alone. If they leave counseling when the immediate pressure is removed, they may be forced to return when they get themselves into further difficulty. Habit patterns developed over many years must be replaced by new biblical patterns. Otherwise the client will leave counseling still programmed (preconditioned) to handle life's next crisis in the usual sinful way. The debilitating or performance problem is simply one example of the underlying disposition to handle problems in such a manner. The preconditioning problem is really a kind of computer problem. The client has programmed himself by his past activity to act in certain ways in response to given stimuli. If he has repeatedly responded to difficulties by becoming angry, and as a result, his parents capitulated to his wishes in order to appease him, he is likely to do the same at work with his boss or when he establishes his own home with his wife. He needs the radical change of personality that only the Holy Spirit can bring through his Word. Dealing with the debilitating or performance problem alone may be equivalent to a change in behavior without an underlying change in personality. It is ceasing to express anger toward one's parents, for example, without acquiring the fruit of the Spirit which is "self control."

While three dimensions of problems may arise in counseling, the presentation problem, the performance problem and the preconditioning problem, sometimes a client may frankly set forth the performance problem, which is the immediate cause of difficulty, *as* the presentation problem. Both of these problems are of great importance and must be taken seriously.

It is also essential to stress the great importance of the third, the preconditioning problem. The preconditioning problem is the pattern which has been established over what often has been a long period of time. It is the pattern of which the performance problem is but one instance. One difficulty already mentioned is that sometimes clients want to settle for something less than full solutions. Once the immediate performance has been altered, thereby bringing relief from immediate difficulty and stress, some clients wish to terminate counseling. They are willing to settle for short-term satisfaction rather than work toward long-range and deeper solutions. Of importance to note here also is the eternal-range problem of man's need for redemption which underlies the other three, and about which more has been said under the subject of Evangelism.

In order to offset this tendency to settle too soon for too little, counselors find it necessary to point out the several strata of problems to each client. It is usually wise to work on all levels concurrently, starting as soon as information is available about each. Probing at all levels ought to be done at the earliest opportunities. As clients are taught along the way that there are different levels of problems, as enough past data is unearthed to demonstrate the existence of hardened patterns, the client can be shown that his problem is not simple but complex, and cannot be solved simply by eliminating one instance of it. He must be shown the need to replace the old by new patterns. He must be shown that God speaks of sanctification not only in terms of being "separated from" but also "separated unto." The old man is "put off," partly, by establishing the "new man." Old habit patterns are crowded out by new ones.

### The Past May Be the Present

Going back into the past is sometimes unnecessary. There are at least two good reasons, however, for doing so in most cases. First, it is important to review the past thoroughly enough to establish the fact that non-biblical response patterns are at the root of one's immediate problems. It is necessary to get a general picture of the shape of the response patterns which the client has developed to meet life's difficulties. He needs to be shown the preconditioning problem at the root of the particular problem which he has presented. The weeds will grow again unless they are uprooted.

The purpose for going back into the past is to take a behavioral history. A behavioral history is concerned about determining the life style of the client, largely from his habitual response patterns.[1] Nouthetic counselors are currently working on a habit-response inventory which may be used in con-

---

[1] It is true that cruel unloving parents may have been the prime instructors in such behavioral patterns. But the crucial point here is not what someone else has done to the client (people will continue to treat him wrongly throughout life), but rather, how he has learned to respond to such treatment. If he has learned non-biblical patterns (imitation of cruelty, hitting back, etc.), he can only be helped by repenting and changing to biblical patterns instead.

junction with other counseling activity, to help determine and classify the behavioral response patterns that have been developed over a period of time. At present a preliminary form of this test is in use. They look forward to its refinement and possible validation in time.[1]

There is a second reason for going back into the past. The client needs to discover and confess any "perfect-tense" sins. The English language does not have the same tense distinctions as other languages. The perfect tense in Greek, for instance, indicates an act in the past which has effects up to and including the present. It is distinguished from another past tense which is called "aorist." Aorist-tense sins are sins that have been dealt with and have been set to rest. But perfect tense sins, sins committed in the past which still have present effects, are sins that have not been settled. Such sins, because they have never been dealt with adequately, are really present-tense sins as well, because they continue to influence the client's life and destroy him. Because of such sins, the past may truly be the present. Such sins must be dealt with before God and before man.[2] Paul speaks of "mourning" over "many of those who have sinned in the past and not repented" (II Corinthians 12:21).

Frequently perfect-tense sins cannot be turned into aorist-tense sins until restitution has been made. Don was a college professor, highly respected among his colleagues, who was suffering from severe insomnia. No matter what he tried, he couldn't get to sleep. Dosages of sleeping pills had been in-

---

[1]Some tests are probably of more value than others. Christians do not always come off well in psychological tests that have been designed to be used with non-Christians. Therefore, we recognize a need for good tests based on Christian presuppositions.

[2]The future may also be the present. Someone may be suffering the effects of guilt from planned sinful future behavior. See the example of "Joe" under the next section in this chapter, entitled "Total Structuring." Cf. also O. H. Mowrer, "Note and Notions," *Dis-Coverer,* Vol. 4, No. 4, October 1967, p. 8.

creased to a danger point. The upshot of counseling revealed that he had been cheating on his income tax. Underneath, his evasion bothered him greatly because he was afraid that the Internal Revenue Service would find out, and he would be exposed as a thief. At night his conscience would not let him sleep. Eventually, Don faced up to his sin and wrote to the Internal Revenue Service, suggesting a plan of repayment and promising to make full restitution. He had no sooner written the letter than he began to sleep like a baby and had no future occurrences of the problem.

Restitution is biblical. Proverbs 6:31 sets forth the Old Testament rule for robbery:

> The thief, when he is caught, must restore sevenfold; he must give all the substance of his house . . .

(i.e., if necessary to pay the fine, he must be willing to make restitution at the cost of losing everything he owns). John the Baptist called for "fruits in keeping with repentance" (Matthew 3:8; cf. also Acts 26:20), and Zacchaeus gave half his possessions to the poor and repaid money fourfold to anyone he had defrauded (Luke 19:8).[1]

## Total Structuring

Many clients do not have scarlet sins in their past.[2] Fre-

---

[1]In Leviticus 6:1-7 and Numbers 5:5-8, the principle of full retribution plus one fifth is set forth. Also, if the party to be reimbursed was dead or for some reason unable to receive the sum, the money was then to be given to the priest. This latter provision shows that in restitution, one's responsibility is met not merely by benefiting the one who has been wronged, but in addition the benefit of the repentant one is envisioned in his making restitution before God and the organized church.

[2]That is, scarlet in the sense that the world calls glaring sins scarlet. In God's sight all sin is equally heinous since it is all a violation of God's law. Sins of the heart, Jesus taught, are as bad in God's sight as sins of performance. Murdering one in one's heart, however, has less devastating social effects, and seems less heinous in the sight of men.

quently the client's whole life has been characterized by irresponsibility. The following instance is a glimpse of such patterning.[1] The alarm goes off at 7:00. Joe picks it up, turns it off, throws it across the room, pulls the covers up over his head and goes back to sleep. Five minutes to eight Joe awakens, realizing what he's done, recognizing that he can never get to work by 8:00. Now Joe has a choice before him. What should he do? First, he can do the responsible thing: he can immediately pick up the phone, call his foreman at work, and say,

> Bill, I did a foolish thing this morning; I turned the alarm off, threw it across the room and went back to sleep. I'm calling you now, Bill, to let you know that I'll be late. I'll be there as soon as I can get my shirt on. I wanted you to know so that you could get someone to cover the machine for me until I arrive.

That's one thing that Joe can do. He won't feel pleasant about what he's done, but the issue will have been set to rest.

On the other hand, Joe may do the very irresponsible thing that so many do. Instead of calling Bill, he may begin to fret and fume and think about how he's going to lie his way out of this situation. In his rush and disturbed condition, he cuts his face shaving. This adds to his anxiety. While getting dressed he is thinking furiously about what he is going to do. Guilt already is mounting because he knows that he's about to do something wrong. In fact, in his heart he has already sinned because he has determined to lie. And so, with a guilty conscience, Joe wolfs his breakfast down, and growls at his wife because she burned his toast. The whole time he is foaming inside about how he can lie his way out of his predicament. On the way to work he nearly hits two other drivers and curses them, knowing full well that the near misses were the result of his own poor driving. When he gets to work he tells Bill a

---

[1] The story also typifies the destructiveness of a downward spiral.

lie which he wonders if Bill really believes. All day he wonders whether he was able to persuade Bill or not. He grumbles at the men who work with him, things seem to go all wrong at work, and when he gets home that night he's a tiger. He takes the family apart verbally soon after he enters the door, and the rest of the evening is turmoil.

Multiply this by a hundred other minor events that grow out of edgy and stressful attitudes due to irresponsible activity, then multiply a day of that sort of living by weeks and years. The result shows why many people, after sustaining this kind of activity and stress day by day, end up in the counselor's office. As a matter of fact, a number of people who can point to no specific act of irresponsibility have lived such a life of consistent irresponsibility that this, itself, is their problem. So many small things in each aspect of such a client's life are wrong that nothing less than a total restructuring of his life will do. He must learn to apply biblical principles of honesty and total responsibility before God and man.

But it is not only those who have lived a life of general irresponsibility who need structuring. Whenever a client's problem turns out to be one large, glaring sin, like homosexuality, he may believe that he has only one problem to solve. He may even be impatient with a counselor who attempts to look at other aspects of his life. "Why don't you get to *the* problem?" he may ask. But in such cases, the problem cannot help but affect every other aspect of his life. Its effects doubtless have bled over into social life, married life, work, physical and financial matters, etc. Structured, or disciplined living is living that conforms to God's commandments. Living a life of love is the goal. Clients and counselors alike should be satisfied with nothing less than the goal of total structuring according to God's law.

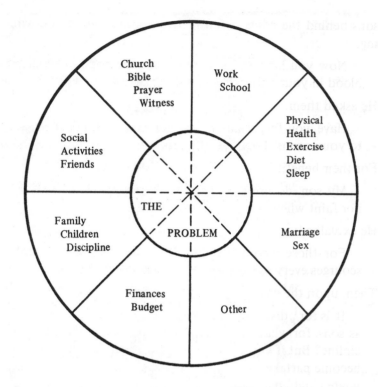

TOTAL STRUCTURING means looking at *the* problem in relationship to all areas of life. The problem affects all areas, and whenever all areas are in proper relationship to God, the dotted lines become solid lines and *the* problem dissolves. The above diagram is not intended to be comprehensive, but suggestive.

## Discipline

The book of Hebrews was written to encourage perseverance on the part of some who had been considering the possibility of defecting from Christianity under the pressures of persecution. The writer compared and contrasted Christianity with what his readers had left. His argument in essence was, "Why go back to that which is inferior?" His key word was, "better." In chapter 12, he addressed himself to the basic reasons behind the contemplated defection. He began by asserting,

> Now you have not yet resisted to the point of shedding blood in your striving against sin (Hebrews 12:4).

He asked them:

> Have you forgotten the exhortation which is addressed to you as sons? (Hebrews 12:5).

For their benefit he quoted Proverbs 3:11, 12:

> My son, do not regard lightly the discipline of the Lord, nor faint when you are reproved by him.

He explained:

> For those whom the Lord loves, he disciplines, and he scourges every son whom he receives (Hebrews 12:6).

Then, upon the basis of this evidence he made his point:

> It is for[1] discipline that you endure; God deals with you as sons, for what son is there whom his father does not discipline? But if you are without discipline, of which all have become partakers (literally, "sharers"), then you are illegitimate children and not sons.[2]

Furthermore, he argued,

> we had earthly fathers to discipline us and we respected them.

Moving from that fact he asked:

> Shall we not much rather be subject to the Father of spirits and live?

The argument so far, then, is that rather than discouraging them, the hardships Christians suffer ought rather to encour-

---

[1] The word *eis* means "for," "unto" or "for the purpose of."

[2] Discipline is the common lot of all genuine Christians, and therefore is one of the marks of a child of God.

age, for suffering disciplines and shows us plainly that we belong to God's family.

Then the writer drew a contrast (vs. 10). He observed that our earthly fathers "disciplined us for a short time" (or better, "for the purpose of achieving short-term goals"). Earthly fathers disciplined (or trained) us to do what in their judgment seemed best calculated to enable us to obtain short term goals.[1] But God disciplines us "for our good (our advantage), that we may share his holiness." The writer was not talking about duration, but direction, when he contrasted the ends for which earthly fathers and the heavenly Father discipline their sons. The former, he said, have in mind such things as social, financial or educational advantages. But these are short-term purposes. God, on the other hand, disciplines his children for their eternal advantage. His purpose is to bring Christians to full participation in his holiness. God disciplines them in order to make his children holy (vs. 10). He wants them to enter into a holiness that reflects his holiness, and which he alone can give.

To discover what "discipline" means, one needs only to

---

[1]Proverbs 22:6 is a very familiar passage. "Train up a child in the way he should go: and when he is old, he will not depart from it." This has been taken by some interpreters to mean that if parents train children properly in youth they will not depart from that training when they grow older. However, this is probably not what the verse means. Literally, the passage reads, "train a child after the manner of his way," that is, after the standard or manner in which *he* wants to be trained. The verse stands not as a promise but as a warning to parents that if they allow a child to train himself after his own wishes (permissively) they should not expect him to want to change these patterns when he matures. Children are born sinners and when allowed to follow their own wishes will naturally develop sinful habit responses. The basic thought is that such habit patterns become deep-seated when they have been ingrained in the child from the earliest days. The corollary to this passage is found in Proverbs 19:18 where the writer exhorts the reader, "Discipline your son while there is hope; do not set your heart on his destruction."

review the first ten verses of this chapter to discover what God has said about it. There discipline is described as corrective punishment called "reproof" and "scourging" (vs. 5). Notice the parallelism between discipline and reproof, and discipline and scourging (vs. 6). Since the kind of discipline that the Hebrew church was enduring was persecution,[1] the writer urged his readers to "consider him who endured such hostility by sinners against himself" so that they might not "grow weary and lose heart" (vs. 3). Christ did not turn back, even when it meant giving his life for us. And in his case, what he suffered was not even designed for his eternal advantage, but for ours. The discipline we endure has an eternal end in view; it is sent to God's sons to produce eternal holiness. Therefore, Christians, who are far from perfect, should not consider it strange that "it is for training" that they have been called to endure (vs. 7). Discipline (training) in holiness comes from enduring suffering. God disciplines in love to correct, to purify, to train, and to structure his children's lives according to his wishes:

> Do not regard lightly the discipline of the Lord, nor faint when you are reproved by him: For those whom the Lord loves he disciplines, and he scourges every son whom he receives.

Finally, again note that discipline proves that one is a son by demonstrating the heavenly Father's concern for those whom he loves.

While it is true that God disciplines his sons to make them holy, there is another dimension that must not be overlooked: discipline is also for their advantage. Holiness is always eternally advantageous. The words used in verse 10 mean, "for our good, for our advantage," indicating that when God disciplines his children he does so to bless and help them (the nouthetic note is strongly sounded here (Note III, p. 49).

---

[1]No blood had yet been shed, however. Persecution had only begun.

Sometimes clients contrast biblical morality and disciplined living with pleasure, and associate structure with boredom. The truth is that morality is not opposed to pleasure but to the abuse of pleasure. Morality simply demands pleasure on the long term (God's terms) rather than on impulse. Morality is concerned with lasting and genuine pleasure.

Structure is the means of moral living. Lives structured according to the Ten Commandments are by the very nature of the case also structured according to the principles upon which God constructed the world. Biblically-oriented lives do not clash with the structure of the world, but rather harmonize with it. Biblical structure tends to bring more deep-seated pleasure and to foster longer, healthier lives.

But is not structure confining? No; exactly the opposite is true. The train is free to run most rapidly and smoothly when it is "confined" to the tracks. The musician who "confines" himself to the laws of music and harmony plays more freely than the one who, in the name of freedom, disregards them. God created man to live fully and abundantly, and he has outlined the structure that will produce abundant life through love.

It is true, of course, that rebellious, sinful men often make the way of believers difficult through persecutions of various sorts. But in the long run, all inequities shall be righted (cf. II Thessalonians 1:4-12). Nevertheless, in considering the peace and joy available to obedient Christians (Philippians 4:4-13), and the promises of Proverbs to those who pursue divine wisdom, even the present life of the Christian must be considered far superior, despite inequities and persecutions.

Holiness always has good results. When an earthly father disciplines his child throughout the early days of his life, he thinks of the child's future and of the part this discipline will play in preparing him to reach his future goals. Likewise, God thinks of their eternal future when he disciplines his children. He is preparing them for an eternal future of holy living with him. But they are already living in God's world and even here benefit from holiness. The earthly father's short-term discipline has certain disadvantages in contrast to the eternal holiness that the heavenly Father's discipline has in view. The earthly father disciplines *as it seems good to him.* But human discipline by sinful fathers is always imperfect. What seems good to an earthly father may not in fact be good for his son. Earthly fathers are sometimes prejudiced or short-sighted; they make mistakes, they are often selfish, and they fail to exercise discipline consistently. But when God disciplines his children, what he does always profits his sons, for he disciplines perfectly.

The life which disciplined disciples endeavor to live is the same life of discipline and training for eternal holiness that Christ, the Son, perfectly lived. The disciplined life (a life lived according to God's commandments) therefore grows out of the same kind of training to which Christ subjected himself. He too "learned obedience" (Hebrews 5:7-10). Hebrews 5:8 through the end of· the chapter speaks of God's sinless Son in relationship to God's sinful sons. Obedience is sometimes viewed only in terms of restraint upon sinners. But specific acts of obedience are not intuitive, even to a sinless son. He had to *"learn"* obedience (Hebrews 5). The desire to obey, of course, was always present in Christ. As a faithful believing child of his Father, Jesus the man wished to obey God. And yet, to obey properly meant that he had to learn God's will. Such knowledge was not intuitive to his human nature, but had to be learned (Luke 2:40, 46). The word that is used in Hebrews 5:8 is the common Greek word for learning.

> Although he was a son, he *learned* obedience from the things which he suffered and, having been made perfect, he became to all those who obey him the source of eternal salvation.

Jesus learned God's will from God's Word which he applied to life. He had to learn how to develop biblical patterns by

162

actual practice in responding to life's problems.[1] This is precisely what clients must do too.

Since obedience is the goal of the Christian life, the writer of Hebrews chides his readers for their lack of such learning. He says:

> You should be teachers by now—but instead you need to be taught the elementary principles of Christianity again.

They could drink milk only and not eat solid food, because they had become dull of hearing (vss. 11, 12). He explained this dullness:

> For everyone who partakes only of milk *is not accustomed* to the word of righteousness, for he is a baby, but solid food is for the mature who *because of practice* have their senses *trained* to discern good and evil.[2]

They were "unaccustomed" because they had failed to "practice" and "train" themselves in holiness. Holy living, then, involves habit. Patterns of holiness can be established only by regular, consistent practice. Just as Christ learned obedience, we too must learn obedience by actual practice.

God's will is often hard to do, even for a sinless son (vss. 7, 8b). In the days of his flesh he prayed with loud crying and tears. And although he was heard because of his piety, yet he suffered, and through suffering was taught obedience. The practice of obedience in a sinful world was difficult. There were other seemingly easier ways (that is, easier for the moment only) that kept presenting themselves. The temptation of Matthew 4 is the classical instance. The Devil tempted

---

[1] Learning in this context goes beyond intellectual comprehension. The text does not say Christ learned the facts about obedience (what it is, how to do it, etc.) but rather says "he learned obedience," i.e., he learned to obey.

[2] (Hebrews 5:13, 14) Italics mine. The italicized words show the importance of establishing biblical habit patterns.

Christ by offering him an easier way to gain all the kingdoms of the world. "Simply worship me" he said. But Jesus refused the easy, sinful way. He likewise refused to succumb to pressure in the Garden of Gethsemane. Obediently he went to the cross, through death, and then rose again from the dead, triumphant.

Sinful sons must similarly learn obedience, and it is all the harder for them. Verses 11-14 indicate that clients must be taught obedience by persevering in its practice in life experiences until obedience becomes the natural course for them to follow. They must be trained by reason of practice to discern between good and evil. The words "senses" *(aistheteria)* and "trained" *(gegumnasmena)* in Hebrews 5:13, 14 indicate that it is in the innerspring of one's actions, in the *heart* of his personality that one must learn by consistent repetition to discern between good and evil. Other translations read: "minds trained by practice" *(Jerusalem Bible),* "faculties trained" (Williams), etc.[1] One must *learn* to do God's will which he has discovered in Scripture. He must practice the good so faithfully that whenever occasions to sin arise, naturally, and without deliberation, he knows what to do and does it with ease and expertness.

There is a purpose behind God's discipline which he has in mind at all times; God disciplines for good *"in order that ..."* (12:10). That purpose, we have seen, is to enable God's children to share in the eternal holiness of God. The question arises at this point: what does sharing in the holiness of God

---

[1]The word *aistheterion* ("senses") speaks of the ability to judge. It refers to discrimination in the sense of "good taste" in the LXX as a translation of טַעַם in Psalm 119:66. In Cicero and Quintillian the word meant comprehension, notion, or cognition in general. Perception by senses alone is a later usage. In biblical Greek, the stress falls upon the judging of sense perceptions rather than upon the act of perception. This judgment is regarded by the writer of Hebrews as becoming perfected by use or exercise. Cf. Kittel.

mean? Is this holiness objective or subjective? Is it the holiness which God gives or the holiness which God possesses? Do God's sons share that which other Christians have from God and thus enter into it themselves (sharing it together with them), or do they somehow enter into the very family holiness which the Father possesses? There is a close connection between both thoughts, since man's holiness must reflect God's holiness. One is innate, the other is acquired. There is a reflection, since Christian holiness is the restoration of the "image and likeness of God" (cf. Colossians 3:10, 11; Ephesians 4:23, 24). All holiness comes from God and reflects his holiness. The question probably cannot be answered more precisely. The idea of sharing in the holiness, by God's holiness becoming a part of our life patterns, is an important goal for Christians. It is the goal which the Father has in mind for them. The goal is love, i.e., love toward God and man through conformity to the commandments of God. Habitual holy living is God's purpose for his sons and, therefore, should be their purpose for their lives, as well.

By its very nature most discipline is unpleasant. The chipping away of imperfections is a painful process. But the fruit of discipline is very pleasant:

> All discipline for a moment seems not to be joyful, but sorrowful: yet to those who have been trained by it . . . . . (Heb. 12:11).

The word translated "trained" comes from the same root as our English term, "gymnastics." The Greek, like the English, means to practice something until it becomes natural. Hebrews refers here to that kind of regular, systematic, habitual practice which makes the work of the Lord natural. Just as the athlete practices until his training makes him expert and his athletic accomplishments are "second nature"[1] to him, so

---

[1]This is a happy expression. Many habits become so strongly ingrained that it is often difficult to separate them from the natural

the Christian by practice must become expert in holiness, so expert that his "second nature" (wrought by the work of the Holy Spirit) is dominant, natural, and easy. As he continues to practice, the pattern is etched out more permanently, holiness becomes easier and he becomes more naturally Christian. Though it is unpleasant for the moment, discipline has in view the joyful outcome of the habitual practice of holiness.

All discipline at the moment seems "sorrowful" (the word literally is "painful"), yet to those who have been "trained by it," afterwards (that is, once they have become accomplished in their training) "it yields the peaceful fruit of righteousness." The word "fruit" means *result;* the peaceful result of discipline is righteousness. Righteousness is called a peaceful result since it brings peace:

> When a man's ways please the Lord, he makes even his enemies to be at peace with him (Proverbs 16:7).

The result of corrective, disciplined and structured living is righteousness. Bite into the fruit of righteousness. It has the flavor of peace. One who tastes the results of discipline enjoys the peace that passes all understanding: peace of conscience, peace of mind, peace of heart, peace of soul, for which men everywhere vainly strive. Righteousness is peace-flavored. And so when Chrsitians sow discipline, they reap righteousness, which in turn results in peace.

The first word of verse 12, "Therefore," shows the logical connection of the former with what follows. On the basis of what has been said about discipline leading to sanctification, righteousness and peace, the writer urges:

> Strengthen the hands that are weak and the knees that

---

*(phusis)* or instinctual drives. Doubtless, much of the confusion and error of Freudian determinists who stress the unconscious as irrational and ethically neutral (leading to non-responsibility) stems from the fact that learned behavior can become as "natural" as the drives that are instinctive (inherent in the *phusis*).

are feeble; make straight paths for your feet, so that the limb which is lame may not be put out of joint; but rather be healed.

The picture here is of an athlete who is out of condition. The basic analogy is to the inefficiency of weak, undisciplined Christians who, like a weak athlete, cannot perform properly. They need to strengthen the weak hands and feeble knees by exercise in godliness.[1] The relaxed arms and the feeble knees pictured in Hebrews represent a condition impossible for participation in competitive sports. An athlete cannot afford to have his hands hanging down limply and knees loose. His whole body has to be in shape. His muscle tone must be honed to a fine edge. Extending and slightly modifying the figure the writer continues by saying:

Make straight paths so that what is lame may not be permanently injured but rather may be healed.

A man with a bad foot who walks among potholes is likely to do himself more harm. Walking on a smooth level path helps assure that one's ankle may not be wrenched or turned out of the way and thus be put out of joint permanently. God laid out the course and in the Scriptures pointed the way, so that man does not have to map out his own road. God's level path is clearly charted in Scripture. To sum up, as good athletes in the race of life, Christians must pursue after peace with all men. They are to chase until they obtain it in this pursuit of holiness.

In order to do this, Christians must

See to it that no one comes short of the grace of God; that no root of bitterness springing up cause trouble, and by it many be defiled (vs. 15).

This "root of bitterness" here was the root of their problem.

---

[1]Cf. also I Timothy 4:7, 8. Paul wrote: "by practice discipline yourself for (or toward) godliness."

In the Hebrew church it seems as if bitterness had mush-roomed. Instead of learning endurance from persecution, com-plainers were saying (or might soon be saying if they did not take heed):

> We made a bad choice when we left Judaism and went into Christianity. All we've had since is persecution and os-tracism. It seems as if we've jumped out of the frying pan into the fire. I wonder if we shouldn't quit; I wonder if we shouldn't go back?

The seed of bitterness had taken root among a few who could cause trouble for the whole church, for by their bitterness many might be defiled. Since the loss of large numbers was a possibility, the writer warned against bitterness. He pointed out that there might be some among them who were not gen-uine Christians at all. He urged, "See to it that no one comes short of the grace of God," i.e., see to it that all of you have truly found the grace of God in Jesus Christ; make sure that you are in the faith. He reasoned, be sure that

> . . . there be no immoral or godless person, like Esau, who sold his own birthright for a single meal. For you know, afterwards, when he desired to inherit the blessing, he was rejected: for he found no place for repentance, though he sought for it with tears (vss. 16, 17).

Esau was sorry, but he was not sorry about what he had done against God. He was sorry only about the personal conse-quences of what he had done, and that there was no way to change the results.

It was only through discipline in holiness that bitterness could be uprooted. That is why this passage stresses the im-portance of discipline. Not all discipline, of course, comes through persecution. God's Word disciplines. Wise are those believers who train themselves to do God's will by practicing those things that God has set forth in the Scriptures. In this way they may strengthen their hands and knees, and make straight paths for their feet. Thus the pursuit of peace along those paths can be rapid and effective. Rather than suffer the imposition of discipline from without, it is better to walk in the "more excellent way" of self discipline. God will discipline all of his children, either through the discipline of the Word, accepted and applied by them, or through the discipline of providential pressures, like the pressure of persecution or sickness.

Clients frequently comment about the important part that insistence upon discipline played in the solution to their problems. At the end of counseling, when the six-week checkup comes around or during the debriefing session which closes regular counseling sessions, they often say something like, "We appreciate the fact that you were rough on us, that you were hard on us, that you did not let us get away with anything."[1] Most people appreciate this because for the first time someone has held them to the commands and the commitments of Scripture. For the first time, their lives have begun to be structured biblically. For the first time the gimmicks, tricks and ruses that they developed to make others pity and coddle them have been penetrated. Clients themselves recognize that this is why they have been helped; and they say "thanks" for it, because they have begun to taste the fruit of holiness.

Barbara and Bob were not getting along very well in counseling. They had made some minor gains. Their financial problems had been worked out. Their counselors had put them on an austerity program, so that they were able to retrieve about $30.00 a week out of a small salary that previously had been draining away and that had caused a sizeable debt. Impulse buying had been curtailed, and their debts were beginning to be paid. Other problems had been solved; but it seemed evident that there was some underlying factor that had not yet come to the surface. Their counselors concluded that Barbara and Bob were dragging their feet; they were not working hard

---

[1] An actual quotation from one case history.

enough at their problems. Around the sixth week of counseling sessions, a re-evaluation usually takes place. So when the sixth week came, the counselors faced Bob and Barbara directly. They were asked about the suspected foot-dragging. They were told that there had not been adequate progress for that length of time. The counselors said, in effect:

Something is wrong, and as far as we are concerned, if you don't tell us what the real issue is and get down to work, we're through. We can do no more for you. We can only work with the data that you give us.

Probing in various areas produced nothing; then one of the counselors asked point blank, "Do you both want to make a success of this marriage?" Bob replied sincerely, "Yes, I do." But Barbara said, "Well, I'm not sure." There was the problem. Barbara was not working hard because she was not sure it was worth it. Bob and Barbara are both Christians, so their counselors again discussed the biblical commands and promises related to their problem. Then they said:

If you don't make a solid commitment to save this marriage we can't help you. You will be in direct disobedience to the will of God and can expect only further difficulty. If you want to do God's will, he will help you. What do you say?

Barbara agreed. "I mean business," she said. "I'm going to make a go of this marriage. I've been sinning." She apologized to Bob; Bob apologized to her for some of his sinful attitudes. "Now you must keep this commitment," said the counselors. They prayed about it. The next week Barbara and Bob returned, transformed people. They had worked hard all week at improving their marriage. They had spent hours talking over every aspect of their problems and praying about them. When they returned it was apparent that a great change had occurred. They were released two sessions later, after making tremendous strides. Bob told his counselors at the final briefing session: "What you said to us at the sixth session was just what we needed. I don't think we would have made it if you

170

hadn't been rough on us and knocked some sense into our heads. Thanks!"[1]

## Break Downs are Break Ups

Counseling is not usually an enjoyable process for the client; hard decisions must be made and painful subjects must be discussed. The discipline of the Lord is not pleasant either but at length it produces the pleasant fruit of righteousness and peace. Sometimes nouthetic counselors talk about taking a person apart and putting him back together again. In one sense, this is what happens. Some clients who come for counseling, however, have already had their lives come ripped apart at the seams. Kazimierz Dabrowski, Professor at the Polish Academy of Science and Director of the Institute of Child Psychiatry and Mental Hygiene in Warsaw, Poland, in a recent book[2] propounds a significant thesis. He holds that a mental breakdown, as it is sometimes called, is really a very advantageous thing. He thinks clients and counselors ought to look upon a breakdown as a breaking up, not a breaking *down*.[3] He says that during such times old patterns, old ways, old habits that have failed are broken up. The client comes to a

---

[1]This case also demonstrates the importance of motivation. Yet it is significant to observe that, as in this case, frequently where motivation is absent, the client may be motivated by the consistent application of nouthetic principles. Nouthetic counseling—of all the approaches—is best adapted to arousing motivation. In the first few sessions especially, when data are being gathered, motivational patterns ought to be noted. Try to gather data to answer the question: "What in the past has motivated the client?" This information may be needed later on in restructuring. However, any motivation used must be biblically justifiable. Every emotion may properly be activated under the proper conditions. But the reasons and circumstances must be considered, since Scripture regulates the use of motivation accordingly.

[2]Kazimierz Dabrowski, *Positive Disintegration* (New York: Little, Brown and Company, 1964).

[3]My phrasing, not his.

recognition that he has not been meeting life's problems properly. And so in frustration the old patterns are abandoned and the client for a time is at sea. To use a different figure, he stands bewildered with many of his past patterns shattered at his feet. While he is standing in the rubble, God affords him an unprecedented opportunity. He may now pick up the pieces and restructure his life in a more thorough manner than he otherwise might have been able to. To put it biblically, by a breakup of the past God affords him the nouthetic opportunity to put his life back together again according to scriptural principles, and to initiate new biblical patterns.

Any life-shattering event affords this opportunity. Periods of serious sickness, grief, financial loss, or breaking of deep ties, are examples of the sort of life-shaking experiences that usually tear a person apart. Grief offers an important opportunity for a pastor to reorient lives according to biblical patterns. Death demands changes; why shouldn't those changes be in the direction of greater devotion to Christ? When one loses a job, when a divorce ruptures a home, when a child gets into serious trouble, when somehow one loses face, when his life seems to be falling apart, when a client is so deeply depressed that he doesn't know where to turn next, the nouthetic counselor senses an important opportunity to serve Christ. When viewed positively, disintegration of the past may be considered an advantage. If the situation is handled properly, when one's life is disintegrated it can be altered much more readily, much more rapidly, and much more radically along biblical lines than at any other time.[1]

---

[1] A study of completed cases at one center has shown that the more serious the problem, the more likely are the hopes of a full rather than partial success. Motivation as well as the complete disintegration of past patterns seems to be a strong factor—"How badly is the client hurting?" may be an important question for the counselor to answer. People who are "set" for a radical change are in a position to make great strides. Jennifer and Larry came for counseling. Jennifer had decided to divorce

Whenever clients come with presentation problems that are also performance problems and preconditioning problems all wrapped up together, counselors know that it is probable that the client has suffered disintegration and is in a state of despair. A person in despair is ideally suited to counseling.[1] Half the process already may be completed. The most difficult cases often afford the most unique opportunities. If pastoral counselors do not confront such people nouthetically they miss some of the greatest opportunities of their ministries. If people do not get help in reassembling their lives according to biblical principles and structure, they are likely to drift into other sinful response patterns and form new patterns just as unbiblical and just as harmful as the first. Perhaps the eventual outcome will prove even worse and lead to deeper and

---

Larry (i.e., she had already determined to make a radical change in her life). He too was "set" to experience radical change. The Holy Spirit used counseling to make radical changes of a different sort in both of their lives and give them a totally new marriage relationship. Both were set for radical change when they came. But the Lord transformed the nature of the change. A sinful course of action was replaced by a radically righteous one. Doubtless God in his providence often readies his children in similar ways. Counselors ought not to despair in such situations; the more radical the nature of the problem, the more sweeping the desired change may be.

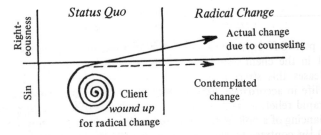

[1]Despair of itself is not necessarily an aid to counseling. "Godly sorrow" which "worketh repentance," however, shows the proper place of despair of one's own efforts in the working of repentance (cf. II Corinthians 7:9-11).

blacker despair. Christ resturctured Peter's life when he was in utter despair, when his life was shattered over his rebellion and denial (John 21). A radical change in Peter's life took place, and from then on he began to live up to his new name, "rock." Likewise, it was in a time of great fear and distress that God chose to change Jacob into Israel (cf. Genesis 32:7-31).

Many clients do not come to counseling in a state of despair. Frequently clients are discouraged but also somewhat cocky about the way that they are handling life's problems. In such cases, it may be necessary to precipitate some sort of responsibility crisis which has been pending but which the client has avoided until now. As an example, if a Matthew 5:23-24 type confrontation between the client and someone whom he has wronged is long overdue, the confrontation might be set up.[1] Not only is the client thereby encouraged to right a wrong, but he also breaks up an old sinful relationship pattern and in its place begins to establish a new biblical one. The client often needs God's law applied to his life with power in order to blast the old patterns loose. Nouthetic counselors do not think that clients need to be led along gently over months or years. Instead, they sometimes find that it is necessary to use God's truth shatteringly to show the person the inevitable hopelessness of his present way of life. They may need to warn him and show him how his present sinful courses of action will lead to nothing but greater discouragement and ulti-

---

[1]Cf. p. 146 ff. It is not necessary to impose stress. Adequate stress is residual in the client's situation. The counselor gathers, concentrates and releases this stress rapidly under control, using it as a force to change life in accordance with the Bible. Such a rapid release of stress brings rapid relief, as well as motivates the client. It may be compared to the lancing of a boil. Better, perhaps, is the analogy of fire (rapid oxidation), in contrast to the gradual process of oxidation which takes place over a long period of time. Stress, gradually released, wears away the person and produces a dry rot in the personality. That is the undesirable alternative to the biblical method of repentance and change.

mate defeat. This viewpoint has been vigorously attacked:

> There are counselors who feel that a quick and complete emptying of sinful facts helps the client to get them out in the open where he can ask for forgiveness. But "yanking" is dangerous and unwise. If you are to be your best in counseling you must let information and thoughts "ooze" out. Why shouldn't counselors yank things out of people? Because it hurts. It hurts both you and the one with whom you are counseling. And the professional counselor is always sensitive to "readiness" when counseling with others.[1]

No one wants to yank teeth unless it is necessary. But in some cases, yanking is not only essential, it is the only thing to do. After all, when a tooth has been bad for a long while, it abscesses and poison runs through one's system. It is more merciful to yank that tooth. Who takes out teeth by stages over a long time? It is far less painful to suffer one bad hurt during the yanking. Then the pain is over and healing can begin immediately.[2] As a matter of fact, the agony of a long drawn out series of sessions is far worse than getting the whole problem out as quickly as possible. It hurts less to cut off the dog's tail with one deft blow than to slowly slice away from the tip end.

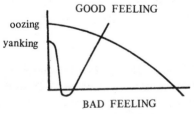

_____

[1]Clyde Narramore (pam.), _Techniques of Counseling_ (Pasadena: n. d.), p. 7.

[2]The incident of the Samaritan woman at the well (John 4) clearly demonstrates this. Christ went to the heart of the matter, and though it hurt, healing quickly followed.

God sent Nathan the prophet to yank a confession out of David. But Narramore protests, "yanking hurts." Of course, yanking hurts; nobody denies that, but abscessed teeth hurt too, and in the long run do far more damage. The point of the psychosomatic Psalms (51, 32, 38), as David clearly indicated, is that God makes us miserable when we hold within the guilt of unforgiven sin. He therefore urged his readers not to be like the stubborn mule that has to be dragged to confession. What hurts most is not the yanking, but the sin which caused the condition in the first place. Wherever sin exists there will be pain. Confessing sin hurts one's pride. It is vain to attempt to avoid this fact, or try to devise some painless method of extracting confessions. Moreover, the way to handle personal problems is not to determine whether one method may be more or less painful than another. In the long run, the "yanking" method must be adopted simply because God calls us to an immediate confession of sin. It is wrong to advise anyone to postpone the confession of sin. Under no circumstances can such advice be justified biblically.

Nouthetic counseling is also preventive. Not only is it important to deal with the tooth that has abscessed and must be pulled, but it is important too to fill teeth and try to preserve them. Both extraction and drilling are painful processes, but both are necessary. Nouthetic counseling is prepared to handle both situations.

## Secondary Matters

Nouthetic counseling, it has been noted, is concerned about total structuring. Total structuring means building a life of love, i.e., a life structured in every respect by the commandments of God. Because of this concern, nouthetic counselors, therefore, are interested not only in basic issues, but also in the secondary effects of problems. Frequently when the presentation problem has been eliminated, when the immediate debilitating (or performance) problem has been solved, and when new biblical patterns have been substituted for the preconditioning problem, some secondary or side effects remain that might have been but an incidental part of the presentation problem.

Tics are one good example. Janet came to us with a facial tic, although she did not mention her tic as part of the presentation problem. Every time she grew tense she twitched her cheek and eye. It was a very noticeable tic that was quite distracting to others and also unflattering to her. During counseling sessions, which had to do with severe marital difficulties, her counselors did the supposedly untactful thing: they called attention to the tic. She was glad that it was mentioned, because she needed somebody to be frank enough to raise this question. She was aware of the tic, and she wanted to get rid of it. She said she prayed and had tried many times. Eventually when it was appropriate to do so (when she had begun an upward cycle), a program was worked out to remove the tic. It took discipline, in addition to prayer, to do so.

First, all of the members of Janet's family were enlisted to pray with her and to work on the problem with her. Secondly, a program of rewards and punishments was drawn up to help motivate her. The family was directed to call her attention to the tic whenever it occurred. Constantly calling her attention to it kept her aware of the tic. Thirdly, she was given an incentive to overcome it. The counselors asked Janet what it was she would like more than anything else if she could have it. Appropriately enough she replied, "A dressing table complete with mirror." This was an ideal request, not only because her husband consented to buy it, but also because every time she looked at herself in the mirror she would be reminded of the victory over the problem. The program was simple: if for one whole week her family could not detect a single tic, her husband agreed he would buy her the table. She got her table the first week.

## Problem Solving through Modeling

In II Thessalonians 3, Paul raised the question of discipline. There were Christians in Thessalonica who, because they had heard (wrongly) that the second coming of Christ was imminent, thought that they could abandon their work. They then went about as busybodies, eating and sponging off others. Paul called their conduct "unruly" (or, literally, "undisciplined"). Paul said, therefore,

> We command you, brethren, in the name of our Lord Jesus Christ, that ye keep aloof (or withdraw) from every brother who leads an unruly life.

The word translated "unruly," means a disorderly kind of life, a life without order or arrangement. Inherent in the word are the ideas of being "out of rank," "out of place," or "out of order." Their congregation was like a column of soldiers with some marching out of step. Paul attacked the problem directly, declaring that every brother who leads an unordered life which is "not according to the tradition which he received from us," should be avoided. It is evident that even in that short visit at Thessalonica, Paul had thoroughly discussed the importance of leading an orderly disciplined life. When he said, "For you yourselves know," Paul meant, "we taught you this; you received it as a tradition (something handed over) from us."

But Paul also said,

> You yourselves know how you ought to follow our example: because we did not act in an undisciplined manner among you.

In that verse Paul used the same term. He said, "We did not live a disorderly life in your midst. Therefore you ought to follow our example." Paul frequently stressed the importance of modeling, or a good example, in learning how to structure living. The importance of showing others how to obey God's commandments through example cannot be stressed too

178

strongly. Role play may also be one valid means of extending the principle that scriptural discipline may be taught by example. (Elsewhere role play as rehearsal has been discussed.) Thus Paul called his readers not only to remember the words that he spoke, but also to recall the kind of life that he and his associates lived among them. Often principles can be most permanently and most vividly impressed upon others by means of example. Reference to example was not something unusual for Paul. Paul frequently used his own behavior as an example for others. This is apparent in passages like the fourth chapter of Philippians. There Paul directed his readers not only to pray and concentrate upon the things that were honorable, right, pure, lovely, and of good repute, but he continued:

> The things you have learned and received and heard and *seen in me,* practice these things: and the God of peace shall be with you ( Philippians 4:9).

In the previous chapter of the same letter, he had already said,

> Brethren, join in following my example, and observe those who walk according to the pattern that you have in us ( Philippians 3:17).

Paul considered his own life a model for new Christians. This emphasis is not limited to Philippians or to the passage in II Thessalonians; Paul also expressed the same thought in several other places. For instance, in I Corinthians 4:16 he wrote, "I exhort you therefore, be imitators of me."

Paul also mentioned modeling when he said, "You also become imitators" (I Thessalonians 1:6). The Greek term "imitator" is the same word from which the English word mimic comes. He wrote, "You became imitators of us and of the Lord." They learned, it seems, how to imitate the Lord by imitating what Paul was doing in imitation of the Lord. Then Paul commended them for becoming models. After they learned how to imitate Paul in imitating the Lord, they themselves became examples for others; "You became an example to all the believers in Macedonia and in Achaia" (I Thess. 1:7).

Peter similarly advised the elders of the church to which he was writing not only to "shepherd the flock of God," but without lording it over those allotted to their charge, to prove themselves to be "examples to the flock" (I Peter 5:3). The word used by Peter was *tupoi* ("types"). Elders are to be types or patterns for their flocks. The idea of the model runs throughout the New Testament.[1]

This idea of modeling also occurs in John's writings, as well as in Peter's and Paul's. In III John 11, John's words show that he assumed that imitation will take place. He says, "Beloved, do not imitate what is evil, but what is good." He said, in effect,

> You're going to imitate. You can't help imitating. As a child you learned how to imitate, and throughout life you are going to continue to imitate others. So make your imitation consciously purposeful and be sure that you imitate that which is good.

The influence of older children in a home clearly demonstrates the importance of example. Younger children pick up their ways of speaking, their words, their actions and their attitudes. The influence of parents is even more striking. And the influence which a counselor exerts in counseling is an important matter, as well. Counselors in all that they do, model, implicitly. At some times they may model explicitly as well.[2]

---

[1] Cf. I Thessalonians 1:6; Philippians 4:9; 3:17; I Corinthians 4:16; II Timothy 3:10; II Thessalonians 3:9; I Timothy 4:12; Titus 2:7; Hebrews 13:7; I Thessalonians 1:7; III John 11, etc.

[2] Cf. especially Christ's words in Luke 6:40b: "Everyone after he has been fully trained, will be like his teacher." Modeling stresses the importance of the "with him" principle of discipleship (Mark 3:14) to which Rev. Kenneth Smith of Pittsburgh, Pa. has forcefully awakened me. Its implications for teaching as well as for counseling are sweeping. Scripture brings teaching and counseling together in the one person, as indeed they should be. Note the close relationship pictured in Colossians 3:16; 1:28.

And so the idea of modeling as a means of bringing about discipline is something which must receive adequate attention from counselors.

Mowrer was involved in very deep personal problems and came to his theories of confession and responsibility by trial and error. In the process, he stumbled upon modeling. Thus he strongly emphasizes what he believes to be a need for always making confession a deeply shared experience. He feels that such modeling helps elicit data from clients. He tries to begin counseling "one down" (rather than one up) on the client, confessing some failure of his own first. Even if "telling one's story," as Mowrer defines modeling, is not needed to elicit a confession from another, Mowrer insists that the counselor must be sure to do so.

Mowrer became aware of the possibilities of modeling by accident. John W. Drakeford explained that while speaking to others "about a personal struggle Mowrer discovered his own story would evoke a response in which the client chimed in with an experience of his own. Much impressed, Mowrer carefully developed the technique and found it so effective that he now refers to it by saying: "Modeling the role is the heart of Integrity Therapy."[1] But Mowrer's strong emphasis on modeling is too strong. Those who work with him, using little or no conscious modeling, often achieved the same results. What one suspects concerning modeling is that it has become the "heart" of Mowrer's theory, not principally because of its usefulness in helping counselees make confession, but

---

[1] *The Dis-Coverer,* Volume 4, No. 4, October 1967, p. 5. What has been said elsewhere about the power of an example or incident that strikes a sympathetic chord in the client equally explains the power of modeling as Mowrer views it. Mowrer stresses modeling as a technique of eliciting confessions, whereas in Scripture the emphasis falls upon modeling as a means of teaching others how to live according to God's Word. That it is not always necessary to "tell one's own story" is apparent from Christ's effective use of parables (about others) that rang a bell with his hearers.

rather because of the beneficial (though temporary) benefits it brings to him as a counselor.

Modeling, as has been shown, is nothing new. It is a useful biblical principle which, at points, counselors will wish to apply. Counseling experience has shown conclusively, however, that *explicit* modeling is by no means an essential element of counseling. In fact, such modeling, as a regular practice, may have grave dangers. The counselor may unnaturally force himself and his own problems into the forefront. Some of those who observed Mowrer and those with him who felt that it always is necessary to tell their story, concluded that for some counselors (not Mowrer himself) modeling often degenerated into story-swapping.[1]

But of far greater importance is the reason why Mowrer may feel the need for modeling so intensely: rejecting Christ's atonement for sin, Mowrer has never experienced the joy of sins forgiven once for all (Hebrews 9:28-10:18) and is endeavoring by good works to effect a "personal atonement" for sin (he uses these very words). But Mowrer's personal atonement is like that of the priest who "stands daily ministering and offering time after time the same sacrifices, which can never take away sins" (Hebrews 10:11). The painful experience of revealing one's sins (for Mowrer it *is* such; for him it could never be a can-you-top-this? story-swapping experience) is an

---

[1]For other precautions about modeling, see Edwin Hallstein, "Integrity Training and the Opening Interview," in *The Dis-Coverer,* Vol. 4, No. 2, April 1967, p. 3. With reference to Promiscuous confession, Richard Parlour, *et al.,* "Rediscovered Dimensions of the Psychotherapist's Responsibility," (unpublished material), suggest some important precautions, p. 15. Group therapy sessions in which confession before persons not involved in the transgression is encouraged, to say the most one can for them, have a dubious biblical warrant for existence. It is questionable whether confession should be encouraged apart from a reconciliation context (except, of course, as a voluntary example for purposes of instruction; cf. David in Psalms cited previously). Cf. especially the introduction to Psalm 32: "A Psalm of David, for Instruction" (Berkeley).

opportunity for Mowrer again to pay a price for his iniquities. Mowrer feels the need and the necessity for somehow punishing himself again and again in order to set his conscience to rest. Watching this fruitless attempt to solve the problem of sin, a Christian cannot help being thankful that "having once been cleansed" by Christ's once-for-all atonement he "no longer has consciousness of sins" (Hebrews 10:2).

## Industry or Institutionalization?

Recent studies illustrate the impossibility of avoiding implicit modeling and the place that such modeling occupies in counseling:

> There is good reason to believe that the most powerful environment for the induction of certain kinds of behavior is to have that behavior exhibited by others. The Schachter experiments show quite clearly that people tend to be euphoric in the presence of a euphoric stooge, that they are angry in the presence of an angry stooge. Recent experiments by Nowlis on mood, demonstrate the general point that the mood represented by the majority of a social group influences the mood of all its members.[1]

These studies illustrate the extent to which the biblical principle of the power of an example extends. They say a lot about the fact that emotions conveyed by gestures and other bodily states and actions growing out of attitudes and moods are catching. The counselor's own attitude in counseling then is important. If he has hope, he will communicate hope; if he is confused he will communicate that.[2] One's belief about the

---

[1] George Mandler in *New Directions In Psychology* (New York: Holt, Rinehart and Winston Company, 1962), p. 312.

[2] Attempts to take a neutral stance are often confusing to the client as they distort one's true attitude. They may convey disinterest or approval when neither are intended. Of one thing the counselor may be sure: something will be conveyed; neutrality is impossible. Moreover, clients need true responses to judge by. One client put it this way: "I

possibilities of solving problems doubtless "comes through." Moreover, it is important for counselors to show proper attitudes, and that means the counselor must be in the best possible state of mind when he counsels others. His own attitudes stemming from personal matters may contradict his beliefs and counteract his efforts to help the client.

II Thessalonians 3 sets forth a further principle of disciplined living:

> For even when we were with you, we used to give you this order, if anyone will not work, neither let him eat.

One must live an orderly, disciplined life in which he works for what he gets. Paul continued, "We hear that some among you are leading an undisciplined life" (vs. 11). As noted, the word "undisciplined" means a life without order and structure. He condemned those who led an undisciplined or unstructured life, doing no work at all, but acting like busybodies. He continued, "Now such persons we command and exhort." Such clients ought to be commanded and exhorted "to work in quiet fashion, and to eat their own bread." Some psychiatrists rather would coddle them all the more. They often put such people in institutions where all they have to do is to lie around on the green grass on the lovely campuses. People who are already lazy thus become more lazy; they become institutionalized and learn to live the institutionalized life where others take care of them, where others work for their bread. Instead, Paul says they must be commanded and exhorted in the Lord to work. "Command" and "exhort" are strong words. He continued:

> But as for you, brethren, do not grow weary of doing good. And if anyone does not obey our instruction in this

---

need to know how this strikes someone who has his head screwed on right." The truly nouthetic response is a biblical response and therefore indicative of God's will in the matter. God is surely not neutral toward sinful behavior. To attempt neutrality, therefore, is to misrepresent God.

letter, take special notice of that man, and do not associate with him, so that he may be put to shame.

Church discipline must be exercised when Christians reject modeling and exhortation and commandments. "And yet do not regard him as an enemy, but admonisth him as a brother" (here the word "admonish" is literally "nouthetically confront" him). The warmth of this word may be seen in its frequent use in contexts which speak of the family relationship. "confront him nouthetically," or better, "confronting him nouthetically" (as the verb form indicates) as a brother.

## Child Training

What do nouthetic counselors have to say about rearing children? First of all, they expect the child to act sinfully. The Scripture indicates that "foolishness is bound up in the heart of a child" (Proverbs 22:15). According to the Psalms, as soon as a child is born "he goes forth speaking lies" (Psalm 58:3) because his mother conceived him in sin (Psalm 51:5). In Ephesians 2:3, Paul plainly stated that "by nature," that is by birth,[1] every infant is a child of "wrath." He is born a sinner, deserving eternal wrath. Since children are born sinners, they will manifest their sinful nature by sinful behavior from their earliest opportunities. Sins by adults do not differ largely in kind from those of children. Consequently, with children, just as with adults, discipline takes the form of a battle against non-Christian response patterns. However, there is one great advantage to child discipline. If one is aware of the kind of patterns that his child may develop in later life, then as a parent he will do all within his ability to instill and structure into his child those patterns which are consonant with biblical living. Wherever he sees the weeds of irresponsibility beginning to sprout forth in his child's life he will seek

---

[1]*Phusis* means the genetic nature inherited from one's parents and thus comes to mean "by birth." Cf. Lysias' *Orations,* "Philo," *hosoi de phusei men politai eisi,* "as many as by birth are citizens."

to root them out and in their place will plant the seeds of responsibility.

Parents (or teachers) should respond to the behavior of children in an honest and appropriate manner. Only by such responses can they provide a standard by which the child may discover the social consequences of his behavior. Such a response will not harm the child as some think. On the contrary, neutral (i.e., distorted) responses and irratic responses confuse and tend to encourage sociopathic attitudes in the child. A child cannot avoid being wronged by people. While a parent should not purposely wrong his child (he doesn't need to work at this, he'll do so naturally), such wronging will not be as injurious as some might think. Throughout life, people will treat him wrongly. It is well that the first wrongdoing he experiences may come from those who love him most, for *if in love* they admit the wrong, apologize and make right what they have done wrong, they teach him much by their example. But also, if they teach him *how to respond* to wrongdoing, they teach him the most important lesson of all. The key in parental discipline is to teach children biblical responses to wrongdoing. A child's problem is not insecurity (as so often claimed) but failure to solve problems properly.

As children grow into their teens, the problem becomes less a matter of the parent structuring responsibility and discipline into the life of a child and more a matter of helping the child to assume responsibility for structuring his own life. Certainly, however, this shift of responsibility must be a gradual process which began many years before. But now discipline becomes almost entirely the responsibility of the child himself. He must become a self structured, self disciplined individual before he leaves his home. He can no longer claim that he is not responsible for his actions. As the teenage child begins to move out from the home and to make decisions on his own, he begins to assume personal responsibility. He may no longer operate according to decisions that have been made for him by his parents. He must recognize his personal obligation to God. He must be taught that the injunction, "If you love me, keep my commandments," is addressed to him. He must build a responsible relationship to God and others through observing God's commandments. He must learn that God requires him to love God and his neighbor. Teen age is the time to grow up. It is a time when one should put away childish ways and put on mature love. It is a time when children in a Christian home should be taught to assume the obligation of self-discipline, a word which frequently appears in Scripture.[1]

In helping teenagers to grow into self-discipline, parents must use much wisdom. When matters come to a head and a decision must be made between a contemplated course of action desired by the teenager but not desired by his parent, the opportunity for a spurt in growth may be present. If the matter in question is one in which serious consequences will follow the youth's action, and he has had few prior opportunities to make such decisions on his own, this is probably not the time to allow him to begin. If the matter is not likely to issue in such serious consequences (e.g., the clothes he or she wants to wear may only embarrass the parents) then this is probably the kind of issue in which to introduce self-responsibility.

Self structuring should be taught carefully. The parent may find it helpful to say something like this:

John, I'm going to trust you to make your own decision about this matter before God. But I want you to do so responsibly. First, I want you to sit down and listen to my point of view as I understand the application of the Scriptures to the question, and I want to explain the consequences of this proposed action as I see them. After that I want you to take a week to think and pray about this matter before coming to a final decision (in a very important matter, or in the first instance of instituting self-discipline, the par-

---

[1]*Enkrateia,* "self-control"; cf. Acts 24:25; Galatians 5:23; II Peter 1:6.

ent may also wish to request written reasons for the decision). Then after you have made it, I'll say no more—but you must be prepared to face the consequences.

During his teens, parents ought to encourage the child to reevaluate his own life. He should reevaluate his standards and performance in terms of the Scriptures. He might well be helped to devise a teen-age program for putting off the old man and putting on the new man for himself. The teen-age period, of necessity, is a time of adjustment. It is a time of physical adjustment and a time of moral adjustment. It is a time when a child assumes new responsibilities and in which he adjusts to a new way of life. It is a time when he must learn to act "not only because of wrath, but also for conscience sake" (Romans 13:5; cf. also I Peter 2:19). It is a time largely for personal evaluation.

As he grows up out of helplessness and dependency, a child must learn to assume personal responsibility for his life. The teenager is a tadpole with legs. He is living in the world. The coalescence of physical and moral maturity in this most crucial period particularly ought to make a child recognize the need to "flee youthful lusts and to pursue after righteousness" (II Timothy 2:22). Unsaved young persons during the teen-age period cannot help continuing in old patterns, or as the result of reevaluation establish new wrong patterns.[1] Without the biblical standard (Scripture) there is no alternative. The teen-age Christian[2] should retain the old patterns which rightly have been established for him according to the Word

---

[1] Rebellion, so characteristic of teenagers is not just a "phase" through which all children must pass, for it is sin. Since this is a period in which he is learning independence and self responsibility, it is hard for the Christian youth to resist the tendency, but resistance by God's help is possible.

[2] The question of conversion in the Christian home cannot be considered here.

of God. He should not be too quick to abandon old ways. But he must also now assume responsibility for judging that each pattern of his life is in accordance with the Word of God. He may not merely assume that all the patterns that his parents have helped him develop are scriptural, even though they are Christians. The teen-age Christian must not repeat the failures of his childhood, but should learn from them. Comparing his life patterns with the Word of God, a Christian youth should determine to live better than his parents did, and better than he did with his parents. But let him be sure that the standard by which he judges any action to be better is God's Word. Each generation of Christian youth should stand upon the shoulders of the last. Children in a Christian home begin life with a heritage. They do not need to start all over again, but in many ways they should begin where their parents left off. This is one of the great advantages of the Christian family's covenantal relationship to God.

## Code of Conduct

Most cases of child discipline may be solved by establishing structure that will lead to the reenforcement of the biblical principles established for the home. To do this, the rules of the home need to be set out clearly. God has given parents full authority to be exercised under the rule of Scripture. The husband is to be the head of the home, the wife is to be his submissive helper, and the children are to love their parents, honoring and obeying them. But these are general principles which must be worked out in terms of the concrete problems children raise. What must be done when a child lies, talks back, fails to come home on time? One good way to determine fair consistent answers to such questions is to draw up a code of conduct. On a sheet, consisting of four columns, each column is headed by the words "Crime," "Punishment," "By Whom," and "When."

## CODE OF CONDUCT

| Crime | Punishment | By Whom | When |
|---|---|---|---|
| | | | |
| | | | |
| | | | |
| | | | |
| | | | |

Each box in the code of conduct chart may be filled in according to the specific problems of individual situations. For example, lying is a crime that can be punished by washing the mouth out with soap, apologizing, and rectifying the situation by telling the truth.[1] The punishment should fit the crime in intensity, and when possible, in kind. In matching punishment to crime, it is helpful to distinguish between failures in performing chores (taking out trash, making one's bed) and overt or rebellious disobedience (back talk, refusal to obey). On the whole, punishments that are productive (work details above and beyond ordinary chores) are the best punishments whenever they can be devised. Ordinary chores ought not to be used as punishments since parents should endeavor to get

---

[1]When soap is used, if the child is old enough, he is first required to do research on soaps by writing to the manufacturing company to make sure that the use of the chosen soap is harmless.

their children to enjoy helping out in the family. Chores may be selected once a week by drawing slips from the family Job Jar. Taking privileges away or keeping children from healthy activity (e.g., "You can't play outside for a week") are among the poorer ones. Frequently such punishments end up as punishments for the parents rather than the children. The punishment is usually administered by either parent at the time the offense occurs. However, there may be instances where some punishments may be delayed until Dad returns home, to emphasize the severity of the crime.

The importance of trying to regulate all four of these items in any given disciplinary situation should be apparent upon reflection. If any one of these items is neglected, confusion and difficulty may result. The important factors in discipline are clarity, consistency, regularity, enforcibility and fairness. In adopting a code, first the parents agree to its terms. Next, the code is presented and explained to the children. They are given opportunity to negotiate any changes they believe would improve the code. Among younger children, these negotiations will largely pertain to determining punishments. Frequently, even very young children will suggest stronger and more appropriate punishments. Parents are the final authority under God, and may veto any proposals. The counselor then goes over the code and helps make suggestions where needed. Using the form provided, the code is then posted somewhere in the home where all can see it, and from that time on is to be observed consistently by the children and the parents. When discipline is set up on such a basis, the parents, as well as the children, must be held to it.[1] If the parents violate the code, they must apologize and rectify the situation.

---

[1] The code structures the parents' behavior as well as that of the children. For instance, there is no place in the code for yelling. If mother screams as well as paddles (as the code provides), she has violated the code and must apologize.

There is nothing inspired about a code of conduct;[1] but this is one useful way of implementing the inspired injunction to "manage" one's household well, "keeping his children under control with all dignity" (I Timothy 3:4). Management ought to be orderly and dignified. In order to assure this, practical measures must be devised. When parents and children begin adhering to a code, the whole household soon settles down, usually in a few weeks.

Even though the children may not like the severity of some of the punishments that are laid down, they at least know the limits; they know precisely what will happen when they violate the code. Children appreciate knowing where the lines are drawn. They have often expressed their enthusiasm for the code to the surprise of their parents. The principle of such a code is biblical. God revealed his will to Adam and told him precisely what would happen if he failed to obey. When Adam sinned, God consistently followed through. "In the day that thou eatest thereof, thou shalt surely die" was the sanction or penalty attached to the prohibition. When the Israelites entered Canaan, God set forth his will, together with the blessings and cursings that would follow in consequence of obedience or disobedience to it. Then, he followed through exactly as he said he would.[2] Penalties made during cool reflection before the crime are normally wiser and fairer than those growing out of the heat generated by the infraction. When children know beforehand what the penalty for a crime will be, and find that parents strictly adhere to it, they learn to live within clearly-defined limits. If penalties for crimes keep changing according to the whims or moods of parents at the time when they are administered, a child soon becomes discouraged and confused, because he does not know the limits

---

[1]Specific items in the code may be renegotiated so long as public notice has been given to all the family. God's commandments and the specific elements in a family code should be distinguished.

[2]Cf. Deuteronomy, chapters 27 and 28.

and the consequences of his behavior. There is no structure in his discipline. If today a child can commit a serious crime with impunity and tomorrow he gets slapped across the room for some relatively minor infraction, he soon comes to the conclusion that there is no consistency in the home. Since the severity of such punishment rarely fits the severity of the crime, and since punishments are unpredictable, he concludes that he might as well do whatever he wants.

There are many important elements in a human code that need to be considered that cannot be discussed here. Perhaps it is important to stress one last factor, however. While the code must be enforced by the parents, they should make it plain that they enforce the code only because they are exercising the authority that God has given to them. Because they have rights and authority delegated to them by God as parents, children must come to recognize that by disobeying parental codes they are really violating God's commandments by rebelling against God's authority. When they break the rules at home, when they show disrespect for their parents, when they do not obey the rules and regulations in their family, their revolt is not merely against parents, but more fundamentally it is revolt against the God who commands, "Obey your parents in the Lord" (Ephesians 6:1). It is important then for parents to tell their children that although family rules of conduct have been devised by their parents and are, therefore, not infallible, nevertheless as parents they have been authorized and commanded by God to exercise discipline in the home. When children obey their parents, they glorify God and bring peace and order into their family.

*Chapter IX*

# SOME PRINCIPLES OF NOUTHETIC TECHNIQUE

## Leading the Client to Self-Discipline

Does directive counseling with its strong structuring lead to dependence? Doubtless the danger exists. But since the goal of Nouthetic Counseling is to lead the client into self-discipline,[1] nouthetic counselors have developed methods for discouraging client dependence. Before turning to these, reflect for a moment upon the successful use of strong structure in a directive context by instructors in all of the arts and sports. The music teacher and the football coach alike use similar methods, and their goal also is the self-disciplined effect to which structure leads. Counselors (who become teachers or coaches in effect) find no more difficulty in making the transition than do they. The passage in Hebrews 12, discussed in the previous chapter, shows the close relationship between training in athletics and training in holiness.

One method, often used, employs transition measures calculated to break client dependence by means of the *cliff-hanger*. In early sessions, counselors often help clients solve their problems by taking the lead in working through some of their problems with them. This does at least two things. First, it enables clients to get early, immediate relief and brings them to an early reversal of the downward cycle of defeat. Secondly, it affords clients the opportunity to see how problems may be solved by biblical means, as the counselor, using the Scriptures, models this for them. But there comes a point where because of the relief received and the instruction given, a transition may be made from counselor to client leadership in problem solving.

---

[1] Cf. Philemon 14 and other such passages to note the general desirability of a transition to self-discipline.

At this transition point the solution to a problem is begun in the office as usual, but purposely not resolved there. Instead, the clients are sent home to continue conferring until they have reached a biblical solution. This means they must learn how to use Scripture on their own to solve problems.[1] This procedure generally moves as follows: for several sessions the counselor helps the clients solve two or three representative problems from a list which the clients themselves have prepared. It is most helpful to have clients compose this list of conflict areas *together* at home, if for no other reason than that by such a project non-communicating persons initiate the regular, daily process of problem-solving communication.[2] In the very process of agreeing upon areas of conflict, both parties begin to work together. Such cooperative effort may itself be the first time that the parties have exerted any genuine *combined* effort toward solving their problems. This alone is a significant step forward.

When the list is brought in, an agenda is drawn up from it stressing priorities. Priorities may be determined by (1) the pressing nature of the problem, and (2) by the ability of the clients to handle problems at the time. Several problems are then dealt with definitively in counseling sessions in an attempt to reach biblical solutions. During the process, the principles of Christian conference are taught by example and explained by precept. The encouragement that comes from solving some problems successfully helps the clients to see that whenever they work at their problems biblically they can find God's answers to them. Hope often grows rapidly. The solutions are reached in the office where the clients themselves

---

[1] While it is impossible to give a course in Bible interpretation during counseling sessions, the counselor must show himself to be an astute interpreter of the Word. And, differing of course according to the background of the client, the counselor must be ready to give at least elementary advice regarding Bible study methods.

[2] More will be said about this list subsequently.

re encouraged to take a larger and larger part in finding solu-ons together. Then, when clients have begun to communi-ate in the office, and they appear to be getting the hang of iblical problem solving, the counselor turns them loose on he first cliff hanger. They take their "solo" flight. Rarely, herefore, do counselors exhaust the list in the counseling ses-ions. It is usually undesirable to do so. When the couple is ent home to complete the solution to a problem which seems o be progressing toward a satisfactory solution, they are in-tructed to bring the results (often written out) to the next ession. In some instances (e.g., matters of great urgency) the ounselor may ask for a phone call in an hour or two when he conference at home has been completed. This is one way of exerting needed pressure upon some who otherwise might ail to complete the home assignment.

At each session the counselor assigns specific problems rom the agenda (or elsewhere) as homework. He writes con-crete suggestions in the client's homework book whenever possible (e.g., "Bring in the shopping list you used with the name and price of each item purchased this week"). A home-work book (8½x5½), entitled *Progress in Problem Solving,* consisting of six drab blue and six bright yellow assignment pages is used. The blue pages represent the first half of coun-seling before the client turns the corner. The yellow pages represent the period devoted to the more positive work of es-tablishing biblical patterns. Yellow pages may be added earlier than the sixth week and blue pages may be added after the sixth week to indicate accelerated progress or the opposite. Structure, with flexibility, enables clients to look at the mile-posts. The homework book has been one of the most valuable assets in bringing hope to and spurring motivation among cli-ents. Homework is regularly assigned each week. Progress and motivation can be gauged by the results.[1] The next session

---

[1] At this point the client may even be allowed to make his own as-signments.

usually opens with a discussion of the homework. Confuse
clients, emotionally distraught, *need* written assignments c
they may forget directions given in counseling. The book als
becomes a personalized textbook to which the client ma
refer in the future for help. Counseling sessions do not sag i
the middle from week to week since the homework book be
comes a daily "counselor" that the client takes home wit
him.

Clients also may use a problem-solution form consisting o
four columns (see diagram). This pink colored form fits int
the homework book (the homework book has an acetate cov
er and a plastic slide binder, providing easy access for counse
or and client), along with other sheets which are often inser
ed. The form may be used to record how old or new prob
lems which arise during the week have been met. The shee
enables the counselor to structure the information he receive
concerning the homework, and also becomes a reminder en
abling him to assess growth and progress. Counselors ofte
know that clients are ready for dismissal when they discove
that they are beginning to solve unassigned problems on the
own initiative. The form frequently captures this or other in
formation which otherwise might be lost.

Often counselors find it necessary to spell out for client
methods for getting things done. They teach them first t
plan their long-range goals. Then they show them how to pla
the short-range goals which must be reached along the way t
attaining long-range objectives. Thirdly, all of the goals ar
then scheduled as accurately as possible. Fourthly, the plan
ning must be followed by doing. The scheduled goals becom
(1) incentives: it is easier to shoot for short-term goals; (2
milestones: goals performance may be checked. When short
term goals are reached on or ahead of schedule, the clien
gains hope; if he drops behind schedule he can be spurred o
to renewed effort before it becomes too late to catch up. Th
double question is: Are the goals reached—on schedule? Cour

197

| PROBLEM - SOLUTION SHEET | | | |
|---|---|---|---|
| What Happened | What I Did | What I Should Have Done | What I Now Must Do |
| Problem (describe) | My Response (describe) | Biblical Response (cite and explain references) | Describe the steps that must be taken to rectify matters. |
| Problem (describe) | My Response (describe) | Biblical Response (cite and explain references) | Describe the steps that must be taken to rectify matters. |
| Problem (describe) | My Response (describe) | Biblical Response (cite and explain references) | Describe the steps that must be taken to rectify matters. |

EVALUATION AND COMMENTS:

selors are careful to help clients assess whether goals are realistic. Is the client shooting too high or too low?

It is often necessary to be specific about many things that are often (wrongly) taken for granted. For example, in teaching children how to obey their parents (in doing a job) counselors might suggest: (1) listen carefully to all instructions (pay attention); (2) ask for explanations or demonstrations whenever necessary (make sure you understand); (3) perform the task at the earliest opportunity (don't put it off). And to this is appended the warning, "Don't get sidetracked." Good advice which fits this picture is, "Whenever you make a decision to do something, *schedule it*" (i.e., schedule at least the first step and a tentative completion date). The example of Abraham's obedience to God vividly emphasizes point three. When God called upon him to perform the most unpleasant duty of his life, the sacrifice of Isaac, "Early the next morning, Abraham got up . . ." He did not put it off.

## Recording Progress

It is a good idea when clients solve problems to have them record the results of their work. Putting down one's thoughts in written form makes him more likely to express his ideas clearly. At least, there is more pressure to do so. One has to be more sure of his ideas if he has to put them down in writing. Because they must agree upon the final wording in which to record the results of their work, clients are less likely to assume that they have reached mutual agreements when they have not. Thus proposed solutions, when written, are themselves heartening evidence of communication, and when solutions are stated in written form, there is less likelihood of later misunderstandings. Moreover, no party can plead ignorance of a written agreement.[1] Parties may more readily be held to their commitments. Also, concrete results of effort preserved

---

[1] Surely the covenantal structure of God's relationship implies this. The written tables of the law served such a purpose.

in tangible form can be reread and reconsidered later. If additions or alterations must be made by renegotiation, the parties involved have something to begin with, rather than starting over again from scratch. Referring back to records is one way of priming the pump for new ideas. Writing and recording is especially important to clients whose lives are unstructured, because the medium itself tends to structure. These are only a few reasons why written records of various sorts frequently ought to be required of clients. The homework book, into which client contributions can be inserted as well as counselor assignments, becomes a convenient and valuable document in which the client may preserve a tangible record of his counseling sessions.

## Generalizing

There is a danger that directive counseling may become mere generalizing, something never found in Scripture.[1] Generalizing has been found to be non-productive. Generalizations, inductively, ought to grow out of specific applications in counseling. Whenever clients fail to deal with specific problems they rarely solve them. One trainee pointed out that the breakthrough in his counseling instruction came when he realized how important it is first to solve specific problems and then to use the solutions as illustrative of the general principles he needed to learn for the future. Handling specific matters also brings hope. Clients see that in one instance, at least, it was possible for them to reach a biblical solution to a problem. Hope then grows that other problems may be solved similarly. Biblical problem-solving soon snowballs positively.

---

[1] Throughout the biblical record, one of the amazing facts that becomes apparent is the concreteness with which even the most profound doctrine is given. The great Christological passage (Philippians 2) was given to stress unity to a divided church by showing the "mind" of Christ who put the concerns of his people before his own welfare. Paul calls the Philippians to emulate Christ in such concern for one another.

Moreover, solving a few specific problems puts clients in a
better position to cope with other problems, since the weight
of guilt and the pressure of some problems has already been
lifted. Through solving specific existing problems, clients best
learn the principles needed to solve new ones.

## Take One Thing at a Time

Counselors sometimes should follow the iceberg method at
the outset of counseling sessions.[1] Clients initially may keep
four fifths of their problems (sometimes the deepest or most
difficult ones) under water. Frequently, however, nouthetic
counselors get a full look at the whole problem in the first or
second interview (possibly in part because of our *Personal Data
Inventory*[2] which is calculated to dig out the roots of problems). But if the counselor wants to get to the deeper problem quickly, he must learn to take seriously the problems clients initially present. The *presentation problem* may be only
a complicating problem which grows out of the *performance
problem* and the *preconditioning problem*.[3] However, the

---

[1] There will be general probing of the total structure of the client's
life, but it is usually wise to let him focus initially on the areas in which
he thinks the most serious problems may lie.

[2] Cf. Appendix A. The P. D. I. ordinarily is taken during or prior to
the initial interview.

[3] We distinguished earlier between three sorts of problems, but perhaps a concise summary here would help: (1) the *presentation problem*
is the first problem presented to the counselor. It answers the question,
"Why are you here?" and usually consists of the recital of symptoms
like, "I'm depressed." (2) The *performance problem* is the specific cause
or causes of the immediate debilitation. Not infrequently clients reveal
the performance problem early in counseling. Sometimes the performance problem ("I've been using drugs and I'm hooked") is stated *as* the
presentation problem. When this takes place, the client is often in despair; at the end of his rope. His defenses are down. (3) The *preconditioning problem* is the long-standing underlying pattern of non-biblical
responses which often stems back into childhood. It is of this general
pattern that the performance problem is but one specific instance. Of

presentation problem should not be ignored, as some seem to suggest. Those who follow such a practice usually assume that the client has little idea of what his real problem is. Therefore the counselor must by-pass the presentation problem and probe deeply to uncover the true problem. His task then is to show the client that what the latter thinks is his problem is not really the problem at all. While it is true that in some cases people may be able to go no deeper than symptoms, most frequently in the opening session of a nouthetic interview the client presents a genuine problem (more frequently several). This is largely because clients are encouraged to focus not on feelings (symptoms) but on behavior. This problem may or may not be the most serious problem. The presentation problem may only be a complicating (or secondary) problem, but even this is usually a genuine problem which, therefore, must be taken seriously. When the counselor takes time to help the client solve this problem, even though it may not be the deepest or the most difficult problem, he has not allowed himself to become sidetracked if he knows what he is doing. On the contrary, he will assure the client that he intends to consider other issues in time, but that he can handle only the data that he has been given, and that he intends to take seriously everything that is presented to him. The counselor may take seriously all that is presented and at the same time orient the presentation of data toward behavior and problem solving by saying something like: "Bill, when you lay out all the facts I shall be able to help you lay out a biblical course of action." Successful solutions to presentation problems have the effect of giving encouragement and hope to clients, who then usually rapidly disclose new facts of

---

course, at bedrock, beneath all three is the sinful disposition with which man is born, the "heart" out of which all else proceeds. Good counseling seeks to solve not merely the presentation or the performance problems, but also attempts to break all non-biblical preconditioning patterns and to replace them with biblical behavior. Sanctification consists of putting off the old man and putting on the new man.

greater importance. Sometimes a client wishes to "test" the counselor's concern, his ability to meet needs, or his method for doing so by the presentation of secondary problems. Taking clients seriously enables the counselor to "sell" clients on further counseling about more crucial needs.

Actually secondary (or complicating) problems usually are smaller and simpler and therefore are easier and often better to handle at first. These are problems like feelings of depression that lead to failure to do the ironing or clean the house. Solving simpler problems quickly by giving early attention to them (not to exclude work on other more complex data) causes hope. Moreover, the solution to any problem (no matter how small) may be used to begin the reversal of the downward cycle which has resulted in these secondary or complicating problems. Presentation problems necessarily involve the discussion of performance problems, since the former arise from the latter; thus a discussion of the presentation problem may be but the first step in digging deeper.[1] In addition, the removal of secondary problems often relieves the client enough to enable him to cope more effectively with more difficult

---

[1] Larger problems (especially preconditioning patterns) may emerge or be clarified by dealing with smaller ones. It is unwise for counselors to wait until all relevant information has been unearthed before beginning to tackle any problem. After all, who ever has all the information but God? But when assignments based upon adequate available information are given from the first session on, patterns and deeper problems tend to surface rapidly as they appear even in the manner in which the assignments are carried out. An analysis of these patterns is often more valuable than the client's analysis, since the counselor can observe first hand how the client responds to assignments requiring biblical problem solving. Moving to action concerning concrete instances not only reveals problems, but at the same time sets up machinery for resolving them. Clients may have difficulty in self-analysis or in communication of data and for various reasons may not make accurate unprejudiced judgments. Beginning with smaller problems first is not an unwarranted extension of the principle in Luke 16:10, since in teaching faithfulness to God, one must learn first to be faithful in that which is least.

problems. And finally, the simplicity of the smaller problems and the consequent simplicity of solutions also allows for clearer teaching of principles.

And so, not everything has to be disclosed before clients can begin to find relief. Problems may be taken up one at a time, but usually several emerge at once. The iceberg method means that whatever is protruding above the surface, even though it be a very small amount of the iceberg, is material for counseling. As the counselor chips away at the top, more and more of the iceberg rises, until eventually the bulk of it is in sight. As a matter of fact, addressing their attention to minor problems first (while assuring the client that they will continue to probe until every relevant issue has been raised), has enabled nouthetic counselors to get to major problems much more rapidly than by other methods.[1]

When counselors offer help from the outset (even though the help may relate to minor matters), clients do not have to wait discouragingly for weeks or months or years until all has been revealed before solutions can be attempted. Such discouragement is counter-productive, and itself becomes a new dimension of the client's problem. Non-productive waiting periods tend to establish patterns of non-help in counseling sessions which become difficult to reverse, while early solutions, even for minor problems, establish patterns of success which tend to persist and snowball. Early snowballing effects take place which culminate in early release from counseling (cf. Proverbs 13:12). Nothing in the Bible indicates that one must wait to change. Everywhere, immediate, if not complete change is pictured as possible. In each session a counselor may say to his client, "God can make things different this very day." Focusing on biblical solutions from the outset is one way of demonstrating this truth.

---

[1] To use another figure, we just keep tapping the wall until we hit all the studs.

## Team Counseling

The use of team counseling has been assumed throughout this book, as may be apparent to the reader. Nouthetic counselors consider team counseling one option. Since it is a method largely used by them with success, something must be said about counseling in teams. Why counsel in teams? First, because in Scripture the principle of team effort is consistently set forth as an effective practice. Christ worked with disciples Paul worked and traveled with a team. Jesus sent out the seventy by twos.[1] Ecclesiastes says that two are better than one for if one shall fall the other shall help him, and that a threefold cord is not easily broken (Ecclesiastes 4:9-12). This idea of mutual help is basic to team counseling. Team counseling provides help of various sorts. While one member of a team is speaking, another member may spend his time thinking and observing. Another can take more copious notes.[2] He can look up passages of Scripture or think about ways in which the rest of the counseling interview may be structured. He can secure handouts without interrupting the session, and can jot down assignments in the client's workbook. The presence of a team counselor enables counselors to participate in more meaningful reviews of the case after the counseling session. Verbatims or notes alone are by no means adequate for that

---

[1]The exact number of counselors in a session may vary. Experience has shown that more than four is cumbersome. Two or three seems to be the best number for a counseling team. Calling for the "elders" (James 5) also suggests a team effort.

[2]Some counselors think it is wrong to take notes in sessions. But nouthetic counselors show the value of notes by reading back quotations, noting priorities, listing items for an agenda, etc. Clients learn to appreciate such diligence in gathering data. "Verbatim" reports written following counseling sessions are too subjective and omit too much vital information. Note taking, far from hindering counseling, is itself a useful tool, when properly used.

purpose. Nearly always post-counseling conferences suffer from the fact that information comes funneled exclusively through the personality of one individual who is very subjectively involved. When everyone gathers facts through him and sees the case through his eyes, if he has gone off on particular tangents, if he has missed important facts, if he has led the session in some wrong direction, there is no way to know so.[1] Any discussion which follows is really quite dependent upon one source and one alone.

Meaningful and very profitable post-counseling discussions can be held where two or more counselors can compare notes. This is a great asset to the counselors themselves. They can fill in gaps in each other's observations, and evaluate one another. The trouble with verbatims and notes is that counselors fail to observe many faults in themselves. Since they never record or discuss these faults, faults frequently get repeated until they become habitual. Precisely what counselors need to learn if they are going to grow is what mistakes they are making. Counselors need to see their own counseling as others do. Of course, for maximum value in cross-evaluation, an open nouthetic relationship must exist between the counselors themselves.

There are other values in team counseling. Counselors can learn from each other's examples. Security is afforded from having a witness present to what was said, especially where sexual questions are raised. Team counseling, like multiple counseling, precludes almost all of the provocative conversation and action which is the stock-in-trade of some female clients. Counseling is hard, tedious work, and can "grow old" rapidly. The encouragements that team counseling affords

---

[1] Taping is one option, of course, but studies have shown that taping has proved to be too great a hindrance to many counselors who tend to play to the audience when they know their words will be preserved for posterity. Taping, too, misses all the nuances of facial expression, gestures, and the other bodily action so essential to good communication and especially to counseling.

help keep one going under difficult circumstances. Team counseling allows also for training others in actual counseling situations.[1]

There are disadvantages. Team counseling means tying up two or more persons per counseling hour. Yet, nouthetic counseling gets rapid results which enables larger numbers of persons to find help. Not every counselor approaches clients in precisely the same way, and this may be good. Individuality has its place in counseling as elsewhere. Yet, unless counselors learn to work together in harmony *as a team,* confusion results. Nouthetic team counselors consider it a prerequisite to be able to work out their differences. They soon learn how to work alternately so that trains of thought begun by one counselor are not interrupted by another. In order to keep from crossing wires one counselor may indicate to another by a gesture or nod that he has finished a line of thought and wishes to relinquish the floor. Another counselor may more directly say to his colleague, "Mark, what do you think of the reply Mary just made?"

It is important for one counselor to take charge of each case. Both the counselors and the client should know who that person is. The responsibility in this way is placed upon a single individual. Yet if, because of sickness or for some other reason, the counselor-in-charge cannot attend a particular session, someone else who has been participating in the case with him can most readily step into his shoes. Thus clients do not have to miss sessions at important points. There may be times when cases should be transferred from one counselor to another. If one counselor is getting nowhere, he should be frank enough to admit this and hand over the case to someone who may be able to do a more adequate job.

---

[1]Pastors and seminary students are now being trained effectively by this method as participant observers. The method, which I hope to discuss some other time, approximates the discipling or apprenticeship method employed by Christ.

# A Pastor as a Team Counselor[1]

Also, there comes a point in counseling where, in some cases, it may be advisable for an outside counselor to call in the client's pastor.[2] Toward the end of counseling a transition needs to be made. Instead of a debriefing session, a transition session then takes its place. The client himself sums up what has happened so far: what his problem was at the inception of counseling, what solutions have been reached, what commitments have been made, what has been learned, and what remains to be done. All this is accomplished under the guidance of the counselor, who supplements as necessary. The pastor must understand precisely where the client is at the moment, how he arrived there and from where he has come.

It is desirable for other counselors to make a transition to the pastor when precise theological problems need answering and where other questions have arisen which might be discussed more profitably by the pastor than by another counselor. Some problems pertaining to the local church make such a transition desirable. This is especially true whenever disciplinary action may be necessary. When a client who has been confronted nouthetically about his sin recognizes his need to confess and repent before individuals or the elders of the church, it is almost always necessary to make a pastoral transition. If, for some reason, calling in the pastor is impossible, the client himself can be sent to inform the pastor. Whenever this takes place, the client should be briefed about

---

[1]It is possible for pastors of two or more adjacent congregations to join together in team counseling and thus reap the benefits it affords. This is perhaps one of the best ways to begin nouthetic counseling. It would be desirable, perhaps, to include various ruling elders in counseling sessions as team counselors also (cf. James 5:14 f.). Presbyteries might also provide for a center staffed by ministers of the presbytery.

[2]This sort of flexibility, as well as team counseling in general, is impossible where transference is used as a tool. Team counseling itself is the deterrent to the evils of transference.

everything he will say, so that he will not miss any vital points. Transition is usually more desirable since it affords a bridge between counseling at a center and future counseling or disciplinary action that will continue in the church. It is helpful, too, for a counselor to interpret facts to the pastor from the counselor's viewpoint. The transition session allows both the counselor and the client to provide a full rundown of the case from both viewpoints.

It is very undesirable for counselors to give information about the client to his pastor privately. It is much better to present any such information to him in the presence of the client. Nouthetic counseling encourages clients to be open, frank and honest with others who are entitled to share in their lives. Counselors themselves should set a good example for clients by refusing to hide information or speak secretly about clients behind their backs. If there is something that needs to be said, let it be said in front of the client. Then there can be no suspicion, no question, no difficulties later on arising from secrecy. All that the counselor is going to say ought to be said, whether bad or good, whatever it may be, in the presence of the client himself. However, permission for the transition interview should first be obtained from the client.

## Non-verbal Communication

It is important for counselors to learn to read faces, actions and gestures, as Paul did. His ability to interpret non-verbal feedback is noted, for instance, in Acts 14:8, 9:

> Now at Lystra there was a man sitting, who could not use his feet; he was a cripple from birth, who had never walked. He listened to Paul speaking; and Paul, looking intently at him and *seeing that he had faith* to be made well, said in a loud voice, stand upright on your feet.

Paul was a keen observer. In the midst of a crowd, while preaching, Paul was able to single out one man who had faith to be made well, by "looking intently" at him.[1] *Seeing* that he had the faith, Paul said, "Stand upright on your feet." There comes a point when a good counselor can see that the client is ready to make a decision or to take action. Sometimes the whole demeanor of the client signals this. Often some particular element of that demeanor gives the clue (e.g., frowning or hesitation indicating decision-making). At this point the counselor, like Paul, ought to challenge the client to take the next step in faith.

Sometimes when a client protests most he is about ready to begin to comply with the Word of God. In counseling, people often behave as they do when they are about ready to buy an automobile. A good salesman knows when the customer is ready to buy. The customer begins kicking the tires, or some such other foolish act. He begins asking questions that are unessential to the purchase. He may even raise strong opposition. Because of his basic perverseness, he feels that he must put up some kind of a last resistance before giving in.

Sometimes when people become most vehement in their insistence that they will not do what God requires them to do, they are really ready to do so. Evelyn insisted that she would not, under any circumstances, make peace with her mother-in-law, although she admitted that she needed to confess long-standing resentments and seek reconciliation. She was a Christian, and agreed that this is what God required of her, yet she categorically refused. Her last word as she left was, "I'll never go!" The next night Evelyn phoned and told her counselor triumphantly, "I went!"

Sally, another recalcitrant client, insisted that she would never return to her church, that her counseling had been useless, and that she was getting nowhere. The counselor recognized that her words and actions looked like tire kicking. So he said to her:

---

[1] There is some textual question about these words.

Sally, it sounds to me as if you don't have many more arguments left to resist the Word of God. Aren't you just about ready to decide to do God's will? Why don't you go back to that church, face those people, and square things off?

Sally replied, "All right, I'll do it." And she did.[1]

Other techniques might be mentioned, but these indicate clearly the general direction that nouthetic techniques, appropriate to and growing out of biblical presuppositions, will take. Method is no more neutral than principle, since the two are so closely intertwined that they cannot be separated. As a matter of fact, conflicts of all sorts occur more frequently about the *how* than about the *what*. It is not usually difficult to reach agreement on noble goals; the difficulty comes in implementation. That is why new ways and means developed from nouthetic principles are continually needed, and offer one of the most fruitful areas for further study.

---

[1] Sometimes the direct question, "Where has your present sinful behavior (or attitude) gotten you?" makes a strong impact upon clients at this stage.

## Chapter X

## COMMUNICATION AND MULTIPLE COUNSELING

### The Present Problem

Sociologists, world statesmen, marriage counselors—all sorts of people—seem to agree that one of our greatest needs today is genuine communication. Communications satellites circle the globe, teletypes clatter away, and even the poorest homes tune in on the world through television and transistor radios. Today more books are published in every field than the specialists can read, and communications experts have begun to discuss the problem of the glut of communication.[1] Yet communication at the most essential level of all, in the direct confrontation of one person with another, has perhaps never been as superficial, unauthentic and unsatisfying. In the midst of plenty, it seems there exists a famine of genuine communication. Why is there water, water everywhere and not a drop to drink? To what can be attributed the fact that people are not communicating?

One answer is that people are not communicating the *truth*. There is a credibility gap, not only in politics, in advertising, in business and in personal relationships, there is also a credibility gap in the Church of Jesus Christ. The problem is not a new one, though it may be exaggerated at this time. All problems of communication go back as far as the Garden of Eden. God chose to relate himself most intimately to man by means of his Word, so he made man in his own image as a communicating being. Every day in the cool of the day God came and talked with Adam. Language was one of the great gifts that God gave to Adam. God's own communicating Person was reflected in this priceless gift. We know of Adam's language capabilities, not only because we read that he spoke with God,

---

[1] The other day I saw on our seminary library shelf a bibliography of bibliographies in a narrow field.

but also because Genesis says he named the animals and his wife. The gift of language implied the duty of communication. God and Adam communicated personally through the use of language.

Into that idyllic situation Satan introduced the first communication problem by casting doubt upon the Word of God. The Father of Lies (that is, the father of all communication difficulties) questioned the word of God. "Hath God said?" he asked in history's first question. Man listened, and questioned too. Satan not only cast doubts, but also distorted and denied the word which God had spoken.

When Adam and Eve fell, communication with God and with one another was broken. Man, a communicating social being who needs others, began to experience the agony of being severed from the relationships in life that really count. Because his social relationships were ruined, man began to suffer the misery of alienation, and also began to show it.[1] As God came walking in the cool of the day and Adam heard the sound of God walking in the garden, he hid. No longer could the two walk in sweet communion. Their relationship was now in shambles since sin had come between them. Man should have turned to God in confession and repentance for his sin. Casting himself upon the mercy of God, he would have found forgiveness and the restoration of communication. But instead, man failed to handle his sin properly, and in so doing further complicated the communication problem. Instead of entering into God's way of salvation by repentance and trust, man responded by half truths, blameshifting, hiding, and attempting to cover up his shame and guilt, thereby further complicating the communication difficulties that had arisen.

Now it should be of more than passing interest to note that

------

[1] Herman Ridderbos has some penetrating comments on the relationship of guilt to misery in his book, *The Coming of the Kingdom* (Philadelphia: The Presbyterian and Reformed Publishing Company, 1962) pp. 211, 213, 214 ff.

every one of the major problems that today are encountered in counseling were present at least in seed form in the garden. Truly, no one's situation is unique! Many of those problems are expressed in terms of communication. For instance, the depressing shame of a guilty conscience that every counselor encounters so frequently today was experienced by Adam. The capacity for self-evaluation that God built into man now activated painful inner sensations. Man had come to know good and evil by personal experience, and the red light on the dashboard was flashing. Man's conscience accused him of sin, painful visceral responses followed, and Adam ran. But instead of running to God, he ran from him and hid.

When God finally ferreted Adam out from among the trees, Adam emerged covered with fig leaves. He had further complicated matters by attempting to handle the difficulty on his own rather than turning to God for the proper solution. Adam had committed a crime, had attempted a getaway, and was now trying to cover up. But God pointed the finger of accusation squarely at him. In spite of Adam's attempts to avoid the problem of his sin, God pressed the issue. God confronted him nouthetically, forcing him to deal with the problem. Even under the pressure of that confrontation Adam lied and shifted blame. He said in effect, "the *woman* which *you* gave me, Lord, she is the one who made me eat." God turned to the woman. She, too, passed the buck: "The serpent," she said, "is to blame for my sin."[1] Neither Adam nor Eve was

---

[1] The Scriptures highlight this sinful tendency. Note Proverbs 19:3, "When a man's folly brings his way to ruin, his heart rages against the Lord" (RSV), or in R. B. Y. Scott's translation, "It is a man's own stupidity which ruins his life, yet he is bitter against the Lord," *Anchor Bible* (New York: Doubleday, 1965). It is important to understand that misery, sorrow, disappointment, heartache, and bitterness, come from one's own stupidity. Others do not make us bitter or miserable, regardless of what they do to us. It is our problem. By wrongly responding, we hurt ourselves. And yet man, in his rebellion and sin, not only rages against others, striking out with blame while excusing himself, but from

214

willing to bear personal responsibility for his rebellion. Instead, each attempted to justify himself by shifting his blame to another.[1] These sinful responses became additional complicating factors in the problem of communication.

And so, reestablishment of communication (between man and God, and man and man) involves not only the sin which

---

the Garden of Eden his heart has raged against the Lord. Adam's words are very plain: they implicate God in the problem which Adam brought upon himself. For he said, "Lord, the woman which *you* gave me, she is the one who gave me to eat of the fruit and then caused me to sin." He sees the woman as the secondary cause, and God as the primary cause of the problem. The Freudian viewpoint finally boils down to this, that God is to blame for the misery and ruin of man. Freudian blame shifting leads to the idea that man is not responsible for what he is or does; others as secondary causes are responsible. This means God ultimately is responsible, since man himself has no choice in these matters. Christians must reject this Freudian point of view.

[1]That others have done much to shape our lives, no one can deny. However, each individual must bear personal responsibility for how he has allowed others to influence his conduct. No one can blame another for his bad behavior, even when he has been taught that behavior from childhood. What he learned may be unlearned. Since we may reshape ourselves, we are responsible for the shape we are in. Even under the most severe pressures Christ taught us that it is one's personal responsibility to respond properly to wrongs and the one who inflicted them upon us. "After all," nouthetic counselors tell clients, "you live in a sinful world in which people will continue to wrong you throughout life. The important thing is how you handle these wrongs." Men are not matchboxes tossed on the sea by winds and currents. If a client complains that her husband is to blame for her problems and bad behavior a counselor may reply, "Everything you have said about him may be true. It may be very difficult to live with someone like that, but that doesn't excuse you for how you have responded to his poor treatment of you. As a matter of fact, let us assume that he is far worse. Let us suppose . . ." After painting a picture much worse than that which the client described, he might continue: "Even if he were a man like that God would still hold you responsible for the way you respond to him. If Christ had not prayed for those who crucified him, he would have sinned."

broke communication, but also the continued baneful influence of sinful response patterns involving downward spirals that complicate everything. Take, for instance, a family in which communication has broken down. The husband and the wife have been at each other's throats for some time, and a situation has developed in which even their attempts to reestablish communication only further complicate matters. George has grown quite upset over the fact that he, as a Christian, has not been able to settle the problems between them. All day long at work he has prayed and thought about the matter. He decides, "Tonight I'm going to try to do something about it." He walks through the door that night and says to his wife, "Janet, about these problems we've been having lately . . ." Before he can get another word out of his mouth, she spits back at him, "Right! Let me tell *you* something about the problems we've had lately! If you continue to act the way you have been, those problems are nothing compared to the problems we're going to have!" Growling to himself he stalks into the livingroom, buries himself in a plush chair, pulls the newspaper down over his head, and turns the TV up. To himself he says, "What's the use! Here I am trying to reestablish communication and she acts *that* way." Meanwhile, in the kitchen, Janet, who has been stirring something at the stove, finds her conscience stirred as well. She thinks about the way that she answered George as he came into the house. Remorseful that she was so gruff, she puts down her spoon and goes into the livingroom to apologize: "George," she begins, "when you came in the door tonight . . ." George throws the paper aside, glares at her and says, "Yes, I know when I came in the door tonight! And I'd better never come home to anything like that again or I may not come home again!" At that Janet turns on her heel, strides back to the kitchen, and vigorously stirs her pot, mumbling to herself, "Well, what's the use?"

Under such circumstances even the very attempt to reestablish communication can widen the communication gap. Genesis 3 exhibits the first instance of this complicating factor. Because of sin men not only break communication in the first place, but also frequently bungle even the attempts to restore communication. So there is a necessity to work at this serious problem on at least these two levels.

Communication breakdown is a serious problem. The basic nature of its divisiveness is evidenced by the tower of Babel where the simple failure of communication by language alteration took place. Communication binds persons together. Moreover, only by communicating can problems between persons be solved. That is why in any difficulty between individuals communication suffers. Therefore, communication is the point at which counselors must begin in restoring relationships between individuals. And yet, the only means by which restoration may be achieved is through communication. This is the communication dilemma: those who are unable to communicate need to communicate in order to solve their communication problem. Usually the only solution to this difficulty is for some outsider to assist the parties in reestablishing communication.

The basis for the restoration of communication is reconciliation with God. Restoration begins with the saving grace of Jesus Christ. For all significant communication of any depth must be communication in him. Communication must be based, as John says in his third letter to Gaius, upon "love in the truth" (vs. 1). Such love exists only in the realm of God's truth. Truth which is held in common, shared, and believed by all of the parties who communicate, is the foundation for all significant communication. All definitions and rules of communication must issue from God in the Scriptures. When the credibility gap between God and man is closed, the gap between man and man may be closed as well. And so in sending Jesus Christ to reestablish communication, God took the initiative in bridging the gap. Because of Christ's death and resurrection, the communication problem can be solved. There is no other adequate solution.

## God's Solution for His Church

Such communication is exactly what the fourth chapter of Ephesians is all about. Paul begins the chapter by saying,

> I therefore, the prisoner of the Lord, intreat you to walk in a manner worthy of the calling with which you have been called.

The figure of walking runs throughout the chapter. For example, in verse 17 he says,

> This I say therefore, and affirm together with the Lord, that you walk no longer just as the Gentiles also walk in the futility of their minds.

Called by Christ, Christians are to walk with him. Adam once walked with God in unbroken fellowship by obedience. The new walk with Christ is possible through restored obedience. Christians must no longer walk as they did before communication was established with Christ. Paul speaks of that former walk as a walk of "futility of mind" in which one's understanding is "darkened" (verse 18) and he is excluded from the life of God because of "ignorance," Because of the

> hardness of their heart they having become callous had given themselves over to sensuality for the practice of every kind of impurity with greediness (verse 19).

Paul's description is the description of the life of the unbeliever who continuing in his sin becomes hardened even to the pangs of his conscience. Paul continues,

> But *you* did not learn Christ in this way, if indeed you have heard him and have been taught in him just as truth is in Jesus (verses 20, 21).

This former manner of life must be changed:

> In reference to your former manner of life, lay aside the old self which is being corrupted in accordance with the lusts of deceit, and be renewed in the spirit of your mind and put on the new self, which in the likeness of God has

been created in righteousness and holiness of the truth (verses 22-24).

The image of God in man was distorted by the fall. Man as a communicating, holy, knowledgeable, righteous being, reflecting God, his creator, became rather a reflection of the Father of Lies. Christ restores the image of God to Christians.[1] Believers are being renewed in the spirit of their minds. The mind because of sin had become futile, the understanding had been darkened, the heart had become hard and callous. All of these conditions, now, are in the process of being changed by the Spirit of God. He renews the spirit of the believer's mind so that the former manner of life, with all of its corrupt habits, patterns, and ways of living called "the old self" or "the old man" may be shed like a tattered, worn, filthy old garment that one throws away. Christians are called to "put on" instead new biblical patterns, new ways that truly reflect the God who created them. This new self must be formed in the image and likeness of God, created in righteousness and holiness of the truth.

When Paul speaks about the "new self" (verses 25 to 32, and in the chapter that follows), significantly, the first thing that he mentions is the restoration of communication through truth:

> Laying aside falsehood, speak truth each one of you with his neighbor, for we are members of one another.

Communication was broken in the garden when God's truth was doubted and denied and man began speaking lies. Every man since Adam (except Christ) has been born a rebel against God's word of truth. He, therefore, speaks lies instead of

---

[1] The concept of the renewal of the image of God is found not only in Ephesians 4:23, 24, but also in Colossians 3:10. This renewal necessarily results in a new manner of life which in both contexts is evidenced by the restoration of communication with God. The renewal affords opportunity for genuine communication between believers as well.

truth. There is a credibility gap. Because of his sinful nature, man does not love the truth. Instead, under stress he thinks first of lying instead of telling the truth. Just as sinful Adam first thought of lying his way out of difficulty, men today lie their way through life. It is perfectly *natural* for the "natural man" to develop patterns of falsehood. New ways appropriate to the new creation must *become* natural to him.

In the fellowship of faith Paul says, "Each one of us must speak truth with his neighbor." The reason he gives is, "we are members of one another." Paul here uses the familiar image of the body. If there is poor communication between the brain and other parts of the body, chaos and confusion result. Imagine the brain sending coordinating messages to the feet and to the arms, but the arms decide to do something entirely different from what the brain directs. The actions of the arms, therefore, will not coordinate with the actions of the feet. The result is disasterous. So it is in the Church. There is chaos and confusion where there is no coordination through communication. Communication from Christ, the head, must be heard and obeyed by each member of his body. Then coordination by meaningful communication between them is possible. Communication must be based upon the truth of God. Otherwise no one can speak the truth.

Men who speak truth speak earnestly in accordance with the standard of Scripture. They speak the truth with their neighbor for his welfare. Christians must willingly unveil their own hearts and share matters of mutual importance with one another, knowing others need information, encouragement, rebuke, correction, etc. They need *one another,* as truly as the parts of the body need each other. Just as in a well-coordinated organism all the parts of the body obey the head, the work of the Church must be coordinated by obedience to Jesus Christ. Each part needs him and needs the other parts of the body. The way in which we are bound together, the way in which we work together, the way in which we serve Christ together is by communicating his truth.

## Anger and Resentment

Paul recognized that there are problems blocking effective communication. In verse 26, quoting Psalm 4, he wrote, "Be angry, and yet do not sin: do not let the sun go down on your anger." All sorts of problems arise in the Christian enterprise which may lead to angry feelings, since the body is composed of sinful members. Yet these problems can be solved. Anger need not persist so that it drives new rifts between believers or enlarges old ones. Instead there is a way of handling anger. Paul says it must be dealt with daily: "Do not let the sun go down on your anger."

Anger is not resentment. Mark 3:5 makes this quite clear. In that passage we are told that Christ was angry. The words used there speak of emotional upset.[1] Though stirred emotionally about the issue, Christ did not allow his anger to turn into resentment. He, therefore, was angry but did not sin. In another place the Scripture is quoted concerning Christ, "The zeal of my Father's house hath eaten me up." "God is angry with the wicked every day" (Psalm 7:11).

Anger in administering disciplinary codes must be thought of as within the code. Modern advice that parents should never administer discipline when angry is not biblical. Because anger is not wrong, one apologizes not for anger, but only, for instance, for losing one's temper in the discipline of children. That is, he apologizes for anger which is out of control; anger in which one does or says things which violate the disciplinary code.

Passages such as Proverbs 14:29 and 29:11 refer to anger which is unjustified and uncontrolled:

He who is slow to anger is of great understanding: but whoever is hasty of spirit exalts folly (Berkeley);

and:

---

[1]*Orge.* The next word, *sullupeo,* strongly emphasizes the emotional factor by indicating that Christ was "deeply grieved, or upset."

A fool gives full vent to his anger: but the wise man holding it back quiets it (Berkeley).

The idea of allowing anger to break out in an undisciplined manner by saying or doing whatever comes into mind without weighing the consequences, without counting ten, without holding it back and quieting it, without hearing the whole story, is totally wrong. Group therapy that is predicated upon the principle of ventilating anger in order to get something off one's chest, is totally out of accord with the verses just cited. Ventilating sinful feelings is simply unbiblical. The words "full vent" (29:11) mean literally "to send forth all of one's spirit." The wise man, according to Proverbs, knows how to check his feelings. Feelings do not have to rule and run a person's life. They can be checked and quieted. Clients should practice holding back and quieting anger rather than ventilating it. Checking anger is neither harmful nor impossible since the Bible commands it.[1]

To the verses above may be added the following:

Have you seen a man hasty of words? there is more hope of a fool than for him (Proverbs 29:20).

A quick-tempered man stirs up strife, and a wrathful man abounds in wrong (verse 22).

One important principle to remember in overcoming anger (and a principle which incidentally extends to other bad habits as well) is,

Do not associate with one given to anger, and with a wrathful man do not keep company: lest you learn his ways and get yourself in a snare (Proverbs 22:24, 25).

The principle is to associate closely with friends whose lives accord with the highest biblical principles. The importance of models has been discussed elsewhere.

---

[1] S. I. McMillen, in fact, shows the dire consequences of giving full vent to anger in his *None of These Diseases* (Westwood: Spire Books, Revell Co., 1963), chapters 10 and 11.

Client after client who comes for counseling soon reveals that he has allowed not only the sun but many moons to go down on his anger. The incident concerning Leo Held cited in an earlier chapter (p. 26) vividly illustrates the importance of dealing with anger before it turns into resentment. Held's problem was that he "had it in" for his neighbors and eventually that which he "had in" came out. Herodias, according to Mark 6:19, also "had a grudge against" (literally, "had it in for") John the Baptist. At length she poured forth her resentment, and had John executed.[1] Sometimes Christian clients come who have carried bitter feelings against another person for thirty years. The very person that such a client so dislikes is the person whom he has been allowing, strangely enough, to control his life by remote control. In reaction to the hated person he has been doing all he does over against that person. He is not free, but is bound by the very person whom he dislikes, and yet his anger burns so intensely that he is blinded to the foolishness of his pendulum action.

Paul's instruction cuts through all of this. He says that Christians must not allow one single day to pass with unresolved anger stored in their hearts. The principle is clearly set forth: "Do not let the sun go down on your anger." In other words, every day Christians must handle the problems that have arisen. This does not mean that others must be confronted about every sin which they have committed. There are many matters that can be covered over by love. As Peter says, quoting Proverbs, "Love covers a multitude of sins."[2] Yet there are some things that cannot be set to rest simply by covering them with love. They continue to rattle around down

---

[1] It is instructive that the very word used in the Scriptures for holding a "grudge" means to "have it in" for someone (*enecho* used here, is translated by Williams, "to have it in for"). In modern Greek, the word means "to contain," a usage which retains the idea of holding in, containing resentment within against another.

[2] I Peter 4:8.

inside; they fester and eat away. Such problems need to be settled daily by personal confrontation. They should not be carried over to the next day. What can't be covered with love, can't be covered with blankets; time alone does not heal. It is more likely to cause the wound to become infected.

Paul speaks in the same spirit as our Lord who said that Christians should not worry about tomorrow's problems because "sufficient unto the day is the trouble thereof." No one's shoulders are broad enough to bear the weight of tomorrow's problems, neither are they able to carry yesterday's resentments. God wants problems handled one day at a time; and every problem must be dealt with on time. Differences must be covered by love or dealt with directly so that the members of the one body may function properly together.

One who harbors resentments within, but acts as if nothing were wrong, lies and does not "speak truth with his neighbor." Significant communication breaks down because he "has it in for" his neighbor.[1] Communication that coordinates efforts for Christ is impossible, and the church functions on a minimal superficial level. The eye cannot be angry with the ear, the hand cannot be angry with the foot, without causing poor coordination and giving the Devil an opportunity to cause confusion in the body of Christ.

Old patterns of living must give way to new biblical ones. Paul gives an example of the kind of change that God expects when one puts off the old man and puts on the new:

> Let him who steals steal no longer, but rather let him labor, performing with his own hands what is good in order that he may have something to share with him who has need (Ephesians 4:28).

---

[1]According to Leviticus 19:17, 18 it is of the essence of love for one's neighbor to avoid grudge bearing by dealing immediately with matters that have come between them. Resentment and hatred are not easily distinguished in Scripture.

God demands an exact reversal of the thief's life style. He once stole; now he is to labor (not just work, but "labor, toil," perspire in his work), with his own hands so diligently that his earnings exceed his needs, and instead of stealing he is able to give to others in need. Paul's call for a reversal of one's "former manner of life," applies as well to those who pile up resentments. Now, instead, they must speak the truth about their feelings and settle matters with others daily, before the issues between them have time to grow larger.

In Matthew 5, Jesus spoke about anger. He said:

> You have heard that the elders were told you shall not commit murder; and whosoever commits murder shall be liable to the court; but I say to you that everyone who is angry with his brother shall be guilty before the court: and whoever shall say to his brother Raca shall be guilty before the Supreme court: and whoever shall say, You fool, shall be guilty enough to go into the Hell of fire (verses 21, 22).

This passage contains perplexing problems about the courts mentioned which cannot be considered here. Christ continues (verses 23, 24) immediately thereafter: "If therefore ..." This continuation shows that the discussion of anger was not concluded with verse 22. There is a progression of thought however from the serious nature of anger against one's brother to directions concerning the method for handling it and the urgency for doing so. Jesus said:

> If therefore you are presenting your offering at the altar, and there remember that your brother has something against you ...

Jesus pictures two believers who have become alienated from one another by anger. Because no subsequent reconciliation has occurred, one while in the act of worship remembers that his brother has something against him. Christ says to him:

> Leave your offering there before the altar and go your way; first [note that word of priority] be reconciled to your

brother, and then [only then] come and present your offering.

It seems clear that Christ considered an unreconciled condition between brethren a hindrance to the proper exercise of worship. For this reason he stressed the priority of reconciliation over worship. The priority is expressed in terms of urgency. The same immediacy called for by Paul in Ephesians is evident in these directions.

It is important to notice who goes to whom. Christ said that when the one presenting his offering at the altar remembers that a brother has something against him (perhaps during worship is when he is most likely to do so), *he* is to go. Whoever recalls that he has wronged another (or that his brother claims he has) is thereby obligated to take the initiative to seek reconciliation.

Matthew 5 presents only part of the picture; Matthew 18 completes it. In Matthew 18:15 Christ directs, "If your brother sins, go and reprove him in private." In contrast to Matthew 5, Christ here postulates a situation in which another has caused the injury, but has failed to observe the injunctions of Matthew 5. In such a case the wronged one must take the initiative. Putting both passages together leads to the following conclusion: whenever estrangement takes place between believers, regardless of who is at fault, both parties are obligated to take the initiative in seeking reconciliation. If one brother injures another, he is to go to the injured party, but if his brother is the one who wronged him, he still must go. Either way, whoever feels concern must go. Thus, Christ ensured the certainty of a nouthetic confrontation.[1]

---

[1] Henry Brandt puts it this way: "Whether you are the one who has the grievance or the one who has caused your partner to have a grievance, it's your move to initiate the process of reconciliation." He says, "It's always your move" (*Happy Family Life.* Lincoln, Neb.: Back to the Bible Broadcast), p. 16.

Christ continues:

> If he listens to you, you have won your brother, but if he does not listen to you, take one or two more with you so that by the mouth of two or three witnesses every fact may be confirmed.

In other words, the goal is to keep the dimensions of the problem as small as possible. The initial confrontation is wholly nouthetic in character; not disciplinary (in the official narrower sense): the object is reconciliation, to win one's brother. But if he will not listen, then a second attempt must be made, taking others along. The possible need for witnesses for a later trial is contemplated: take two or three, i.e., enough people to be witnesses of the efforts made toward reconciliation. Verse 17a seems to indicate that these witnesses also should play an arbitrating role. They first serve as a nouthetic counseling team. If there is a refusal to listen to them, the matter must be brought to the church. If he refuses to listen even to the church, if he does not accept the mediation of the church, he is subject to the results of official discipline. Let him be tried, and if he persists, excommunicate him (let him be as a Gentile and tax collector, i.e., outside the church). So then, in either case, whether the problem was largely his fault or if it is a problem for which someone else is to blame, whoever becomes concerned about a problem must be the one to initiate the process of reconciliation.

Frequently people think differently about reconciliation. They seldom think, "John has wronged me; I'd better go to him." They are more likely to say, "John has done something wrong; let him come to me." But Christ gave no support to such an attitude. Since it is possible, of course, that John does not realize that he has offended anyone, if the usual non-biblical response is followed, reconciliation is not likely to take place. John doesn't think that he has done anything wrong, and perhaps he has not. Possibly it only seems to Tom that he has. But in any case there can be no misunderstanding if under all circumstances the biblical procedure is followed. Whoever feels the problem keenly must take the initiative. Ideally, both should meet on the way to see one another.

Now what does one do when he approaches another after a rift has occurred? One of the first things he must do, according to Matthew 5:23, 24, is to confront the other party and confess any sin. He is to acknowledge that he has wronged his brother. He is to acknowledge that he has sinned against God, and he is to ask his brother for forgiveness. One of the problems that has already been mentioned in another context is that people sometimes assume that they have secured forgiveness without specifically asking to be forgiven. Nouthetic counselors stress the importance of saying specifically, "Will you forgive me?" When attempting reconciliation, not only is it important to ask specifically for forgiveness, but it is also useful to attempt to get a clear statement of forgiveness like, "Yes, I will forgive you." The goal is reconciliation built upon forgiveness. If the forgiveness is uncertain, so is the reconciliation.

If forgiveness cannot be obtained, the one taking the initiative has done all that he can do under those circumstances. His task was to follow the rule in Romans 12:18: "So far as it depends on you, be at peace with all men." The writer of Hebrews put it strongly, "*Pursue* after peace with all men" (Hebrews 12:14a). As far as his part is concerned, one is obligated to do everything he can do to bring about reconciliation. However, he cannot predict how the other person will respond to reconciliation overtures. All he can do, all that God requires him to do, is to confess any known sin, ask for forgiveness, and earnestly seek to make restitution wherever necessary and possible—all in order to bring about reconciliation.[1]

---

[1] It may be that this impasse eventually will require going again officially with others, as just noted in the discussion of Matthew 18, for now the other party has committed an offense against the first by refusing to extend forgiveness. The goal is reconciliation, and the process is directed toward that end.

How does one know when to approach another nouthetically? One very important principle to guide in the matter is found in Proverbs 17:9:

> He who covers an offense seeks love; but he who brings up a matter again alienates a close friend (Berkeley).

The idea of love covering a multitude of sins means that, whenever possible, love lets offenses go by. Whenever love can cover sins, there is no need for nouthetic confrontation. If it were necessary to confront one another about every problem that occurred (especially in a home), there would hardly be time for anything else. When we learn to love, we also learn to cover, to forget, and to overlook many faults in others. But whenever something cannot be overlooked, whenever something rankles inside, and it is obvious that it will be carried over to the next day, the problem must be dealt with and not covered up. Only love truly covers; anything else is but a cover up. But he who learns to cover an offense seeks love. It is important to remember that love is a forgetting kind of forgiveness (when sins are covered by love, they are not "brought up again"). One can forgive and forget if there is love in the heart. Nouthetic confrontation in love also seeks to cover sin.

## Attacking Problems instead of People

Paul continues the discussion of communication by the new man among new men begun in Ephesians 4:25. The example of the thief (vs. 28) was just that; it was an example to illustrate the need for a radical reversal of communication patterns. He says:

> Let no unwholesome word [the Greek is literally "rotten" or "putrid" word] proceed from your mouth (vs. 29).

Paul is talking about words that tear people apart. Such speech consists of unkind words, words that cause and complicate problems rather than solve problems. These are words that cut and slice, the kinds of words that were natural to the former manner of life. But now the believer is a new man who is engaged in laying aside the old patterns. He must reverse his life style. Just like the thief, he is to behave in the opposite way. In circumstances where he used to use cutting, harsh words against others, now he must begin to use "only such a word as is good for edification, according to the need of the moment that it may give grace to those who hear."

These verses paint the picture of a different sort of man, one who confesses his sin and does not harbor it. Christians must go directly to those they have wronged, tell the truth, and ask for forgiveness and help. If he believes another has wronged him, a Christian must not let the sun go down on feelings of anger. He must not hold resentments inside, but in love must voice his concern directly to the individual involved. If he has become bitter because he failed to deal with the problem, he must ask forgiveness for having allowed himself to become bitter and resentful. He must set this matter to rest before God and man. Then, having asked forgiveness, having dealt with his anger and his resentments, he can help restore his brother. But the way to approach another who has done wrong is to begin by making sure that all of one's own sins have been confessed and forgiven. He must remove the log in his own eye before he attempts to pluck the splinter from another's eye.

Instead of using unwholesome, rotten, cutting words, a Christian must speak words that "edify" (build up). They should be constructive rather than destructive words; they should build up instead of tear down. This work of edifying can be accomplished only by words that are "according to the need of the moment that give grace to those who hear." Translating that freely, wholesome words are those which are directed toward the problem that has arisen (literally, "the present need") in order to help those who hear. If a brother has been doing something wrong, he needs help. He doesn't need tearing down, he needs building up. So instead of directing one's words in anger and accusation toward the *person,* he must direct his energies and words toward the *problem.* Talking about the problem and giving help in solving problems to those who hear, puts one on the right track. Then words build up and help. Christians must learn to attack the problem at hand, not each other. This is real communication.

Paul stressed the importance of maintaining proper communication. The Holy Spirit dwells within every believer as God's securing and identifying seal, marking them for the day of redemption. He is the proof that God has purchased them. He is a kind of downpayment, a mark that believers belong to God and some day will be redeemed to himself. Believers should thank God for the Spirit and prize him as God's greatest present gift. But Paul warns that Christians grieve the Holy Spirit whenever they fail to communicate as they should. Lying, resentments, bickering and sharp words all bring grief ("pain") to the Holy Spirit. The Spirit was given in loving mercy to bring assurance and comfort. It is tragic that Christians should grieve the one who seeks to bring comfort and joy to them. That is why Paul insists:

> Let all bitterness [the resentment, deep-seated anger that builds up day after day] and wrath and anger and clamour and slander [screaming, yelling, arguing, fighting] be put away from you, along with all malice (verse 31).

Then he delineates more fully the ingredients of wholesome speech:

> Be kind, instead, to one another, tenderhearted, forgiving each other, just as God, in Christ, also has forgiven you.

There is, of course, a difference between the forgiveness which may obtain among others outside of the household of faith, and that of which Paul is speaking. This is a redemptive forgiveness. This is a forgiveness that reflects the forgiveness of God. This is a forgiveness that stems from the forgiveness of Christ. Not only love for God, but all Christian love is reciprocal: "We love[1] because he first loved us" (I John 4:19). We

---

[1] "Him" is not in the best texts.

love "in ("in the sphere of" or "within the context of") the truth" (III John 1). Forgiveness toward a brother does not depend upon the goodness of that brother, but rather it rests upon the mercy and kindness of the Christian who forgives. Because Christ gave himself for them, forgiving them in kindness and grace, Christians must forgive their brothers and sisters in Christ in the same way. No Christian has the right to withhold forgiveness from his brother when he seeks it in repentance (Matthew 18:22).

## The Conference Table

One practical method of helping clients achieve the goals of Ephesians 4 is to encourage them to set up a conference table. Families are directed to sit down at the table (preferably one that is not frequently used for other purposes[1]) each evening and confer about their problems. A table is important for several reasons. Tables tend to draw persons together. Writing can be done easily at a table. The time it takes to get to the table may be important for cooling tempers (cf. Proverbs 15:28; 14:17, 29), and it is harder to walk away from a discussion when the parties are seated. The table soon will become a symbol of hope, a place where previous problems have been solved successfully. Few persons who come for counseling have been in the habit of solving interpersonal problems *daily*.[2] That is one reason why they are having difficulty. People who have been nursing grudges and building up resentments for a long time find concrete structure helpful in changing old patterns and establishing new ones. Commitments to biblical response patterns are aided by structure erected to insure the discipline required to establish them. Setting aside a definite period of time toward the end of every day for the members of the family to meet together and talk

---

[1]Some families set up a card table each evening for the purpose.

[2]Christ represented Christian growth as a daily enterprise: "take up your cross *daily*" (Luke 9:23).

over the day's problems seems to be one of the most realistic ways of resolving difficulties that have arisen.

In instituting the conference table, as in the establishment of any new habit, regularity is most important. It is preferable to meet at the same table every day. A student who regularly studies at the same desk finds after a short while that the act of sitting down tends to put him in the proper mood for study. Students who sometimes study at the desk and at other times lie on the bed make the task unnecessarily difficult for themselves. Not only do they fail to associate any one place with studying (and lose the benefits of mood-setting through proper association) but on the contrary, they engage in counter-productive activity since beds are associated with sleeping. Lying on the bed automatically tends to produce the attitudes of sleep, which are certainly not conducive to study. The student who refuses to do anything but study at his desk can reinforce the study mood-association if when he finds his mind wandering or starts daydreaming, he gets up immediately so that none of these things becomes associated with that desk. Likewise, the conference table should become the place where the family meets to solve problems by Christian communication. They should never allow anything else (particularly arguing and sharp words) at the table. After a period of time (usually three or more weeks), they will find that simply sitting down automatically helps bring about a proper frame of mind for discussion.

The rules for the conference table must be kept simple. The father calls the conference, and in general, as head of the home, is in charge of the meeting.[1] Mother often acts as recorder or secretary, and does any writing necessary. The conference is opened and closed with prayer. The Bible is studied

---

[1] One of the most prevelant problems in marriage is a reversal of the roles of husband and wife. Counselors must not only deal with this matter directly, but should take every opportunity to structure the proper relationship.

during the conference to discover God's will concerning the questions before them. At this table everybody *begins* to discuss the problems of the day in terms of his own responses to them (first setting right his own failures; thereby often preempting possible accusations by others around the table). He begins by telling the others how he has wrongly responded to them, if he has been jealous, how he has felt bitter, how he has acted spitefully, etc. He may also mention wrongs done toward others outside the home and may seek advice and help on how best to deal with them. He admits his own sins first and asks for forgiveness and for help. The request for help is important for the avoidance of similar problems in the future. The family should discuss the problem and make suggestions for keeping such temptations to sin from arising in the future. Frequently, means for direct daily help can be devised and specific persons can be assigned tasks to be carried out. As one begins to talk about himself and directs attention to his own failures, fears and sins, communication opens up. If he had begun by confronting someone else at the table about what he had done wrong, a clash might have resulted, blocking significant communication. But when one begins to talk about himself (the same person that the other person is already quite anxious to talk about), he opens communication on the same wave length.[1] Both parties are looking in the same direction and focused on the faults of the same person. When one begins by discussing his own problems, others often respond by doing the same. Conditions have been structured so that everyone finds it easier to talk about himself.

When members of a family begin to confess sins to one another, they also find that they can ask for and receive the help they need. Without such communication little help can be

---

[1] As John Bettler, a nouthetic counselor in Hatboro, Pennsylvania frequently says: "When you want to strike out at someone who is willing to acknowledge his sin, it's like punching a pillow."

given. They discover that confession and forgiveness allows them to shift the focus from persons to problems. Getting rid of the personality aspect of the problem allows the family to move on to discuss solutions to the problem itself.

If during the conference someone forgets the rules, feelings start to run high and he begins to argue, something must be done. Communication can break down even at the conference table. One simple means of solving this problem is to adopt a prearranged signal. The minute that anyone at the table recognizes that something is going wrong, he stands up. He does not say a word; he simply rises quietly in his place. This is a signal which has been prearranged to notify everyone at the table that, in the opinion of one member, someone has stopped conferring; someone has reverted to pre-Christian attitudes and patterns. Whenever anyone stands up the other participants recognize that one of them may have transgressed the rules of Christian behavior found in Ephesians 4. If one who is seated finds himself in the wrong, or even misinterpreted as violating the rules of the conference table (it doesn't matter which), he immediately should say something like this, "All right, I understand what you are saying. Please sit down, let's talk about the problem instead of arguing and getting upset." If he thinks he has violated the rules he will want to apologize.

The conference table does not exist in order to tell others off. After each one handles his own failures, he raises other issues that have arisen during the day. He speaks the truth, but always in love (verse 15), and always with the intention of helping. All this may seem unnatural and very difficult at first. In fact it may seem foolish to go through such proceedings. And yet, most activities that now seem perfectly natural were awkward at first. Clients are reminded of how foolish they felt the first time they tried to ice skate, ride a bike or drive a car. There was nothing "natural" about that. It doesn't take very long to establish a habit (and soon the unnatural feeling vanishes) by regular consistent daily repetition. Whenever one learns to drive a car, he at first feels awkward and foolish and wonders how he can ever learn to coordinate his eyes, hands and feet. Yet in a few months after he has been driving, he can slip into his seat in pitch darkness while debating an abstruse point of theology and without conscious thought slide the key into its slot without a scratch on the dashboard. Three or more weeks of regular effort at the conference table ought to make conferring quite natural. The structure needs to be framed up only until the concrete firms up.[1]

Husbands and wives who have had difficulty in sexual intercourse often discover that many of their problems in bed at night stem from difficulties during the day which have never been resolved. A nightly conference table, at which they settle problems that have bothered them during the day, frequently makes a great difference in their sexual relationship.[2] One young couple that had had serious problems in sexual relations wrote:

> We have learned a new habit. We never let the sun go down on anger . . . The conference table was a wedge which opened up discussion and brought us closer and closer to-

---

[1] The principle applies in many areas. One highly successful twelfth grade teacher (and there aren't many around) put it this way: "I crack down hard during the first part of the year until the patterns are established, then I can let up along the way; the same kind of pressure will not be necessary throughout."

[2] We cannot deal here with the many sexual difficulties that are presented in counseling, nor with the financial, social and interpersonal relationships of family life. Hopefully, in a future volume marriage and family problems can be treated in depth. The purpose of this book is but to touch upon the whole field of counseling from a presuppositional viewpoint, becoming concrete enough to give some idea of counseling techniques and procedures. Granted these are spotty, and the balance is not always the best; but this book is viewed as but a beginning. We hope that much more can be written about specific aspects of counseling in detail with greater comprehensiveness.

gether. Gradually our sex life improved until it reached a point of almost unbelievable success.

Counseling often reveals the existence of a communication breakdown. Nouthetic counseling, in which all of the involved parties are usually counseled together, enables clients to reestablish communication (or establish communication for the first time) in the counseling session itself. One memorable case might be mentioned. The family consisted of three teenage children, two boys and a girl, and of course the parents. The parents originally came with the oldest boy with whom they said they had lost all communication. The counselors discovered that there never had been any significant communication in the parent-child relationship. They explained the principles behind the conference table. But the parents doubted whether any such conference was possible, and questioned its value. In order to demonstrate the value and feasibility of the conference table, the counselors began to open and moderate discussion between the parents and their child right on the spot. The interaction which occurred was so significant that one astounded parent said, "I never knew that my boy believed that," and the other said, "Well, I'm amazed to hear what he has to say, too." The discussion proceeded so well that the counselors soon sat back and listened. After a while they sent the family home to continue conferring. About an hour later the phone rang, and the mother was on the line. She said,

We're still sitting around our conference table having a good discussion. The only problem is that our daughter now wants to get in on this discussion and she doesn't know the rules. Will you please explain them to her?

The daughter was instructed over the phone and the whole family has been talking ever since.

## Multiple Counseling

This is as good a place as any to say something about the type of counseling which has been described throughout this book. One-to-one counseling has its place, and, of course, in many situations not everyone who is involved in a problem can be enlisted for counseling. However, multiple counseling is to be preferred as the rule rather than the exception. Since most people with personal problems get into difficulty because of sinful behavior toward God and man, the counseling structure should make recognition of this fundamental interpersonal dimension. God must be brought into relationship to every aspect of counseling, and insofar as possible all other individuals involved. The number of participants who ought to be included seems to be as great as the number of individuals who are intimately involved in the problem.[1]

There are many implications of multiple counseling. Solutions to difficulties often are reached much more effectively, much more permanently, and much more rapidly when all of the parties of a controversy are included in counseling. If, for instance, the wife is the one who comes with the presentation problem, nouthetic counselors also try to include the husband. Why? For one reason, when communication breaks down, as it frequently does regardless of what the underlying problem may be, multiple counseling provides the best conditions for re-establishing communication. Communication is an essential tool for solving other problems. When communication is established, the members of the multiple counseling

---

[1]This seems clearly to be the import of the word "alone" in Mathew 18:15. Here, the stress is on keeping the problem as narrow as those involved in it. Christ's stress seems to eliminate group counseling of the sort that encourages uninvolved parties to participate. Much damage may be done in Oxford Group type meetings, sensitivity training groups, etc., where sins are freely confessed to mixed audiences and where the presence of uninvolved parties is encouraged. Christ is concerned about confession leading to reconciliation; therefore confession to uninvolved persons is confession used for an unauthorized purpose. Confession always must be made within a reconciliation context, i.e., to those who are estranged, for the purpose of reconciliation (cf. Matthew 5, 18).

group can talk to one another about problems that they have been unable to settle before. When a conference table is set up, for instance, families often find themselves capable of reaching many solutions on their own.

Secondly, when the husband comes to counseling with his wife, the family is not divided. One-to-one counseling, in contrast, may be quite divisive. One-to-one counseling often raises suspicions on the part of other members of the family. It frequently encourages one party to talk about another behind his back. Nouthetic counselors scrupulously avoid letting clients do this. Not knowing what is happening in counseling, a husband suspects that the counselor has sided with his spouse against him, and that false information is being given and decisions based upon it are being made without his knowledge. In other words, because he is not in on the counseling, he may suspect (often rightly so) that the counseling may be adverse to his best interests. He rightly recognizes that since he hasn't been there to fill in the picture, the counseling *is* one-sided. He knows that the counselor is not getting a full view of what has happened, and so he correctly is dubious about such counseling. Where people have already been driven apart and where communication has broken down, one-to-one counseling usually widens the communication gap. Bringing both parties in, however, allows both sides of the question to be presented. When both or all parties (if there are other individuals involved such as children, parents or grandparents) have a say, counselors get a fuller, more accurate picture. The presence of other interested persons keeps any one party from grossly misrepresenting facts. Quite frequently one person presents what seems to be a persuasive, clear-cut, seemingly airtight story. Yet ninety per cent of the story has to be rejected after hearing a refutation or explanation by the other person involved. A client may seem quite convincing when some other person is not present to supplement. He may seem less convincing afterwards. Violet with great emotion and tears represented her husband as having refused to support her for fiv years. But a thorough discussion with the husband, who was present, made it clear that he had only stopped paying for permanent waves and a few other items, and on top of that, she, rather than he, had been the one who effected the financial change in the first place.

Counselors should take to heart Proverbs 18:17 and 14:15: "He that is first in his own cause seemeth just; but his neighbor cometh and searcheth him" and, "The simple believeth every word: but the prudent man looketh well to his going." Cross-talk between the members of a multiple counseling group helps keep true data before the counselor. Triangulation between counselor and clients provides a check which not only allows for a truer picture of the situation, but also insures a fuller picture as well. Details may be filled in as well as challenged.

Since no counseling is an end in itself, the methodology should conform to and promote the end in view. The biblical goal is love to the glory of God (cf. *supra*, pp. 54-55). Love issues not only from confession but from confession leading to reconciliation (cf. Matthew 5 and 18). Confession apart from attempted reconciliation is unbiblical, because as such confession is but a self-centered catharsis in which one gets something off his chest for his own benefit. Multiple counseling more readily leads to reconciliation while one-to-one counseling more readily leads to catharsis. The biblical concern for love through reconciliation should lead toward maximizing the conditions for reconciliation by doing counseling in a reconciliation context.

Often clients are amazed at the information that emerges when communication takes place during a multiple counseling session. Jenny accused Fred of being a thief. She said he had been holding back money from each pay, and that she could prove it. The counselor said, "What about it, Fred? The way to get on top of a problem is first to get to the bottom of it. Did you take the money?" Fred admitted he had, pulled out his wallet, produced the money, and explained that he had been saving (not stealing) it to buy her a fine present for their 10th wedding anniversary.

A Christian man and his wife had been seeing a Rogerian psychiatrist (who is also a Christian) for over a year. The psychiatrist saw husband and wife separately. The husband was severely depressed and felt that it was necessary to discontinue his work. Because there had been no progress in all this time, and as a matter of fact the situation had worsened, they came to a nouthetic counseling center where for the first time they were counseled together. At the beginning of the initial interview one of them said, "We've heard that this is the place where you get things done fast; that's why we've come, we need help now."

During the interview the counselor took them seriously whenever they made comments about their sin, exploring every such suggestion with evident concern and making a Christian response to each. The husband was evidently surprised and encouraged by this, and when it became apparent to him that there was a truly Christian counseling milieu, he suddenly turned to his wife. "I want to tell you something I've never said to anyone before: Cynthia, I don't love you. In fact, I don't know whether I have loved you in all these years we've been married."

Many elements, doubtless, entered into John's decision to tell Cynthia his long buried guilty secret at that first meeting. But one prime element certainly was her presence itself. For the first time in more than a year's counseling he had the opportunity to unburden his heart to her in the presence of someone who could help them work out the problem. John had been suffering from the pain of this intolerable secret for many years; years that were unnecessarily expanded by counseling which made it easy for John to go on with his sinful non-disclosure. But multiple non-Rogerian counseling by it very nature encouraged him to bear his soul to Cynthia. Subsequently, misunderstandings of love were cleared up, many problems solved, and the family was brought together in a entirely new relationship of love. The multiple approach is one more reason why nouthetic counseling "gets things done fast."

## Clients as Counselors

Multiple counseling also has the advantage of allowing counselors to enlist other parties as assistants. Often they make valuable contributions. Another reason why nouthetic counseling moves so rapidly, why people are changed so quickly, and why their lives are affected so radically, is because of assistant counseling. Multiple counseling makes this possible. When the other parties know what is going on in counseling, they potentially become assistant counselors, who day by day may help carry the counseling into the rest of the week. Counseling need not sag in the middle from session to session. The counselee does not have to return to counseling in order to get another shot in the arm. His dependence upon the counselor is lessened. Instead, someone else is present daily to remind him of the commitments that were made in the counseling session and to help him keep them. The "assistant counselor" day by day, in addition to holding the other party to his commitments, can help maintain an atmosphere conducive to carrying out homework assignments. Knowing what is expected also helps keep him from unwittingly working at cross purposes. As A. A., Weight Watchers, and a number of other groups have shown, it is easier to stick to new programs when one does it together with others. In addition to all this, it is likely that more than one of the parties may have problems, even though when counseling begins, it is assumed by the clients that only one party needs counseling. This is frequently the case. Counseling rarely remains one-sided. When other persons can be enlisted as helpers in counseling, all parties grow, and as they grow, they grow together. They learn to do things together, and they work together so that there is a change in the total environment.

Multiple counseling also affords opportunities for crucial

joint decisions. Tom and Mary had led rather despicable lives. Each had engaged in extra-marital sexual affairs. When they married neither was a Christian; until very recently they had known nothing of Christianity. But now in the eighteenth year of their marriage they became Christians. Tom, over the last year, had been seeing another woman. He didn't want to give her up. Mary found out about it and made Tom promise to break the relationship. He agreed; but he didn't do it. For nearly a year Tom's broken promise and double life had eaten away at him, and the more his Christian faith had become a pressing reality, the more the guilt of his actions weighed upon him. What could he do? He came for counseling. He came under the guise of talking about his son, but in the first interview it was not long before the discussion turned to the real problem. "Tom," his counselor said,

> you've got to give her up. If you want to straighten out your marriage you're going to have to tell your wife about it. You'll have to tell her that you've been lying; that you really have been seeing this woman. You'll have to ask her forgiveness, assure her that this time you mean business, and ask her to help you stick to your promise.

Tom said, "I can't do it." "Tom, we can't help you if you don't." After some discussion of God's commandments and his grace, Tom agreed: "All right, I'll do it." Tom asked God's forgiveness and help. The counselor prayed about the outcome. Tom scheduled another visit for that afternoon, and brought Mary along.

During this counseling session Tom told Mary the truth. He confessed that he had lied and that at this very moment he had the keys to the other woman's apartment in his pocket. Mary was shattered, but she was gratified that he had told her, and she took it well (she probably took it better because it happened in the presence of a counselor who was able to help them take the next step). She said, "What can we do?" Tom said, "I want you to forgive me and help me to become the kind of Christian husband I ought to be." Mary said, "Well, I will forgive you, Tom, if you mean it, if you really want to save our marriage." Tom said, "I do" (it sounded almost as if he were taking his marriage vows again). So Mary forgave Tom. As a matter of fact, before the session had ended, Mary too had asked for forgiveness for some previous escapades of her own, and had received it. "What do we do next?" Tom asked. Everyone talked this over. It was decided that Tom should phone the other woman and tell her he would not see her again.

The next week Tom and Mary came back for further counseling. During the week an issue had arisen between Tom and Mary about those keys to the other woman's apartment. Both agreed that he should dispose of them—but how? Should he take them back to the woman and give them to her? Should he throw them away? What should he do about them? Everyone felt that it was important to do something immediately. The matter disturbed Mary considerably. The counselor said, "Tom, hand over those keys right now." He did. Dramatically he placed them one after another on the table in a solemn commitment that helped Mary know that he meant business. She was a new woman after that. This very act, this burning of his bridges, meant a great deal to her. Those keys are in the counseling files to this day, as evidence that Tom meant business. Sometime in years to come, if it is ever necessary to do so, those keys could be shown to Tom or to his wife as a reminder of the commitment he made that day. It probably won't be necessary to do so. The keys remain as a landmark in their lives; they are like the pile of stones which the old patriarchs erected noting a milestone along the road of sanctification.[1]

---

[1]Cf. God's use of "reminders" in Numbers 15:37-41. His people were to wear tassels on their garments as a reminder to obey his commandments. One client was helped by affixing a large "T" (constructed of masking tape) to his front door to remind him to take out the trash as he left. Masking tape is a nearly universal aid in counseling!

Nouthetic counseling files contain many interesting symbols of various sorts. One file may boast the wrapper from a package of cigarettes where someone who has been fighting the habit and wanted to break it that very night handed over his cigarettes. Another contains the picture of a married woman that should have been disposed of when her marriage to another took place. Giving up the picture was one way of saying that a commitment to abandon the practice of engaging in sinful thoughts about that person had been made. A third contains a razor blade that a minister removed from his wallet on the first visit, saying, "If I hadn't received help here today, I would have used this on myself." Thus, some concrete evidence of a person's change is often a useful adjunct to decisions about making a break with the past. And in each of the cases cited, the object given up itself was a temptation to sin.

The concept of multiple counseling is not new. The values and significance of family counseling should not be a surprise to Scripture readers, since the Bible plainly reveals God's purpose and determination to work covenantally with families. Multiple counseling is so much a concern of nouthetic counselors that they hope some day to conduct summer family camping based on the principle that whole families can be radically changed for Christ and sent back home as newly-functioning units. One of the problems with camping for single members of families is that often on returning home, other members of the family who did not climb the mountain and did not share the mountain-top experience tend to dampen their enthusiasm. Counseling of entire families for a week in a family-living context (possibly in tents) seems to afford one of the greatest opportunities for utilizing the advantages of multiple counseling to the fullest.[1]

---

[1] Anyone wishing to finance such an endeavor may contact the writer.

### If Only One Will Come

Sometimes only one of the parties involved in a problem will be willing to come for counseling. This was true in the case of Bill and Jane. Bill came saying that Jane had asked him for a divorce for the second time, and she was now really pressing the matter. They had been married for over twenty years, the children were grown and were beginning to leave the home, and going off to establish their own homes. Jane then told Bill, "I've lived with you as long as the children were at home, and now I want a divorce; I can't stand living together any longer. You don't love me and I don't love you." Bill didn't want the marriage to break up. He did love Jane, and subsequently it became evident that Jane really loved Bill. But she had given up; she had given up trying to communicate with Bill, trying to get through to him, trying to talk about the things that mattered to her. So at the first session Bill came alone. He said he wanted to save his marriage but he didn't know how to do it himself. The counselors asked Bill to bring Jane along next time, since marriage is a two-way proposition. Bill said, "She'll never come. I asked her but she refused and insisted, No, I want a divorce; it's too late, there's no hope."

How can a marriage be saved with only one party present? His counselors told Bill, "We can't guarantee anything, but why don't you go home and talk to your wife in a different way from the way that you have talked to her in the past?" Together they took an inventory of Bill's life and found that he had deep resentments and bitterness toward his wife and that there were some specific matters that especially bothered him. They pointed out to him that resentment is sin, and ought to be confessed regardless of whether his wife would respond positively or not. He needed to get these matters settled before God and his wife. After prayer in which Bill made a full confession of his bitterness to God, he went home to square these things off with his wife. He was told:

Bill, we can't guarantee how she'll respond. We've never even met her. But one thing we know. You'll feel better because you will have done what God commands you to do; you will have been pursuing peace; you will have been trying to do all that you can to set these matters straight and to bring about reconciliation. The likelihood is that when you talk to your wife about your failures and sins and faults, she will be interested, because you will begin to communicate. When people begin to talk about their own sins they're pointed in the same direction, they're headed in the same direction as the other person is. She has been focusing on your faults for some time. Now you will both be talking the same language. Instead of driving her off as you do when you begin to talk about her instead of yourself, you're likely to find that your wife will be drawn near.

Well, Bill went home. He was dubious about the whole matter. But an hour later he called and said exuberantly:

My wife is coming for counseling! Do you know, you said that if I talked to her about my problems and opened communication in this way, and I confessed my sins and asked for forgiveness, that she'd come near?

The counselor replied, "Yes, we remember, Bill."

Well, she did, literally! I entered the house and she was standing at the sink. I went over and told her, "Honey, I'm sorry that I've been such a bad husband. I've failed in many ways." Then I detailed many of these matters, and said "I've been to blame. I want your forgiveness. Will you forgive me and will you help me to become a better husband?"

He added: "She turned and she literally rushed to me. I had to step back to keep her from knocking me down." Subsequently Bill and Jane not only patched up their marriage, but began a new life for themselves; many questions were settled and they began to look forward to the days ahead when the children would be gone and they could enjoy life together.

Another husband who remarked that he came to counseling only because his wife had apologized and asked for forgiveness said, "I came because I never thought I'd ever hear her say she was sorry." These, and many similar instances, are merely illustrative of Peter's words in I Peter 3:1, 2 where he stresses the need for influencing by "conduct" when another will not listen to words.

It is not uncommon for nouthetic counselors to make several attempts to enlist other parties if necessary, since they consider multiple counseling so important. Their success in making enlistments is high.

## Daily Devotions

An attempt is made to establish regular Bible study and prayer in every client's home. Problem solving is a means of growing in love toward God; the use of Scripture, prayer, etc., must never be viewed merely as the means by which one overcomes his difficulties and makes life more pleasant for himself. Unless one maintains vital contact with God, he cannot grow properly into the image and likeness of Christ, because he cannot solve the problems that stand between him and a joyful fellowship with God. Daily devotions help maintain contact with God through his Word and prayer.

The morning is one of the best times for devotions. Often the whole family can gather together at this time. Of course, members of the family must discipline themselves in order to get up early enough to do all the things that need to be done and also to have time for devotions. Brief Bible reading that centers upon a small portion of Scripture in which one principle seems clear is probably the most beneficial practice to establish wherever Bible reading is new. It is better to read and understand one verse than to read one chapter or one book of the Bible without understanding. Someone who is trying to establish habits of Bible study and prayer for the first time must read briefly if he wishes to read with understanding. When one clear point emerges he may then stop at that point and think about that particular principle. He may ask, "Does the principle embody a promise, a command, a duty, a warning, or what?" He may then pray about the day to come in terms of the principle, asking God to help him live according to it. He should think about this principle throughout the day and let it filter down into his living. If he has read the verse that says, "Do good to those who despitefully use you," he may think about how this applies to John at work. He is to do good to his wife, who fussed at him when he came from work. He is to do good to his next-door neighbor, who even after repeated reminders that his children have been putting rocks down the gas tank of his automobile, has refused to discipline them. Whatever the problem may be, the principle must be applied wherever it can be. Perhaps one of the reasons why the reading of Scripture has become academic and irrelevant, influencing life so little, is because people have read it as a book apart from living. The Scriptures are full of principles (usually connected with or imbedded in concrete situations) that really can be put into practice. Verses come alive as they become part of one's life.

## Compatibility in Marriage

In this chapter something has been said about marriage and marriage problems. A final word or two should be appended. Only adultery and desertion can break marriage.[1] Apart from these exceptions, marriage is for life. Incompatibility, one frequently alleged ground for divorce in our country today, has no legitimate status before God. Yet the issue of compatibility has become so significant that it might be well to ask, what is compatibility in marriage? Is it really important? How can it be determined? Is it frozen and unchangeable? What can a Christian do about being compatible?

---

[1] Cf. John Murray, *Divorce* (Philadelphia: Presbyterian and Reformed Publishing Company, 1961), for the exegetical basis of this statement. Murray's work in I Corinthians 7 is exceptionally valuable.

Society built on romantic love is relatively new. From biblical times until very recently marriages mostly were arranged by parents. And so the Bible says relatively little about romance. Yet there are several indications even in the Old Testament that there was a romantic love between individuals often leading to marriage (cf. the record of Jacob in Genesis 29, and the Song of Solomon). But the question remains, is compatibility important? Of course compatibility is important to a marriage. But compatibility is not something which is native to two persons. While all the studies show that people of the same economic, social and educational level seem to get along better, such external compatibility is not absolutely essential to a good marriage because it is not basic. The studies also mention religion as a significant factor. One's belief is an absolute essential of compatibility: Christians should marry "only in the Lord." Believers cannot disobey God by marrying unbelievers and expect their marriage to go well. There is no other factor which is really essential for compatibility. Race, age, social status, everything else is secondary, although there may be desirable qualities within the one basic requirement of Scripture. Yet the Scripture itself makes no such distinctions. The backgrounds which two people bring into a marriage may be quite distinct. These backgrounds have contributed to the personalities which each marriage partner has developed through memory, associative bonds, and the response patterns he has developed. If both the man and the woman have developed biblical habits of response to life's problems, *regardless of what their background may have been*, they have more basic compatibility than two persons who had nearly identical cultural backgrounds but were not Christians. Because they will know how to sit down and work out their differences, they will at length learn how to use the diversity of their backgrounds to enrich their marriage. That means that nouthetic counselors never tell clients, "You can't make it because you are incompatible; you would be better apart than together." If both parties are Christians, or if they become Christians, they can make a success of their marriage if they are willing to work hard at it according to biblical principles by the means of grace.

One woman said, "My husband knows and understands people he works with better than me—his own wife—even though we've been married for 14 years!" Counseling uncovered the fact that the difference was that he worked at knowing the people at the office harder than he had worked at his marriage. Sitting down at a daily conference table for a week would be the first time for many couples that they had spent five to seven successive days making any joint effort at solving the problems in their marriage.

The most important fact to remember when thinking about compatibility is that personality is changeable. Personality is the sum total of what we are at any given moment. From one's genetic makeup, humanly speaking, an almost infinite number of possibilities for using the genetic makeup itself arise. People are a combination of the genetically-determined *phusis* (nature), and what they have done with that *phusis*. By nature, the unsaved man will respond sinfully. But the Christian knows that a third factor, the Person of the Holy Spirit, enters the picture to enable Christians by his power to respond in accordance with the commands of God. Personality, then, is nature and nurture. But Christians by the Spirit have become more than "natural" men (cf. I Corinthians 2). They have been changed and may continue to change their personalities by the work of the Spirit.

Bad habits develop that have become "second nature." Clients who lack consideration or concern for others have developed bad habits that will be disturbing factors in marriage. All habits are brought into marriage of course. But habits are changeable factors. A language is learned in one's home, but one can move to another country and learn to speak a new language. So too a person may leave his earlier habits behind, if he is willing to work hard enough, and can adopt, instead, habits of courtesy, intimacy, and consideration. If two Chris tians properly talk over all of the things that disturb them, seek to do God's will about them, and work together prayerfully, they can solve those problems.

When Phil goes to the bathroom he leaves the door open (a habit which was not in vogue in Mildred's background and which is offensive to her). If real communication exists in the home, loving Christian consideration can be established. Mildred will mention the fact that his habit is offensive, Phil will thank her for telling him, and in love they will work out a solution which is satisfying to both. In other words, when two people create a new decision-making unit they cannot maintain intact all of the customs and habitual ways of living that each knew before. Neither one should expect the other person to make all the changes, but both parties should together think through how they are going to create a new decision-making unit.[1] In doing so they should consciously take the best (i.e., the Christian elements) from both of the backgrounds. In that way, their marriage will become a third, distinct thing, better than the home from which either came.

Communication problems, because they stem back to the Garden of Eden, can never be solved by Rogerian, Freudian or behaviorist methods. Only the God who made man can show him the path back to paradise.

---

[1] It is essential for the man to "leave" his father and mother and to "cleave" to his wife (Genesis 2:24) or he can never become the head of the new decision-making unit as pictured both in Genesis and in Ephesians 5. Much needs to be said about the husband-wife relationship that cannot be mentioned here. Misunderstandings about the husband's loving headship have often led Christian men to exercise a crushing tyrannical rule over their wives which is entirely out of accord with the spirit of Ephesians 5 and Proverbs 31 (in which the woman's gifts are shown to be fully exercised for the benefit of her entire family).

*Chapter XI*

# CHRISTIAN SCHOOL TEACHERS
## AS NOUTHETIC COUNSELORS

All that has been said thus far concerning Christian counseling is applicable to nearly *every* form of relationship in which Christians come together. This, after all, was the point of Colossians 3:16, where Paul urged all Christians to nouthetic confrontation.[1] But if it is true that in every situation Christians may successfully use nouthetic principles, this is especially true of the teacher-pupil relationship in the Christian school. Built into this relationship are all of the essential elements of good nouthetic counseling. The only difference between the classroom and the counseling room is that the Christian classroom context affords so much more opportunity. That is why it is important to devote a chapter to a consideration of how to tap this hitherto nearly untapped potential.

The Christian teacher (not a counseling specialist) is the key to counseling in the school. If the teacher is qualified to be a Christian school teacher, given the conviction and a minimum of the right sort of training and experience, that teacher can do more effective counseling than the self-styled experts. The counseling principally described in this book is not only entirely applicable to the school, but can be carried on more thoroughly and can obtain results more consistently and more rapidly than in counseling offices. Let us try to understand why this is so.

Like other Christians, the Christian teacher may draw upon all of the resources of God: Scripture, prayer and the church, in the context of the Holy Spirit. But beyond this, consider the fact that the students with whom the teacher works are

---

[1]Cf. also Hebrews 3:13; 10:24, 25 and Galatians 6:1, 2 on this point.

252

younger than those who ordinarily seek counseling. Patterns
are not yet so firmly set; many are being learned for the first
time. The pliability of childhood and youth is clearly a plus
factor.

The classroom context is ideally suited to counseling conditions. It is perfectly adapted to establishing and changing life
patterns. First, it is a total environment milieu such as that
described in Deuteronomy 6:7, 11:19. Secondly, there is a
daily, sustained influence of precisely the kind it takes to establish or alter patterns. Thirdly, the penalty and reward system inherent in teaching, if used under the authority of God,
provides ample motivation for most students. Lastly, the
school reaches the student during the most productive hours
of his day, when his greatest energies and resources are available, and can demand and obtain from him his utmost output.
These factors are but a few of the many reasons why it is not
too farfetched to say that few—if any—situations are more
suited to counseling than the Christian classroom.

The potential impact of the Christian school teacher is im-
mense. There is little doubt that he can in most cases probably
do much more to help his students in much larger ways than
he thinks. Referral is surely a serious question for the school
teacher, as well as the pastor. Why should a teacher refer a pupil *out* of the milieu which is most ideally suited to helping
him? The only answer to that question is that Christian teachers have seldom been taught to recognize this potential, and
consequently do not believe that they can help. Hopefully,
this book will inform and encourage them to begin to actual-
ize this potential.

### Begin with Proper Assumptions

Where does a teacher begin? Perhaps it is best to restate
two of the assumptions that have already been suggested in
this book in terms of the teacher-pupil relationship.

1. Every child (like every teacher) has unsolved problems,
sins every day, needs God's grace to be saved and helped to
grow into the Holy Spirit's methods of problem solving. This

assumption is founded on a more basic one: that the biblical doctrine of original sin is true. This chapter is no place to give a full exposition of this doctrine, which for present purposes will be considered axiomatic. The goal toward which these assumptions point is that the Christian teacher should endeavor to see every student changed for God's glory by the development of biblical patterns of problem solving through his classroom experiences.

2. The problems of "problem" students do not differ essentially from those of other students, or, for that matter, from those of their teachers. Not all problems are exactly alike in all respects, of course. The features of every problem differ in details from every other. Age and experience structure both the level and the complexity of the form in which the problem emerges and takes shape. But at bottom, no case is unique; problems do not differ in kind. The support for this assertion has already been given in the discussion of I Corinthians 10:13.[1] The implications of this assumption are clear. First, there should be real hope: if God does not allow his children to face tests greater than they can handle,[2] there is genuine hope that the teacher can do something to help each one of his pupils solve his problems in biblical ways. This should enable him to bring a humble confidence to the task. If the teacher's problems do not differ essentially from those of his students, and he is truly qualified to be a Christian teacher (one essential element of that qualification being the fact that he is successfully solving his own problems), then he is acquainted already with the basic Christian principles and methods for problem solving. He can help his students to use God's resources in the same ways that he has discovered how to use them in his own life. He already knows what to do; there is no esoteric body of knowledge for him to acquire.

---

[1] Cf. p. 85 ff.

[2] Of course, as they handle them in a biblical manner.

But if he has the resources, then he is a debtor; he must use them. Every privilege carries its own corresponding responsibility. He is obligated to help his students and may not shirk this responsibility or pawn it off on another. With these two assumptions to build upon, let us attempt to state a tentative operational definition of counseling.

## Definition of Counseling as Help in Problem Solving

Counseling in the Christian school context is concerned with helping students[1] to solve problems God's way. This includes (1) problems they bring into the school milieu, (2) problems that grow out of the school milieu and hopefully, as they learn to carry over biblical patterns by extension (3) problems that arise after leaving the school milieu.

Students will tend to solve new problems according to old patterns. When they encounter new problem situations arising within the school milieu (and school is one of the chief places where new problems arise for children), the student will naturally address himself to such problems in ways to which he has already become accustomed outside the school milieu. These patterns of problem solving may or may not be biblical, but the teacher may be certain that many—if not most—will not be. The Christian school teacher cannot avoid the interpersonal relations that develop from such patterns, for the student's patterns will affect not only his relationship to his peers, but to the teacher himself. If the teacher does not help his students develop new patterns and change wrong ones and thereby influence the activity of the child both within and without the school milieu, the wrong patterns he brings from

---

[1] All students, not just irritatingly "problem" students. Quiet, submissive, docile students *may* have more serious problems than their more volatile classmates. They already may be developing avoidance patterns in which they are running from problems rather than facing them. Apart from this possibility, our first assumption is that all sin and need help. Cf. *Infra*, p. 266.

256

without will exert a harmful influence within the classroom. There is no escape; the teacher's stance must be: *attack or be attacked*. The nouthetic purpose of the Christian school teacher then must be to turn the dynamics of habit into the asset that God intended rather than to allow poor habits to become a liability through sin.

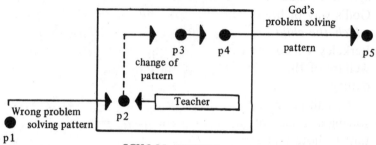

SCHOOL MILIEU

Explanation of diagram: Wrong problem solving pattern developed outside school milieu in confronting problems (p1). Student responds to problem arising out of school milieu (p2) according to previously developed pattern, but pattern is successfully countered by school teacher using resources of God so that a change is effected and new pattern established. New pattern applied not only to other problems within school milieu (p3, p4), but also carried over to problems without (p5).

## Dynamics of Habit as Asset

One major task of every Christian school teacher, then, is to help his pupils establish proper problem solving methods and to change improper ones. This is simply assuming his role as an agent of God's Spirit in His work of sanctification as he helps Christian students put off the old man and put on the new man.

But is such activity legitimate for a Christian school teacher? Most decidedly yes. All of the mandates to parents to teach their children to walk in the ways of God (e.g., Deuteronomy 6) are immediately pertinent, for the Christian teacher receives his commission to teach *in loco parentis.* If he truly stands in the place of the parent who has for those hours delegated his rights and obligations to the teacher, the latter has agreed to assume the obligation of instructing the child in God's way of life *during the very real life situations through which the child lives at school* (cf. Deuteronomy 6:6, 7; see Berkeley Version especially). Not only is such concern for the welfare of the student's life legitimate, but, indeed, it is mandatory.

This all points up the need for teaching Christian problem solving as a part of the teacher's education. And, it is important to note that Deuteronomy lays upon parents (and so by extension, teachers) the double duty of both the formal (didactic) and informal (life situational) teaching of God's commandments. This would seem to indicate that Christian schools also might wish to include in the curriculum some formal instruction in the subject of biblical problem solving.

Where is there a better opportunity to demonstrate both the purpose and the meaning of Christian truth to covenant children than in the Christian school? For it is here that the integration of information and vital problems (some of the youngster's biggest problems involve school and the persons associated with it) can so dramatically occur.

## Integration First in the Teacher's Life

Counseling must move—as often it does not—from principle to practice first in the life of the teacher himself. Proper principles can be conveyed most forcefully when they are taught in the form of a living demonstration day after day in the life of the Christian teacher. Wilmer R. Witte is correct when he writes: "Children are excellent imitators. Much of their education is gained through imitation."[1] The teacher cannot avoid becoming a model (for good or bad). He must, therefore, consciously make every effort to embody the way of life he intends to inculcate (including, significantly, the way he handles his own sins and failures). Secondly, new biblical life styles can be developed by the teacher-pupil relationship itself. This may happen both informally and formally in their relationship to one another as Christians and in their relationship within the authority and learning structure as teacher and student. Lastly, the patterns of Christian problem solving may be established and enforced by classroom structure erected for this purpose.

The word *nouthesis* is of importance to the teacher, as one who is *in loco parentis,* not only because of its peculiar familial nature, but also because the term is so closely linked with *didasko* ("to teach"). Each is on the other side of the coin (cf. again Colossians 1:28; 3:16). The two go together. It is questionable whether there can be successful teaching without nouthetic confrontation. Certainly the least that can be said is that in Romans 15:14, as well as Colossians 3:16, Paul considers nouthetic contact as an intrinsic part of the ordinary relationship that should exist between believers in Christ. So then, even on this lowest level, it may be said that the intimate student-teacher, teacher-teacher, and student-student relationships that develop in the Christian school milieu demand it.

### The Discipling Method

What has been said already about the discipling method (modeling by the teacher) must surely strike every school teacher with force, for students actually are his disciples (pupils). While the classroom and total school milieu are ideal for

---

[1]Wilmer R. Witte, "Imitators and Examples," (*The Banner,* October 3, 1969), p. 10.

teaching the principles and practice of Christian problem solving, unfortunately this potential is often untapped. Many new teachers wonder how they can get through to their pupils; how they can establish a close, personal relationship with them. One of the most important answers lies in the concept of modeling.[1] Christ used the discipling or apprenticeship method for teaching. In Mark 3:14 Jesus set forth this intention by choosing the twelve to be "with him," i.e., to become his disciples. In Luke 6:40 he clearly states his views about teaching by this method: "Everyone after he is fully trained, will be like his teacher."[2] Notice, he did not say, "will believe what his teacher believes," but his words go further: "he . . . will *be like* his teacher." Christ considered teaching to include much more than merely the communication of knowledge. And it is clear that his method was successful, for in Acts 4:13 their enemies take note of the fact that the knowledge and behavior of the disciples clearly indicate that they had been "with Jesus."

That this is all quite pertinent to the Christian school teacher must be apparent. But concretely, how does it work out in the modern school context? Really, quite literally. Students and teachers live a large share of their lives together. They are not only teachers and pupils in the narrower sense, but they are Christian human beings handling life's problems in each others' presence. Students must, really, live *with* their teacher, and it is certain that in ways more numerous and frequently more subtle than either may recognize, the teacher does model and the student does imitate and does become "like his teacher." Such modeling is not always conscious, to be sure. But it is nonetheless effective.

A teacher has been brought together with his pupils for a purpose larger than lecture. Both teacher and pupil need one

---

[1]You may wish to refer again to pages 114-117.

[2]Note the same emphasis in Matthew 10:24, 25.

another for life. Each furnishes much of the content of the other's life during these hours, days and years together. Relationships exist, grow, change, develop, break down. The patterns by which these are formed and reformed are either biblical or not. They either exhibit the loving (i.e., responsible) relationship God bears to his children and calls them to bear toward him and one another by the keeping of his law, or they do not. The teacher cannot afford to ignore this matter.

There is no dichotomy between teaching (viewed as theory) and doing (practice). It is not a matter of attempting to integrate these. Whether we like it or not, theory and practice are by the very nature of human life already integrated in the teacher himself. A teacher teaches theory (perhaps not the theory he consciously wishes to teach) all the time by his practice, and in this he inevitably communicates well. What the teacher does, says, what his (her) attitudes, moods, etc. are, all are a part of teaching *by modeling*. The teacher is the integration of principle and practice.

To become quite concrete, how does the teacher handle his own interpersonal relations with his peers and his students? How does he handle his sins? Has he taught his students to cover up and make excuses for their sins by doing so himself? Or, have they learned the biblical principles of repentance and reconciliation by hearing their teacher apologize to them when he recognized his wrong? Have they been taught the urgency of reconciliation by a teacher who promptly settles matters before the final bell rings (cf. Ephesians 4:26)? Or have their sinful patterns of resentment been reinforced by discovering that their teacher has been nursing a grudge for years against another teacher down the hall? The simple question is, does the student learn God's ways of solving life's problems from his teacher?

Discussion about questions arising out of the milieu from time to time also may be developed by a teacher into seminars. In a non-moralistic manner which always points to Christ and his forgiveness, the teacher, like the Lord, thus may instruct more formally out of the milieu (cf. Mark 9:28, 29). Christ trained his disciples by holding interpretive seminars following field work and lectures. This also seems to be a part of the thrust that is made in Deuteronomy 6.

Particular students, or classes in general, may be set on courses of action with the help of the teacher and/or the student's peers. Such structure, affording daily practice in the classroom under supervision and with encouragement and help may exert a powerful influence.[1] The influence may be so strong that it is important to emphasize once again the warnings in James 3:1: "Let not many of you become teachers, my brethren, for you know that we who teach shall be judged with greater strictness." The teacher must be careful at all times, however, to limit the number of persons to those actually involved in the problem. Classrooms should not be turned into Oxford Group Meetings, or Sensitivity Training Sessions.

Mention of such powerful influence on the part of the teacher naturally raises the question of the qualification of teachers. Such power must be delegated carefully by parents. Three elements, goodness, knowledge and wisdom, have already been discovered to be prime biblical prerequisites to effective Christian counseling (cf. pp. 59-62). In the choice of teachers, Christian school boards can settle for nothing less—despite the many pressures that may be upon them to "get a teacher before September." These prerequisites, in addition to those academic and doctrinal requirements now already determined by Christian schools, ought always to be considered.

### How God May Use the Teacher

Much has been said about the fundamental ways in which God may use a Christian teacher as a model for his students. Now, however, it might be useful to note several more con-

---

[1]Cf. Mark 6:7-13, 30; Luke 9:10 for examples of Christ's policy of teaching not only through example and seminar, but also by discussion, practice and critique.

crete ways in which counseling can be carried on by the Christian teacher in the classroom.

## Disciplining through Structure

Discipline in the school is closely related to nouthetic confrontation. Enough has been said already about parental discipline that need not be repeated here. The principle to be stressed, however, is that *structure for desired behavior must be introduced early*. God introduced the rules of the kingdom at the formal beginning of both its Old Testament and New Testament phases. Before entering the land he gave his people the Ten Commandments, which he spelled out in detail. And along with these he also made clear what the sanctions and rewards would be (curses and blessings, Deuteronomy 11:26-32; 26:16 - 28:68). At the foundation of the New Testament church, Jesus set forth with clarity the rules of the kingdom in the so-called Sermon on the Mount. In both cases there was immediate follow-through by rigid enforcement: cf. Numbers 15:32 ff. and Acts 5, where God took the lives of the Sabbath breaker and Annanias and Sapphira because of violations. God's swift, severe action was calculated to show that he meant what he said.

The importance of taking advantage of the newness of the situation at the beginning of a semester also should be apparent. The children are set for a change. What better time is there to introduce change? They will test the sincerity of the teacher and the limits of the rules. The class will settle down into the teacher's pattern as soon as the students clearly understand it and are assured by the teacher's actions that he intends to enforce every rule he has set forth.

## Few Rules Needed

This leads naturally to a discussion of how many rules there should be. Discipline often breaks down because a well-meaning teacher has set up so many (often also such unrealistic) rules that he cannot possibly enforce them. Anarchy results, because the teacher's enforcement necessarily becomes spotty and arbitrary. God summarized all he required of man in just *ten* commandments. The point is that no rule should be set up unless there is every intention to enforce it. Every rule must be policed and enforced. If it cannot be monitored, it is a bad rule. If it cannot be enforced it is a poor rule. Rules that are not policed and not enforced tend to keep classes confused and confusing.

So that the teacher is not run ragged and is not turned into a full-time police officer, it is desirable to shave the number of rules down to a bare minimum. My colleague, Dr. John Miller, has said, "If you act like a warden, your students will behave like prisoners."[1] Setting up few rules, rigidly enforced, removes the necessity for minute-by-minute policing of students and eliminates the warden image. The strict enforcement of as few rules as possible most effectively leads to the basic lesson that the teacher wishes to teach: obedience and respect for God's authority.[2]

Rather than proliferating rules, it is more advisable to set broad policies which may be distinguished from rules by the fact that no penalties are attached to them. Instead, early in the semester, the teacher may explain these—setting them off from the few absolutely necessary rules—and endeavor to enlist commitment to the policies on behalf of the class. The presence of unenforced (or rather, self-enforced) policies as well as rules (other-enforced policies) enables the teacher to point out the concern he has for the class to learn to shoulder personal responsibility through self-discipline.

Commitment to policy clearly places a lighter disciplinary load upon the teacher and a heavier one upon the student.

---

[1] In an address to the 1969 convention of the National Union of Christian Schools in Ambler, Pennsylvania.

[2] See pp. 188-192 for information concerning rule making.

Obviously there ought to be more rules for children in lower grades than in higher ones.[1] Even so, it is wise to make only a few new rules at a time, firmly establishing those before introducing others. It is important for students to assume increasingly heavier loads of responsibility so that when they graduate from high school there is not suddenly thrust upon them a back-breaking load of responsibility that they are unprepared to carry. Maturation is fundamentally the process of learning to discipline one's self and to carry personal responsibility.

However, when responsibilities are shifted from the teacher to the student, the latter should—along with the responsibility—be taught (formally and by coaching) how to handle the new responsibilities biblically. Scripture injunctions, the explanation of consequences of various courses of actions, advice, etc. are all needed at such transition points. In some cases, particularly in lower grades, it may be wise to spread out the transition over a period of time, perhaps at times even requiring a written essay by the student giving his reasoned biblical opinion upon how he may carry out his new duty in a way that is pleasing to God.

## Interpersonal Relations in the Classroom

While this chapter cannot delineate in detail what to do in all situations, certain important principles may be mentioned. These can be applied to various sorts of concrete instances.

Much has already been said in this book about the importance of avoiding resentment and bitterness by dealing with interpersonal problems on a day-by-day basis. Teachers may take a leaf from the "conference table" techniques suggested earlier. In some manner, differing of course according to ages and personal preferences, the teacher may set a time (formal-

---

[1] This conforms to God's dealings with his church in the days of its infancy (Old Testament) and maturity (New Testament).

ly or informally) to handle daily issues that have arisen. How this best may be accomplished will require the ingenuity of each teacher. But it is important that students and teachers not carry unresolved problems home from school or go home angry. In structuring this the teacher *cannot* settle the hundred and one personal problems that arise among the students themselves. It is probably best to handle difficulties of two sorts, hoping that the principles involved may carry over to the many other problems each student has with his peers. First, any problems between the teacher and the class as a whole (or any segment of it) that have become public matters by the nature of the circumstance itself, should *always* be handled before the class is dismissed for the day. Secondly, any problem between the teacher and a child (or children) which is a private matter ought to be settled privately before that day is over. In this category may also be classed those private matters between students that particularly have been brought to the notice of the teacher, e.g., "Teacher, John stole my ball." Again, since such questions do not involve the entire class, they must not be settled publicly, but privately, confining the number of parties to those actually involved.

In all such interpersonal relations, principles previously set forth in other sections of this book are applicable. The teacher must be careful to stress the urgency for reconciliation, the need for forgiveness and help, the importance of first removing the log from one's own eye, and the necessity for attacking problems rather than people.

## Communication

Communication problems exist not only among married couples. The teacher ought to be aware of bad communication (and other poor problem solving) patterns that are beginning to be adopted by his students, and must learn how to help them to "speak the truth in love." Discussion of Genesis 3 has shown that loving relationships depend upon adequate communication.

One child, in particular, ought to be noticed by the teacher. "Problem child" ought not always be defined as the obstreperous, loud-mouthed child, who becomes such a problem to the teacher. He, of course, is solving life's problems in an unbiblical manner, and needs help to change. But some of those seemingly docile, quiet, and very manageable children who are never a problem to the teacher, may possibly be a serious problem to themselves. It is possible that some (not all) of them (like Leo Held[1]) have already developed patterns of storing up resentments inside. Such children are in as great a need for help as the others who make their need evident in more obvious ways. The danger of course is to find problems where they do not exist. As a general rule, it may be said that any child with which a teacher has not been able to have at least one heart-to-heart talk during the first semester (provided that he has made proper and serious attempts to do so) is probably having a communication problem (at least with the teacher) and may need help. Ways of breaking through communication problems have been described previously in this book.

## Multiple Parent-Teacher-Student Conferences

Discussion of multiple counseling has stressed the importance of bringing in all of the involved parties, and not talking behind the backs of any parties. Has the pattern of parent-teacher conferences, which usually excludes the student, been thought through carefully enough? Does it help bring all parties closer together or does it rather tend to estrange them? Does it create suspicion, even when there is no need for any? When both child and parent know what the teacher says, all three sides know all others know, and it is easier to enlist total agreement to do something about problems. Neither parent nor teacher is able to misrepresent facts (either intentionally or unintentionally) as easily. In general, without further

---

[1] Cf. p. 26 f.

discussion, let us throw out the challenge—why not give it a try?

Much more could be said in this chapter about matters like teaching children how to study, what to do with those who fall behind in their work, etc., but this sort of discussion probably should be published by teachers as the outgrowth of their nouthetic activities in the classroom. Application of the general principles enunciated are probably numberless. The one major point is that Christian teachers should assume the obligations of nouthetic relationships to their pupils. Training in this approach may be available in the near future.[1]

---

[1] See resolutions relative to this matter adopted by the 1969 Convention of the National Union of Christian Schools.

# CONCLUSION

In this volume, I have tried to show that the minister, Christian workers, and indeed every Christian, may consider himself at least potentially competent to counsel. I freely acknowledge that some counselors are more effective than others,[1] and I fully recognize that many ministers have not been trained to counsel biblically. But to agree that for one reason or another (mistraining, lack of training, etc.) Christian workers are not *now* competent to counsel, is not the same as saying that they cannot *become* so. Given the qualities mentioned in Romans 15:14 and Colossians 3:16,[2] plus the proper convictions about counseling, any Christian worker may become a helpful counselor in the place where God has called him to serve. That the work of counseling should be carried on preeminently by ministers and other Christians whose gifts, training and calling especially qualify and require them to pursue the work, I do not doubt. Moreover, in the course of counseling, every counselor will encounter difficult cases and special problems which go beyond his present competency and which therefore indicate the need for referral to some other Christian counselor.[3] Medical problems demand close cooperation with a physician (preferably a Christian).[4] Yet, to say all this in no way denies or detracts from the competency of the Christian counselor to counsel, *so far as his*

---

[1] Counseling is an art that requires skill. Some counselors therefore always will be more skillful than others. In order to teach the art, our center trains counselors by participant observation in actual counseling sessions under supervision and criticism.

[2] Cf. the discussion on pp. 59 ff.

[3] Most counselors cannot be experts in testing, for instance; some marriage and family problems may require specialized information; teachers will want to call in ministers, etc.

[4] It is a wise precaution for counselors to insist on medical checkups for most clients before counseling.

*ability and training* legitimately allow him to do so. He should see no need, therefore, to defer to a self-appointed caste of men called psychiatrists who have pontifically declared that their province necessarily extends beyond his own.[1]

I am aware of the sweeping implications of the changes that I advocate. I am willing to refine my position if I have gone too far. I want to alter any or all of what I have written provided that I can be shown to be wrong *biblically*. I am not interested in debate which moves off non-Christian suppositions, or debate based upon supposedly neutral, objective empirical data. All such evidence, in the end, is interpreted evidence. There is no such thing as brute uninterpreted fact. Data are collected and related and presented by *men,* all of whom are sinners and subject to the noetic effects of their sin. In God's world, all men are related to him as covenant breakers or covenant keepers (in Christ). The judgments of unbelievers, therefore, are arrived at and presented from a point of view which attempts to divorce itself from God. Such judgments must be understood, weighed and examined in this light. I have attempted to reexamine counseling (suggestively, but not exhaustively) in a biblical manner, and I ask, therefore, that my work shall be similarly criticized.

Jesus Christ is at the center of all truly Christian counseling. Although the counseling I have described in this book attempts to recognize and honor him in this rightful place, it certainly contains many defects and inadequacies in doing so. I would welcome enthusiastically the kind of critique which would point out how nouthetic counseling could become more biblical in theory or technique.

Are Christians competent to counsel? Of course they are—

---

[1]If full-time Christian counselors wish to call themselves psychiatrists, I shall not quarrel with them, so long as they do not claim exclusive counseling rights over others with training different from theirs. However, I think the designation is confusing, and therefore unfortunate.

but not enough of them, and some are not as competent as they might be. These days of uncertainty, confusion and transition among many psychologists and counselors afford an unprecedented opportunity for Christians to take the lead rather than to lag behind in this vital area of life. The opportunity must not be lost. But to seize it demands courage and forthrightness. Therefore, let Christian counselors resolve that by the grace of God they shall endeavor to become the most thoroughly competent counselors that can be found.

# PERSONAL DATA INVENTORY FOR USE OF
## C. C. E. F. ONLY

Instructions to Administrator: Please explain to the client that this confidential information form is for the use of the counselor only. Ask him to help you to complete it as carefully as possible. If both husband and wife are coming for counseling, each should fill out a form. If the form pertains primarily to a minor, the parents may need to provide most of the answers.

## IDENTIFICATION DATA:

Your Name _____ Address _____

City _____ State _____ Zip Code _____ Phone _____

Occupation _____ Business Phone _____

Sex ___ Birth Date _____ Age ___ Height _____ Nationality or
Ethnic background _____

Marital Status: Single ____ Going Steady ___ Married ___ Separated ___
Divorced ____ Widowed ____

Education (circle last year completed):
Grade School 1 2 3 4 5 6 7 8 9 High School 10 11 12
College 1 2 3 4 5 6+
Other training (list type and years) _____

_____

Referred here by _____ Address _____

## HEALTH INFORMATION

Rate your physical health (check): Very Good ____ Good ____
Average ____ Declining ____ Other ____

Your approximate weight _____ lbs. Recent weight changes:
Lost _____ Gained _____

List all important present or past illnesses, injuries or handicaps: _____

_____

Date of last medical examination _____ Report: _____

_____

Your Physician _____ Address _____

Have you used drugs for other than medical purposes? Yes___ No___
What? _____

Are you presently taking medication? Yes___ No___ What?_____
Prescribed by _____ Address_____
Have you ever had a severe emotional upset? Yes____ No____
Have you ever had any psychotherapy or counseling? Yes____ No____
If yes, list counselor or therapist and dates: _____
_____

Are you willing to sign a release of information form so that your counselor may write for helpful social, psychiatric, or medical reports?
Yes_____ No____
Have you ever been arrested? Yes____ No____

## RELIGIOUS BACKGROUND
Denominational preference: _____
Church Attendance per Month (circle): 0 1 2 3 4 5 6 7 8 9 10+
Church attended in childhood_____
Baptized? Yes____ No____
Religious background of spouse (if married) _____
Do you consider yourself a religious person? Yes___ No___ Uncertain_
Do you believe in God? Yes____ No____ Uncertain____
Do you pray to God? Never____ Occasionally____ Often____
Are you saved? Yes____ No____ Not sure what you mean____
How much do you read the Bible? Never___ Occasionally___ Often___
Explain recent changes in your religious life, if any _____
_____

## PERSONALITY INFORMATION
Circle any of the following words which best describe you now: active
ambitious self-confident persistent nervous hardworking impatient
impulsive moody often-blue excitable imaginative calm serious
easy-going shy good-natured introvert extrovert likeable leader quiet
hard-boiled submissive self-conscious lonely sensitive other_____

Have you ever felt people were watching you? Yes____ No____
Do people's faces ever seem distorted? Yes____ No____

Do colors seem too bright? \_\_\_\_\_ Too dull? \_\_\_\_\_

Are you able to judge distance? Yes \_\_\_\_ No\_\_\_\_

Have you ever had hallucinations? Yes \_\_\_\_ No \_\_\_\_

Are you afraid of being in a car? Yes\_\_\_\_ No \_\_\_\_

What difficulties do you have in hearing (if any)? _____

MARRIAGE INFORMATION: (if never married, check \_\_\_ and omit this section)

Name of spouse _____ Address _____

Phone _____ Occupation _____

Business Phone _____

Is spouse willing to come for counseling? Yes \_\_ No \_\_ Uncertain \_\_\_\_

Have you ever been separated? Yes\_\_ No \_\_

Have either of you ever filed for divorce? Yes \_\_ No\_\_ When? _____

Date of this marriage _____

Your ages when married: Husband _____ Wife _____

How long did you know your spouse before marriage? _____

Length of steady dating with spouse _____

Length of engagement _____

Give brief information about any previous marriages: _____

_____

Broken by divorce \_\_\_\_ Death \_\_\_\_

Information about children:

| PM* | Name | Age | Sex | Living yes-no | Education in years | Marital Status |
|-----|------|-----|-----|---------------|--------------------|----------------|
|     |      |     |     |               |                    |                |
|     |      |     |     |               |                    |                |
|     |      |     |     |               |                    |                |
|     |      |     |     |               |                    |                |
|     |      |     |     |               |                    |                |
|     |      |     |     |               |                    |                |
|     |      |     |     |               |                    |                |

Your spouse's age \_\_\_\_\_ Education (years) \_\_\_\_ Religion _____

_____

*Check this column if child is by previous marriage.

PARENTAL FAMILY HISTORY

If you were reared by anyone other than your own parents, briefly explain: _____

Answer this section describing your own parents or parent substitute:

Still living? (yes, no)  Father _____        Mother _____

Religious affiliation  Father _____        Mother _____

Church attendance per month  1 2 3 4          1 2 3 4

Occupation  Father _____        Mother _____

Are your parents still living together?  Yes ____  No ____

If not, cause of separation _____

When separated _____

Rate your parents' marriage: Unhappy ___ Average ____ Happy ____
          Very Happy _____

As a child, did you feel closest to your father ___ mother ___ another ___

Rate your childhood life: Very happy ___ Happy ___ Average ___
          Unhappy ____

How many brothers and sisters do you have? _____

How many *older* brothers ____ sisters ____ do you have?

BRIEFLY ANSWER THE FOLLOWING QUESTIONS

1. What is the main problem, as you see it? (Why are you here?)

2. What have you done about it?

3. What can we do?

4. Describe your spouse's personality in a few words (selfish, loving, etc.)

5. As you see yourself, what kind of person are you? describe yourself:

6. Is there any other information we should know?

# GENERAL INDEX

280

Preaching, 22, 54, 55, 61, 97, 208
Preconditioning problem, 54, 103
   148 ff., 172, 175, 200 ff.
Presbytery, 207
Presentation problem, 148 ff.,
   172, 175, 200 ff., 237
Presupposition, xviii, xxi, xxii, 18,
   19, 78, 81, 82, 86, 100 ff., 152,
   210, 235
Prevention, 175 f.
Priesthood of believers, 42, 60
Priorities, 194, 204, 224 ff.
Problem solving, 61, 70, 72, 73,
   82, 85, 88, 96, 119, 129, 130,
   133, 135 ff., 145, 147 ff., 151,
   161, 168, 183, 193 ff., 199,
   213 ff.
Propaganda, xii, 4, 19, 27, 28
Psychiatrist; see Psychiatry
Psychiatry, xii, xiv, xv, xvi, xx, xxi,
   xxii, 1, 2, 3, 4, 7, 8, 9, 11, 12,
   14, 17, 18, 21, 27, 31, 33, 36,
   38, 48, 66, 74, 95, 105, 110,
   122, 139, 142, 183, 239, 269
Psychoanalysis, xxii, 2, 3, 6, 8, 9,
   11, 13, 14, 16, 19, 105, 106
Psychologist; see Psychology
Psychology, xiv, xv, xvi, xxi, 1, 2,
   6, 12, 61, 96, 152, 270
Psychoneurosis, xv
Psychopath; see Sociopathy
Psychosis, xiv, sv, 2
Psychosomatic problems, xiv, 31,
   114, 115, 116, 120, 123
Psychotherapy, xvii, xviii, 9, 12,
   37, 57, 79, 81, 84, 181
Punishment, 7, 44, 50, 138, 159,
   176, 181, 187 ff.

Qualifications, 59 ff., 252, 254,
   261
Questions, 212
Reality, 31
Reconciliation, 96, 101, 108, 111,
   112, 114, 181, 209, 224 ff.,
   226-251, 260, 265
Records, 198 ff.
Referral, 11, 12, 18, 19, 21, 62,
   253, 268
Regeneration, xviii, 20, 73
Relationship, xx, 36, 55, 62, 64,
   67, 69, 86, 92, 97, 111, 113, 12
   127, 156, 205, 211, 212, 236,
   242, 252, 260, 264 ff.
Repentance, xiii, 48, 55, 69, 70,
   101, 107, 111, 116, 120, 121,
   141, 147 ff., 151, 153, 167,
   172, 173, 207, 212 ff., 231,
   260
Repression, 10
Resentment, 27 ff., 36, 101 ff.,
   113, 143, 148, 213, 220-251,
   264 ff., 266
Resocialization, 11
Responsibility, xiv, xv, xvii, xviii
   xix, 4 ff., 8 ff., 13, 15, 17, 27,
   33, 40, 55, 56, 58, 66, 67, 74
   79, 83, 84, 88, 89, 96, 102, 12
   141, 143, 145, 148, 154, 155
   165, 173, 180, 184, 185, 187
   188, 206, 211-251, 255, 264
Restitution, xv, 96, 152 ff., 227
Restructuring; see Total structur
   ing
Reviews of cases, 204 ff.
Rich young ruler, 56, 141

282

# SCRIPTURE INDEX

284

# INDEX OF NAMES

287

INDEX OF NAMES

24-401

This book may be kept
N DAYS

39854